Studies in
African Literature
NEW SERIES

NGUGI WA THIONG'O
Decolonising the Mind

ELDRED DUROSIMI JONES
The Writings of Wole Soyinka

SIMON GIKANDI
Reading the African Novel

SIMON GIKANDI
Reading Chinua Achebe*

EMMANUEL NGARA
Ideology & Form in African Poetry

ADEOLA JAMES
In Their Own Voices
African Women Writers Talk

MILDRED MORTIMER
Journeys through the French African Novel*

KEN HARROW (EDITOR)
Islamic Elements in African Literature*

HEINEMANN Portsmouth (N.H.)
JAMES CURREY London
HEINEMANN KENYA Nairobi

* not yet published

Ideology & Form
in African Poetry

Other titles by Emmanuel Ngara

Stylistic Criticism & the African Novel
(Heinemann 1982)
Art & Ideology in the African Novel
(Heinemann 1985)
Socialism, Education and Development
(Zimbabwe Publishing House 1985)
Teaching Literature in Africa
(Zimbabwe Publishing House 1984)
Bilingualism, Language Contact and Planning
(Mambo Press 1982)

Ideology & Form in African Poetry

Implications for Communication

EMMANUEL NGARA

*Associate Professor of English
& Pro-Vice-Chancellor
University of Zimbabwe*

James Currey
LONDON
Baobab Books
HARARE
Heinemann Kenya
NAIROBI
Heinemann
PORTSMOUTH (N.H.)

James Currey Ltd
54b Thornhill Square, Islington
London N1 1BE

Baobab Books
PO Box 1559
Harare

Heinemann Kenya
Kijabe Street, PO Box 45314
Nairobi

Heinemann Educational Books Inc
361 Hanover Street
Portsmouth, New Hampshire 03801

British Library Cataloguing in Publication Data
Ngara, Emmanuel
Ideology & Form in African poetry : implications for communication.
1. Poetry, African writers — Critical studies
I. Title
800.1
ISBN 0-85255-525-3

Library of Congress Cataloging-in-Publication Data
Ngara, Emmanuel.
Ideology & Form in African poetry : implications for communication
Emmanuel Ngara.
p.   cm.
Includes bibliographical references.
ISBN 0-435-08045-8
1. African poetry—History and criticism.   2. Ideology in
literature.   3. Social problems in literature.   4. Philosophy, Marxism in
literature.   5. African poetry—Study and teaching.   I. Title.   II. Title:
Ideology and form in African poetry.
PL8010.4.N48   1990   90-30115
809.1'0096—dc20   CIP

Set in 10/11pt Paladium
by Colset Pte Ltd., Singapore
and printed in Britain by
Villiers Publications, London N6

Dedicated to
My wife Teboho
My daughter Rutendo
My sons Shingai & Tapiwa

Contents

Contents

PART THREE

POETRY AND THE AFRICAN
LIBERATION STRUGGLE   93

Contents

Preface

This book has taken long to materialize. I first thought of writing it as far back as 1984 as a contribution to the ongoing debate on and the search for the most appropriate approaches to the criticism of African literature. However, pressure of work prevented me from writing the book until September 1987 when I was on sabbatical leave. By then the first drafts of four chapters had been written as three conference papers. The original drafts of the rest of the chapters were written at the University of York, England, where I was an Honorary Visiting Fellow for three months from the end of September 1987.

The impact poets make depends on the significance of what they say about social reality and on how effectively they communicate their vision to their readers. What they say about social reality depends largely on their social vision (authorial ideology) and how successfully they communicate that vision is largely a matter of the effectiveness of their stylistic stance (aesthetic ideology). The burden of this book is to explore the possible link between social vision and aesthetic stance on the one hand, and, on the other hand, between style and the ability of the poet to communicate with the reader. This entails the development of an aesthetic which can adequately account for both content and form in poetry. Within that framework it becomes possible for the critic to help readers and students of poetry understand and appreciate the forces that have shaped the content and forms of African poetry since the rise of Negritude. Consequently, one of the objectives of the book is to show some of the major trends in the development of African poetry over the last four decades.

The book is divided into four parts. Part One sets out the theory and critical apparatus on which the analysis of poetry in the rest of the book is based. These two chapters, chapter 2 in particular, are very important. The theory of Marxist stylistic criticism developed in *Art and Ideology in the African Novel* is applied to poetry in this volume. But Part One goes further by not only defining the role of the critic and the goals and limits of criticism, but also by explaining in much greater detail than its predecessor the relation between authorial ideology and aesthetic ideology on the one hand and that between aesthetic ideology and aesthetic effects on the other. In chapter 2 the book also addresses the problematic of interpretation and the relationship between the text and the reader.

In Part Two the poetry of representatives of 'the first generation' of African writers is analysed. Each one of these poets represents one of the tendencies that critics have discerned in modern African poetry. Christopher Okigbo is a representative of what has been referred to as 'Euromodernism', by which is meant the poetry of Okigbo, Wole Soyinka and John Pepper Clark and others who are believed to be influenced by the modernist trend in European and American poetry. Mazisi Kunene and Okot p'Bitek are categorized as 'traditionalists', while Okara is regarded as belonging to neither of these groups. My analysis has revealed that Okara in fact belongs squarely in the traditionalist group, which comprises those poets who incorporate material from oral traditions in their English-language poetry. There are other tendencies, and Negritude, represented here by Senghor and David Diop, is regarded as a distinct tendency in this volume. Obviously, some prominent names have been left out, including Kofi Awoonor, John Pepper Clark and Lenrie Peters.

The reason for this omission is not that they are not considered worthy of the critic's attention, but that the book only sets out to demonstrate the efficacy of the theory and method adopted and to show that Marxist criticism can help the student and reader of poetry acquire a deeper understanding and appreciation of the genre than the conventional liberal humanist approaches used by most critics of African poetry today.

Part Three deals mostly, but not exclusively, with poetry that was written in response to liberation struggles in Angola, Mozambique, Guinea Bissau, Zimbabwe and South Africa. There is one major exception, Wole Soyinka's *Ogun Abibiman*. The poem was written as a response to the dynamics of the liberation struggle in Southern Africa and I thought it appropriate that chapter 8, which analyses the poem, should take its place among those that address this major African phenomenon. Some of the poems by Musaemura Zimunya and Chenjerai Hove do not exactly relate to the war situation in Zimbabwe but were included because of what they reveal about the two Zimbabwean poets.

The first three chapters of Part Four are studies of poets who have become prominent in the 1980s and are likely to influence the future development of African poetry. It was my original intention to include in this section the poetry of Ifi Amadiume, author of *Passion Waves* (Karnak House, London, 1985), but I finally decided against her inclusion. This was because I was not quite convinced that she was a pacesetter in the same sense as the other three. However, Amadiume is a poet who deserves commendation despite the unfortunate front cover design of her book which at first gives the impression of a pornographic writer, which she is not. The last chapter of Part Four closes the book with a review of some of the major issues that arise in the study and a discussion of some new ones. The chapter is of relevance to both students of literature and budding writers. Indeed as a book which is concerned not only with the content and form of poetry but also with poetics, the entire volume is intended to help students and readers of African poetry as well as young writers who may wish to derive wisdom from the strengths and pitfalls of their elders.

Some of the poets discussed in this book have been commented on again and again by other critics and there should be no surprise that much of what is said here about them has already been said in other works. Even so, I believe the theory and critical apparatus employed in this volume will shed new light on these same authors. On the other hand, some poets are receiving serious attention for the first time. The major claim of the book is not so much that it explores virgin territory but that it provides new insights into African poetry by applying the principles of Marxist aesthetics. In the final analysis whether or not a theory is relevant to African literature or any body of literature depends on what its concepts and method reveal about particular works of art. 'By their fruits ye shall know them.' The claims of the approach adopted in this book lie in what it reveals about the social vision and aesthetics of African poets over the last forty years. Naturally, the book has in some cases managed to raise questions without providing definitive answers to them. As author I shall be satisfied if my readers are convinced that the questions are worthy of the critic's consideration.

It remains for me to express my gratitude to the University of York for granting me the status of Honorary Visiting Fellow, a status which enabled me to use the University's library and accommodation facilities while I wrote the book; and to the British Council, which generously awarded me a Senior British Council Fellowship and thereby provided the necessary financial assistance.

E. A. Ngara

PART ONE

THEORETICAL STUDIES
IN POETICS
& CRITICISM

1

The Functions
of the Critic
& the Goals of Criticism

The Functions of the Critic

In their monumental work, *Toward the Decolonization of African Literature*, the *bolekaja* ('come-down-and-let's-fight') critics have summarized the functions of the critic as follows:

1. Writing advertising jingles for publishers.
2. Exploring themes and ideas, thereby illuminating the layers of meaning beneath the surface of a given work; evaluating the work and situating it within the African literary tradition.
3. Exploring the relationships between African art, the African artist, and African society.
4. Criticism of craft for the purpose of:
   (a) nurturing talent by encouraging and discouraging tendencies among African artists;
   (b) educating the taste of the African public.[1]

Chinweizu and his colleagues should be commended for at least thinking about the functions of the critic and attempting to define them. Very often the role of the critic is taken for granted and yet the approach a critic adopts is crucial because it influences people's views about poetry, fiction and drama. All critical approaches implicitly or explicitly define the nature and functions of literature. It is therefore necessary that in this volume we spell out what is expected of the critic of poetry.

By and large the views of the *bolekaja* critics on the functions of the critic as expressed in the passage quoted above are acceptable to me. There is also a commonality of interest between their book and this volume, and if there is any book that should be recommended to all readers of African literature it is *Toward the Decolonization of African Literature*, and I find it necessary to refer to it precisely because it constitutes an important statement on African literature. However, their approach is a nationalistic one, while this book presents a Marxist and dialectical analysis.

The professional critic, namely, the critic who takes time to write books or major publications on literature, has at least three functions. The first function of any critic, liberal humanist or Marxist, is to elucidate works of art so that readers can understand and enjoy them. In developing countries there is yet another function – to help in the development of taste and of a rich literary tradition. In a world where so much is being published it becomes necessary to distinguish between wheat and chaff, between genuine art and poor literary productions. As someone who is willing to devote some time to literature, the critic, working hand in hand with the publisher, helps to weed out that which is unwanted.

For the Marxist critic there is a third and most important function. Marxism does not subscribe to the philosophy of art for art's sake, neither can it advocate an approach to criticism whose sole objective is the elucidation and enjoyment of works of art. For a Marxist critic to engage in the act of criticism is to participate in the process of liberating humanity. The Marxist critic therefore hopes to raise the reader's consciousness and to contribute towards a fuller understanding and appreciation by the public of the forms of literature and its functions in society. Progressive literature helps us to understand the world we live in: its beauty and its ugliness, its predicament as well as its potential. Good literature helps us to see more vividly the struggle between the forces of oppression and those of liberation and progress. Good Marxist criticism cannot be expected to do less. On the contrary, it is the duty of the Marxist critic to probe into the rhetoric and silences of the text so that the reader can acquire as full an appreciation of its concerns and methods as possible. By making the text more explicit in its depiction of the world around it the critic participates in the writer's task of raising social consciousness. In saying this I am by no means suggesting that the Marxist critic should act as a propagandist. A work of art that degenerates into political propaganda is alien to socialist aesthetics. Engels discouraged open didacticism in his letter to Minna Kautsky as long ago as 1885.[2] Similarly, a critic who sets out merely to indoctrinate cannot succeed as a critic. Just as a work of art moves the reader by its artistry and ideological content, so does the critic convince by the soundness of his or her judgements and revelations.

Having explained the functions of the critic we need now to look more closely into how he or she performs the central function – that of elucidating works of art. What does literary criticism entail?

Much of the work done by critics of African poetry, both African and western, is of an interpretative nature. Some of the critics seem to be concerned mainly with making students and teachers of poetry 'understand' the work of a poet. Thus Ken Goodwin's book is actually entitled *Understanding African Poetry*.[3] Much of the deconstructionist criticism that is in vogue in the West is preoccupied with interpretation. Interpretation is at the very centre of such works as *Deconstruction and Criticism*[4] by Bloom, de Man, Derrida and other leading exponents of the theory of deconstruction; and it forms the core of Christopher Butler's *Interpretation, Deconstruction and Ideology*.[5] In fact deconstruction, like structuralism before it, has generated an obsession with the interpretation of the text in literary circles. It goes without saying that interpretation is central to the study of literature, and deconstruction has undoubtedly done much to enhance our understanding of the nature of written discourse, but the critic does more than interpret the text. The critic is also a judge of effective communication and seeks to explore the soundness of the artist's assumptions about the world. It is my contention that, in order to perform his or her task satisfactorily, the critic must be in a position not only to tell us what the poet says but also to comment on the value of the poet's message and how effectively it is communicated. This is why in our scheme of things the term *critical analysis* is more appropriate than *interpretation* because critical analysis subsumes analysis, interpretation, evaluation and appreciation. A critical approach that has any claim to adequacy must include all these four elements. Focusing on interpretation alone leads to the absolutization of one element at the expense of others, equally important. It can also be argued that while critical approaches based on interpretation may be fascinating and intellectually challenging they tend to present a partial view of the nature of poetry and of how poetry functions.

It is also worth noting that there is a danger in applying the methods of disciplines such as philosophy and linguistics to the study of literature. I have explained elsewhere that, while advances in linguistics have had a salutary effect on literary criticism, there is a limit to which the methods of linguistic analysis can be applied to the study of literary texts.[6] With regard to philosophy, it goes without saying that the works of such scholars as Louis Althusser and Jacques Derrida whose academic discipline is philosophy have had a tremendous impact on literary criticism. This is partly because literature and philosophy have much in common with each other. That said, we must go on to distinguish between, on the one hand, a guiding philosophy like Marxism which illuminates the study of literature and of all social phenomena, and, on the other hand, philosophy as a discipline. As a discipline, philosophy is the kind of subject that lends itself to interpretation without appreciation; for in philosophy we are concerned with the essence of things, the whys and wherefores, and not with aesthetic considerations. The language of philosophy is necessarily referential, for in philosophy we are concerned with the relationship between signifier and signified, between sign and sense. In other words the student of philosophy is more preoccupied with what words mean than with how they convey their meaning. In literature, on the other hand, and in poetry in particular, how words say what they say is just as important as what they signify. As we shall see in the next chapter, form is no less important than content in poetry, and so the reader's appreciation of form is no less important than his or her evaluation of the content.

A true understanding of a work of art by the reader requires coming to grips with both its content and form. A work of art is not like a scientific text whose content the reader must understand literally sentence by sentence. Or, to take another example, understanding a poem is not like translating a passage written in a foreign language. Students of Latin used to pore over a text, analysing this word and that, this structure and that structure, teasing out the meaning until they could jump with joy at their discovery. Literature does not function in that way. The understanding of a poem does not only consist in an interpretation of its semantic meaning or its theme. A poem contains both a semantic and an aesthetic meaning, and to understand it is to appreciate both. This matter, which I have put rather crudely here, will be explored in greater depth in the next chapter, but it has important implications for the practice of criticism.

A critic who engages in interpretation alone gives an important but extremely partial view of a work of art. That form of criticism equates the understanding of a poem with an interpretation of its semantic meaning. Sadly, it is the form that prevails in our universities. It does a disservice to poetry because it gives students the impression that as long as they are able to tease out the meaning of a poem, identify and discuss its theme, they have done all that is expected. The approach followed in this book avoids this limited view of poetry. An exploration of authorial ideology leads us to a deeper understanding of the content of the poet's work. An examination of aesthetic ideology enables us to appreciate the dialectical relationship between content and form. By focusing on the aspect of poetic communication we are able to judge to what extent a poem has succeeded as a work of art. In this way, we hope to enable the reader or student of poetry to regard a poem as a complex whole, and to avoid the absolutization of one dimension. As a result, the student of poetry will realize that the effectiveness of a poem does not depend on the mastery of only one feature. Ours is a dialectical approach to the criticism of poetry.

The Purpose and Limits of Criticism

In helping the reader to understand and appreciate poetry, the critic cannot and need not say everything. The critic selects those crucial elements that will enable the reader to see for him- or herself the beauty or inadequacies of a poem, its major stylistic features, the ideological imperatives that shaped it, the gaps that need to be filled and so on. It goes without saying that, in a volume which seeks to treat authors rather than individual poems, the amount of attention given to each poem will partly depend on the extent to which it represents the trends and features the critic is seeking to explain. Accordingly, some of the poems analysed in this volume are treated in greater detail than others.

A work of criticism is not a scientific account of how a poem was composed and cannot contain every detail about the meaning and sound of every word, its place in the poem and its relation to every other word, the structure of every sentence, etc. By the time the critic has finished explaining every detail he or she will have bored the reader beyond reasonable limits. It seems to me that the information given to the reader by the critic should be just enough to let the former get on with the task of reflecting upon and enjoying the poet's work. This is where I am extremely suspicious of Sunday Anozie's *Structural Models and African Poetics*.[7] Anozie goes on and on *ad nauseam* talking about Senghor's little poem 'Le Totem' until even an experienced reader requires the services of a critic to summarize for him or her what the author is trying to say. There is a real danger of scientism in Anozie's structural models and as I have explained elsewhere literature is one of those subjects that cannot be reduced to a scientific analysis and remain alive.[8] T.S. Eliot was a bourgeois critic and one of the fathers of humanist criticism, but what he said in 1956 about what he called 'the frontiers of criticism' is a good warning to those inclined to follow the structuralist model or other exhaustive linguistic approaches to criticism.[9]'

The Merits of Marxism

Having explained the functions of the critic and the purpose of criticism it still remains for us to justify the philosophical basis of our method. What are the merits of Marxist criticism as opposed to, say, liberal humanist criticism or indeed *bolekaja* criticism, which is, after all, guided by an active nationalist consciousness?[10]

Does the critic who adopts a Marxist approach to African poetry not get trapped in a universalist theory which has no direct relevance to the African experience? Or, to examine the problem from a different angle, what advantage is there in abandoning the hegemony of the West inherent in the liberal humanist tradition only to embrace a philosophical approach, which, according to some champions of Afrocentricism, entails getting trapped in the hegemony of the Russians? In a review of *Art and Ideology in the African Novel* Chinweizu has charged that 'Marxist aesthetic theories have little to offer for the study of African literary style, which is why Ngara has to resort to non-Marxist stylistic criticism to evaluate the work of African novelists'.[11]

The first point to make in response to these charges is that Marxism is not a preserve of the Soviets. Indeed the greatest advance in Marxist criticism in the second half of the twentieth century has occurred, not in socialist countries, but in the West. One need only cite the impact of the works of Louis Althusser, Raymond Williams, Terry Eagleton and Fredric Jameson, to make the point. Secondly, there is no necessary contradiction between Marxism and Afrocentricism in literary criticism. While Marxism originated in Europe historically, it is a truly revolutionary theory which is well suited to the task of liberating African literature and criticism from Eurocentricism. Frantz Fanon became such an eloquent and powerful spokesperson of the oppressed black peoples of the world precisely because his analysis of the plight of 'the wretched of the earth' was based on Marxist principles.[12] Similarly, by using a materialist analysis, Walter Rodney has produced the single most impressive account to date of how the peoples and economies of Africa have been retarded and destroyed for the benefit of Europe.[13] It is the peculiar advantage of Marxism that while it has a global vision, while it seeks to encompass the entire field of humanity and to take in its stride the totality of human history, it also emphasizes the absolute necessity for the critic to analyse any literature in relation to its historical context. Consequently, a Marxist analysis of African literature cannot but emphasize the historical and social conditions which have given rise to African literature. A Marxist analysis of African literature cannot turn a blind eye to the problems attendant on Africa's encounter with Europe. There is, therefore, no sense in which a serious Marxist analysis of African literature can avoid an Africa-centred consciousness, for that would be contrary to the methods of Marxism. Marxist aesthetics does illuminate African lives, contrary to Chinweizu's claim that African writers 'find it strange that the aim of socialist art is not to illuminate African lives and conditions.'[14]

With regard to the objectives of the present book, it is appropriate to state that Marxism is a theory of ideologies and as such it is capable of analysing itself and other ideologies. Only a Marxist-inspired analysis can give us sufficient insight into the wide spectrum of ideological stances adopted by such a large number of writers as this work deals with. Marxist criticism is capable of unveiling ideology; it is capable of revealing the ideology of the text whether it is overtly or implicitly expressed. This is due, in part, to the fact that Marxism reveals the relation between the text and external reality, between authorial ideology and the dominant ideologies of the epoch. In other words, Marxism presents a dialectical analysis of literature. In this connection, Butler has correctly observed that 'It is this attempt to reveal hidden implications of the text consistent with their ideology that is crucial to much Marxist interpretation.'[15]

The burden of this book is to explore the relation between form and ideology on the one hand, and form and aesthetic effect on the other. This is by no means a simple task; it requires the application of dialectical criticism whose objective is, to quote Fredric Jameson, 'to reconcile the inner and the outer, the intrinsic and the extrinsic, the existential and the historical, to allow us to feel our way within a single determinate form or moment of history at the same time that we stand outside of it, in judgement of it as well, transcending that sterile and static opposition between formalism and a sociological or historical use of literature between which we have so often been asked to choose'.[16] Marxism enables us to do this because it requires that we interpret and evaluate literature in relation to history, that we relate the ideology of the author to historical conditions, that we cannot study the style of a work of art in isolation from the circumstances in which it is produced, that form is social experience artistically recreated, and that we regard the author not just as a product of history but also as a maker of history. This is the lesson we learn from dialectics and historical materialism, the Marxist theory of social development.

Notes

1. Chinweizu, Jemie O. and Madubuike, I., *Toward the Decolonization of African Literature*, Volume 1, Washington D.C., Howard University Press, 1983, pp. 286–287. In the Preface, Chinweizu and his colleagues explain that *bolekaja* means 'Come down let's fight'. The term indicates something of the aggressive tone and filibustering approach of the book.
2. For a full discussion on partisanship in literature see Emmanuel Ngara, *Art and Ideology in the African Novel*, London, Heinemann Educational Books, 1985, pp. 10–13.
3. K.L. Goodwin, *Understanding African Poetry*, London, Heinemann Educational Books, 1982.

The Functions of the Critic

4. Harold Bloom, de Man, P., Derrida, J., Hartman, G., Hillis Miller, J., *Deconstruction and Criticism*, New York, The Continuum Publishing Corporation, 1979 (Sixth Printing, 1987).
5. Christopher Butler, *Interpretation, Deconstruction and Ideology: An Introduction to Some Current Issues in Literary Theory*, Oxford, Clarendon Press, 1984.
6. See Ngara, op. cit., pp. 2–3.
7. Sunday O. Anozie, *Structural Models and African Poetics : Towards a Pragmatic Theory of Literature*, London, Routledge and Kegan Paul, 1981:
8. Ngara, op. cit., pp. 2–3.
9. See T.S. Eliot, *On Poetry and Poets*, London, Faber and Faber, 1957, pp. 103 ff.
10. See Chinweizu *et al.*, op. cit., p. 5.
11. See *Times Literary Supplement*, June 13, 1986, p. 663.
12. See Frantz Fanon, *The Wretched of the Earth*, Harmondsworth, Penguin, 1980.
13. See Walter Rodney, *How Europe Underdeveloped Africa*, London, Bogle-L'Ouverture Publishers, 1972.
14. *Times Literary Supplement*, June 13, 1986, p. 663.
15. See Butler, op. cit., p. 112.
16. Fredric Jameson, *Marxism and Form: Twentieth Century Dialectical Theories of Literature*, Princeton, New Jersey, Princeton University Press, 1971 (Paperback ed. 1974), pp. 330–331.

2

Ideology, Form
& Communication
in Poetry

Introduction

One of the strengths of Marxism and dialectical thinking is that the instruments of analysis, the concepts that form the framework within which our critical appreciation takes place, should themselves be subjected to analysis. In this regard the argument advanced in *Stylistic Criticism and the African Novel* is pertinent, namely, that for a theory of literary criticism to be an adequate theory it should give an account of the nature of works of art and provide the student of literature with a framework of analysis and a method of evaluation.[1] To that end stylistic criticism aims at being more systematic than conventional criticism, by which is meant liberal humanist criticism. This volume explores the relationship between ideology, form and communication in African poetry. These three are the concepts that inform our analysis in the chapters which follow. It is therefore necessary that these categories be reflected upon and defined at the outset.

Ideology

The concept of ideology is discussed in fairly great detail in *Art and Ideology in the African Novel*, particularly in chapters 3, 5 and 11.[2] It is therefore not necessary to go over the same ground but some key issues will be clarified here. The following definition of ideology will serve as a starting point:

Ideology, Form & Communication

Ideology refers to that aspect of the human condition under which people operate as conscious actors. Ideology is the medium through which human consciousness works. Our conception of religion, politics, morality, art and science is deeply influenced by our ideology. In other words, what we see and believe largely depends on our ideology, ideology being the medium through which we comprehend and interpret reality. Reality itself exists objectively outside our consciousness and independently of any particular individual, but how one sees and interprets it depends in part on one's level of ideological development.[3]

Proceeding from the concept of ideology as the medium through which human consciousness operates, we shall single out three categories of ideology which are crucial in the criticism of African literature: the dominant ideology or ideologies, authorial ideology and aesthetic ideology. By the dominant ideology of an epoch we mean the beliefs, assumptions and set of values that inform the thoughts and actions of a people in a particular era. Following Louis Althusser we shall note that the ideology of a ruling class is projected through ideological state apparatuses (ISAs) such as the religious ISA, the educational ISA, the political ISA and the cultural ISA, which includes literature and the arts.[4] In colonial Africa the dominant colonial ideology, which was bourgeois, was projected through the various ISAs, principally the educational, the religious and the cultural ISAs. This has an important bearing on African poetry as most of the poets discussed in this book were subjected to the heavy influence of the various colonial ideological state apparatuses.

Before we end our discussion of the dominant ideology it is appropriate to make the point that in class society the dominant ideologies such·as those of colonial rulers will inevitably be threatened by oppositional or competing ideologies such as nationalism. This is of special relevance to the task of this book, as much African poetry derived its sustenance and energy from a tension that was the result of the conflict between the interests of colonial rule and capitalist exploitation on the one hand and the pressures and ideological imperatives of nationalism on the other.

In a situation such as the one depicted above where conflicting ideologies are symptomatic of a class struggle, a writer will project an ideological stance which may or may not be homologous with one or the other opposing ideology. As part of the African petty bourgeoisie and of an oppressed race, most writers wrote from a nationalist standpoint, but, as is the case in any such situation, the ideological stance of each writer will in part depend on his or her level of political consciousness. A poet may adopt a moderate or radical nationalist standpoint or even display symptoms of what has been called 'the colonial mentality'. Whatever stance the writer takes constitutes his or her authorial ideology. Now authorial ideology is what determines the poet's perception of reality. Whether or not a poet presents an accurate analysis of social reality, whether or not a poet presents a view of society characterized by false consciousness, depends largely on authorial ideology.

Aesthetic ideology refers to the literary convention and stylistic stances adopted by the writer. Thus Romanticism, modernism, realism and socialist realism are aesthetic ideologies. There are, however, some aesthetic ideologies which are not describable in terms of literary movements like Romanticism or realism. These operate more or less at a personal level, as in the case of Achebe, to whom the incorporation of Igbo cultural elements is an important principle of artistic creation. Thus while operating within the broad convention of realism Achebe adds this other dimension to his aesthetic ideology and to the ideology of the social class to which he belongs. It is an expression of the author's nationalism, which is in the same breath a criticism of colonial cultural domination. Aesthetic ideology can therefore be seen to have several layers. A poet may operate within the broad parameters of a literary movement such as Romanticism which cuts across various literary conventions like the sonnet form, the lyric and the ballad, and as a result of certain ideological imperatives adopt a method of composition which contradicts the normal rules of Romanticism or the sonnet convention.

The question that arises here is whether aesthetic ideology is consciously formulated. Does the writer deliberately use a style with features characteristic of Romanticism, realism, modernism or socialist realism? In other words, are the distinctive features of Romantic poetry consciously engineered by the individual poet, or does authorial ideology give rise to certain stylistic features whether the writer is conscious of these features or not? This question is one that can only be answered after a close examination of the styles of a wide variety of authors who profess different ideologies. It is a question we shall return to in the concluding section of the book.

Form

In *Stylistic Criticism and the African Novel* I found it necessary to make a distinction between the concepts 'form' and 'mode'. I described mode as the 'genre' of a work of art, such as the novel, the short story and poetry. I explained that at a more specific level poems can be sub-categorized into, for instance, epic poems, lyrics, ballads, praise poems and sonnets. Each of these modes to some extent determines the linguistic structure of any particular poem. For example, lyrics are written in the eternal present tense while epics are constructed upon certain conventions which are not normally found in ballads, sonnets or lyrics. 'Mode' therefore refers to the external structure of a poem, which usually affects the internal structure. 'Form' on the other hand has a more general application, referring to both the external and the internal structure. In this regard the use of images, symbols, allusions, peculiar idioms and other poetic devices such as repetition and parallelism are part of the internal structure of a poem, part of its 'form'.

For our purpose in this volume the distinction that is being made between the concepts of 'mode' and 'form' is partly for convenience and partly as an indication that our main focus will be primarily, though not exclusively, on the formal elements of African poetry and not on its modal characteristics. Our emphasis will therefore be on elements of style and on any innovations that are seen to have a direct or indirect relationship to authorial ideology and the author's class ideology.

It is appropriate at this juncture to point out that, while writers are relatively speaking independent of history, form is socially conditioned. Styles arise as a result of historical and social factors. If there is anything that *Stylistic Criticism and the African Novel* has demonstrated it is that the styles of such writers as Achebe and Okara are products of a particular historical moment. As a member of the African intelligentsia brought up and educated in Nigeria in the 1940s and 1950s Chinua Achebe could not avoid using English as a medium of artistic expression. On the other hand, he started writing at a time when the winds of change were blowing across Africa; when nationalistic sentiments were in the air among the progressive members of the African intelligentsia. Hence the inclination to incorporate African cultural elements into English-language novels, such as the use of Igbo proverbs and modes of expression in *Things Fall Apart* and *Arrow of God*. Many of the poets analysed in this volume wrote at the same time as Achebe and are likely to share the novelist's nationalistic sentiments. We can therefore expect that the styles of at least some of these poets will be marked by the use of traditional cultural elements and oral forms. Such aesthetic ideologies are an expression of class struggle. They are an instance of the ideological struggle between the African nationalist petty bourgeoisie and the colonial bourgeoisie. At the same time such poets as Okara, Musaemura Zimunya and Leopold Senghor are obviously using the free verse mode which was developed by western poets, although at times modified by forms found in African orature. There is therefore a love–hate relationship between European and African cultural and literary elements in the works of these poets and the so-called 'conflict of cultures' becomes a source of strength for the African poet. By the time we come to the liberation poetry of Mozambique, Angola and South Africa, there is a shift in ideological orientation among some of the authors; there is a new and radical social vision which goes beyond nationalism, and this may be reflected in the style of these poets.

Be that as it may the point must be made that, just as the authorial ideology of one writer is not necessarily identical to that of another writing in similar circumstances, so also are aesthetic ideologies different. While form is determined by social and historical conditions, differences in ideological orientation, perception and creative talent will give rise to different styles among writers of the same generation.

Discussion of form necessarily leads to consideration of the relationship between form and content. The question arises then as to what is meant by content. In liberal humanist criticism content is understood to be the subject matter and/or theme, in other words the *what* of the poem as opposed to the *how*. In dialectical criticism content cannot be restricted to considerations of theme and subject matter only – it includes these as well as the historical conditions which give rise to the poem and also to the ideological dimension. We can, for instance, talk about the ideological content of a poem. The subject matter of a poem and its ideological content cannot be separated from the social and economic conditions under which it is created. Although works of art have an autonomous existence and the writer enjoys relative independence from history, all works of art have a more or less direct relationship with historical developments. By content therefore we refer to a complex interaction of historical and social factors, subject matter, theme, ideas and the ideological element. In dialectical criticism there is no simple separation of content and form. A perfect work of art is a synthesis of content and form in dialectical interaction. It is for this reason that I have sought to explain the various elements of fiction in the following terms:

> We abstract in order to comprehend the object of discussion fully, in order to be able to talk about it. It is therefore convenient and useful to talk about content and form in art; it is also convenient and useful, albeit justifiable, to talk about content, character, narrative structure and linguistic format. *In fact the content is only definable in terms of the artistic creation as a whole,* in terms of the total aesthetic effect of the work of art, an effect that is the result of a dynamic and complex interaction of events, people, ideas and words.[5]

This formulation was made with special reference to fiction but it will serve the purpose of explaining the point I am making about the unity of content and form.

Communication and Interpretation

In our discussion of the aspect of communication in poetry we should keep in mind the fact that like any language act, a work of art is a communicative utterance produced by the author and received by the reader (or hearer if the poem is read aloud). But a poem is not like everyday speech in that it is patterned in order to give its communicative effect a greater impact than everyday language. As a unity of content and form poetry appeals to the reader or listener by the weight of what it says (content) and how it says it (form). If content is a complex interaction of historical and social factors, subject matter, theme, ideas and the ideological element, then form or the aesthetic dimension can be defined as that dimension of a poem which includes the mode, the linguistic structure, imagery, symbolism, tone, rhythmic patterns and sound devices. The impact of a poem on the reader comes from the totality of the poem, from the weight of its message combined with its emotional, intellectual and imaginative appeal. In the final analysis, however, the aesthetic component, or, to put it in the language of stylistic criticism, the linguistic format, is the determining factor in influencing its reception by the reader or hearer. Let me reiterate that the impact of a poem partly depends on the weight of its message. However, a poem on a weighty subject which is badly written may be less effective than a well-written poem on a more mundane subject.

This explanation serves to emphasize the fact that artistic communication takes place primarily in and through the aesthetic dimension, the linguistic format. Whether or not a poem is going to communicate effectively with the reader is determined largely by the poet's craft, i.e. by his or her handling of mode, linguistic structures, imagery, rhythm and sound devices.

Para-linguistic affective devices such as myth, allusion and irony can be extremely effective instruments of communication, and we shall see that some African poets use myth extensively as a communicative device. The degree to which the poet is master of form comes out in how effectively he or she is able to communicate with the reader. Art which fails to communicate, however important its content, is not good art because by its very nature art must be able to speak naturally to the beholder, hearer or reader. It must have an appeal or else it is not art. A piece of sculpture or a beautifully woven Ethiopian basket speaks for itself. The beholder sees it and is immediately struck by its beauty. A melodious song announces itself – one does not have to be told that it is a melodious song. Similarly good poetry should appeal to the reader. Poetry that is so difficult that the reader tries but gives up the effort to understand it, or so simple and flat that it makes no impression on one or bores one stiff is not good poetry.

I must hasten to clarify one point here. The fact that a poet is obscure does not necessarily mean that he or she cannot communicate. There are poems in which the meaning is obscure but the aesthetic dimension so powerful that the reader feels the aesthetic appeal in the same way that one can be attracted by the melody and rhythm of a song without a full understanding of the meaning. This was one of the achievements of T.S. Eliot. His poetry is obscure but highly effective in its ability to make an impression on the reader. His influence on some African poets is an indication of his ability to communicate.

We have so far emphasized the point that the onus to communicate with the reader is on the poet and the poem. This should not be understood to mean that the reader is a passive receptacle into which form and content are poured and 'deposited' like money in a bank. In reality, the poet and the reader are engaged in a discourse. Using the metaphor of the communicative utterance we can say that the poet produces the utterance, the reader receives, interprets and transmutes the utterance, and is affected by it as a consequence of both what comes from the poem and what the reader makes of that which is given.

Here we come to two crucial principles regarding the interpretation, appreciation and evaluation of literary texts. The first principle is that a poem is not a self-explanatory mathematical proposition. The proposition that $2 + 2 = 4$ is obvious to anybody who has any notion of arithmetic. All that one needs to confirm the validity of the proposition is to know the value of 2, the meaning of the addition sign and the value of the resultant answer. But poetry does not work in this simple and logical manner. The understanding of poetry requires an understanding and appreciation of historical and social conditions, ideological factors, literary forms and devices and, of course, a sufficient mastery of the language in which the poetry is written. The second principle is that the meaning of a poem does not necessarily correspond exactly to what the author intended to say. In the process of creating a poem a dialectical process goes on between meaning and form. The author intends to say something but he or she is also concerned with sound, imaginative, emotional or intellectual appeal, its forcefulness and so on. The poet will find it necessary to modify the poem, to change a word here, a structure there, or the order of lines . . . In the process, the poet is altering the meaning to a greater or lesser extent. We can therefore see that in the creative process there is a tension between content and form, between the *what* and the *how*. The success of a poem partly depends on the resolution of that tension. However, the point being made here is that because of this process the poet cannot claim that the finished product means exactly what he or she originally intended to say. Sometimes the poem ends up conveying quite a different meaning from that originally intended by the creator. The end result of this is that the poet cannot claim to have the final word on the interpretation of a poem. The critic can have a different and equally valid interpretation. The poem enjoys relative independence from its creator.

In the process of reading, the reader and the text also enter into a dialectical relationship. There is no one-sided cause and effect relationship. The text bares itself to the reader, exposes its multiple layers of meaning and aesthetic effects and the reader responds by not only receiving what the text offers but also by injecting into it something of his or her perceptiveness, ideological insights and sensitivity. The reader and the text enter into a relationship similar to that of a man and woman making love.

Interpretation leads to the problem of the theory of language in relation to poetry. Harold Bloom sees two valid ways of conceiving language in poetry. These two are what he calls linguistic nihilism or 'an absolute randomness of language' on the one hand, and on the other hand 'the Kabbalistic magical absolute in which language is totally over-determined'[6]. We might refer to these two extremes as the tyranny of language and the bird in a cage theory of language respectively. Critics who subscribe to the theory of the tyranny of language, such as the deconstructionists, see language or words as completely indeterminate and incapable of being interpreted. According to this theory words slip between the reader's fingers like water. According to the opposite theory words have definite meanings. They can be reduced to mathematical formulae like $2 + 2 = 4$, or held captive, like birds in a cage.

Consider, for instance, the meaning of the word 'boy' in the opening lines of Chenjerai Hove's poem, 'A Boy':

When brother will you be?
How will you be?
For you are not yet.
A 'boy' you are called
by milk-plastered lips
and you undo your hat
to bare that musty dome.
Yet a 'boy' you remain.[7]

Following the bird in a cage theory of language we can say that the word 'boy' in this poem literally means 'a young male human being', for that is the technical meaning of the word. But we know that in poetry words work by suggestion and acquire meanings in relation to other words. Consequently when used in poetry and other forms of discourse words cannot be reduced to technical explanations as in linguistics. Thus in the context of Hove's poem the word 'boy' assumes a wider meaning than its technical one. The word shows something of white Rhodesians' attitude to Africans before Zimbabwe was liberated – the attitude that Africans are immature, inferior beings. At the same time this attitude is being subjected to satirical commentary. The tenor of discourse suggests that the protagonist is attacking the racist mentality of white Rhodesians.

My position as a critic is that the two opposing theories – the tyranny of language theory and the bird in a cage theory – are both extremes that contradict the Marxist view of the world. The one advocates chaos while the other spells complete absence of flexibility and inability to attain freedom. Between these two extremes is a theory that advocates freedom with order. True, words are not imprisoned like birds in a cage, but their freedom has limits just as human freedom has limits; their freedom is controlled in the same way as moving things are controlled by the law of gravity. Words define and restrict each other's meaning by the manner in which they relate to each other. While polysemy is an undeniable feature of words and language, and while the privilege of poetic licence exists, a poet who shows complete defiance of the laws governing relations between words lapses, not so much into endless meanings, as into meaninglessness. Thus the utterance: 'Colourless red thoughts walked the car' is meaningless.

A poet can go too far in attempting to juxtapose words and ideas that do not go together. This also has implications for translation from one language into another. Transliterating the idioms of one language into another can be an exciting and worthwhile exercise, as in Gabriel Okara's novel *The Voice*, in which Ijaw idioms and modes of expression are incorporated into the English narrative.[8] However, at times it can hinder effective communication, as we shall see in our analysis of the poetry of Mazisi Kunene, Okot p'Bitek and Chenjerai Hove.

What we are driving at is that, provided his or her usage conforms reasonably to the rules of language, the works of a poet will have a common core of meaning for readers belonging to different epochs and different ideological persuasions. The value of the insights that the critic brings to the reading of a poem will, however, depend on other factors, namely, the usefulness of the theory the critic employs and his or her own talent and sensibility as a literary critic.

In this context, it is useful to consider Tony Bennet's claim that 'value is not something which the text has or possesses. It is not an attribute of the text; it is rather something which is produced for the text'.[9] The difficulty with this position is that, taken to its logical conclusion, it suggests that the text has no value outside what the reader or critic brings to it, so that we cannot distinguish between good works of art and poor ones, and that there are no texts of lasting value, no classics appealing to readers of different historical epochs and ideological persuasions. I am perhaps putting Bennet's position too crudely here, but the comment quoted above should be seen in the context of Bennet's idea, borrowed from Pierre Macherey, that 'the concept of the *text* must be replaced by the concept of the concrete and varying, historically specific *functions* and *effects* which accrue to "the text" as a result of the different determinations to which it is subjected during the history of its appropriation'.[10] While I agree that a materialist theory of literature sees different ideologies and social formations giving rise to different perceptions and even interpretations of the same text, I cannot accept Bennet's extreme view. I must argue that, examined from whatever ideological position under whatever social formation, the gospels of Luke, Matthew, Mark and John will always maintain their differences in the accounts they give of the life of Jesus Christ. Indeed, though the interpretation of Frei Betto,[11] a twentieth-century radical theologian, will differ significantly from that of St Augustine, because their reading of the four texts takes place under very different social conditions and is guided by radically different ideological factors, to both St Augustine and Frei Betto each of the four gospels presents a unique account of Christ's life and teaching. This is because the texts have always been and will always be different. There is therefore a common core in the literary text which stands the vicissitudes of time, history and ideology.

Notes

1. Emmanuel Ngara, *Stylistic Criticism and the African Novel*, London, Heinemann Educational Books, 1982, p. 14.
2. Emmanuel Ngara, *Art and Ideology in the African Novel*, London, Heinemann Educational Books, 1985.
3. F. Chung and E. Ngara, *Socialism, Education and Development: A Challenge to Zimbabwe*, Harare, Zimbabwe Publishing House, 1985, p. 28.
4. Louis Althusser, *Lenin and Philosophy and Other Essays*, New York and London, Monthly Review Press, 1971, p. 143.
5. See Ngara, *Stylistic Criticism and the African Novel*, pp. 28-29. The italics are mine.
6. See Harold Bloom, de Man, P., Derrida, J., Hartman, G., Hillis Miller, J., *Deconstruction and Criticism*, New York, The Continuum Publishing Corporation, 1979 (Sixth Printing, 1987), p. 4.
7. Chenjerai Hove, *Up in Arms*, Harare, Zimbabwe Publishing House, 1982, p. 23.
8. See Ngara, *Stylistic Criticism and the African Novel*, Chapter 4.
9. T. Bennet, *Formalism and Marxism*, London and New York, Methuen, 1979, p. 173.
10. Ibid., p. 148.
11. Frei Betto is a revolutionary Brazilian priest and author of many books, probably now best known as author of *Fidel and Religion: Conversations with Frei Betto*, Sydney, Pathfinder Press/Pacific and Asia, 1986.

PART TWO

CONTRASTING RESPONSES TO COLONIALISM – FROM NEGRITUDE TO KUNENE

3

Idealism
& Realism
in Negritude

The Two Schools of Negritude

Any discussion of the ideology of African writers in the 1950s and 1960s presupposes an understanding of the psychology of colonized peoples and how it relates to the psychology of the colonizers. Any analysis of Negritude as an ideology presupposes some familiarity with the policy of assimilation that was practised by two major European powers in the heyday of colonialism, namely, France and Portugal. In terms of the policy of assimilation members of the black intellectual elite who rejected their African identity could be accorded the status of French or Portuguese citizens. In French territories assimilated Africans were expected to speak French, to think French, to look French in dress, to behave like French people – in short, to be French in everything but colour. It was not enough to accept colonial rule; it was necessary to imbibe and live colonial ideology. But colonial ideology did not go unchallenged. Sooner or later French and Portuguese colonial ideology came face to face with African nationalism. In French Africa members of the African intelligentsia came up with the philosophy of Negritude, a term that was coined by the Caribbean writer and politician, Aimé Césaire, author of *Return to My Native Land*,[1] but which came to be most closely associated with Léopold Senghor of Senegal. Negritude asserted African values and sought to stand French colonial ideology on its head. Negritude is therefore a very appropriate starting point in any analysis of the cultural and literary response of the African to European colonialism.

In this chapter we shall endeavour to make a comparative study of two major African exponents of the movement – Léopold Senghor and

Idealism & Realism in Negritude

David Diop. The burden of the chapter is not only to explore the relationship between authorial ideology and aesthetic ideology in Negritude poetry, but also to demonstrate that by analysing the works of these two poets we can show that Negritude was not a monolithic movement, contrary to the assumptions of many a literary critic. There were in fact two movements, the idealist and the realist school of Negritude. True, the difference between the two is not absolute and can be explained in terms of tendencies, but it is a significant difference and cannot be ignored in a serious study of authorial ideology.

The Idealist School of Negritude – Léopold Senghor

A movement that emerged at the dawn of a new era in the history of black people in Africa and abroad, Negritude will always remain one of the most significant literary movements to have arisen in Africa. As a protest movement, Negritude was a product of concrete historical factors. Kinfe Abraham has explained the rise of black protest literature most forcefully, pointing out that, whether for the individual or society at large, awareness begins with history:

> The black protest writer thus dwells on his past partly because of an attempt to escape contempt due to the long history which has demeaned his person and belittled his culture. But it is also partly because of a strong desire to negate the pernicious propaganda and non-truths which have haunted him over the years. In writing about his past, therefore, the black writer has the twin tasks of responding as the insulted party and of explaining as the spokesman of his own past and present.[2]

In outlining the laws of literary development David Craig suggests the following, among others:

1. The rise of a literary genre is likely to occur with the rise of a class (Law I).
2. The emergence of such a new genre is likely to take place at a time of social upheaval and rapid change (Law 4).[3]

In my account of the rise and development of modern African literature I have explained that the class that was emerging was the African intelligentsia, the product of colonial missionary education. I have also pointed out that the time of social upheaval was the time of agitation for independence.[4] But the period 1957–1967 was not only a decade of intense political activity, but was also a decade of lively artistic creativity. The mission-educated intellectuals, who were at one time so effectively colonized that they worshipped at the altar of colonial languages and culture and despised their own languages and African identity, were also destined to be the champions of mental decolonization at the time of Africa's re-awakening from the deep sleep of colonial domination. It was the bourgeois intellectual elite, the intelligentsia, which came out with such philosophies as Negritude and the African personality. Negritude is thus a product of a critical historical moment in Africa, and marks an important development in the political consciousness of the French African intelligentsia. It marks that high point of African political awareness when, after years of colonization and self-abnegation, the African elite was pleasantly surprised to realize that Africans had something to be proud of after all – that they need not be ashamed of their race and colour as Europeans had led them to believe. In other words the African intelligentsia was beginning to question the dominant colonial ideology and to use literature to attack it.

But Negritude was not only an African phenomenon; it was also the rallying cry of the black intelligentsia of the African diaspora, particularly in the Caribbean. Much of the poetry was therefore preoccupied with the problem of colour: the beauty of the Negro race, the courage of black people, the warmth and humanity of the black race and so on and so forth. It became the philosophy of a race rather than simply an African literary movement. As Frantz Fanon puts it:

> The Negro, never so much a Negro as since he has been dominated by the whites, when he decides to prove that he has a culture and to behave like a cultured person, comes to realize that history points out a well-defined path to him: he must demonstrate that a Negro culture exists.[5]

As an extremist response to an extremist situation, a nationalist reaction to the distortions of European cultural imperialism, Negritude was in danger of lapsing into romantic idealism. This is true of the writer whose name has become synonymous with the movement – Léopold Sédar Senghor. One of the most well-known African poets, Senghor praises the virtues of the African race in the most magnificent and lavish terms, just as he levels criticism at Europeans for their inhuman treatment of Africans and their lack of those qualities which make black people fully human and natural. In 'Murders' he sings songs of praise to statues of Senegalese gods who have been 'captured' and made prisoners in France. These statues, which symbolize the black race, are 'the flower of the foremost beauty' in a world deprived of beauty. They are the very womb of humanity, the origin of human life, the life principle itself, which is victor over fire and thunder:

> In vain they have chopped down your laughter, and the darker flower of
> your flesh
> You are the flower of the foremost beauty in stark absence of flowers
> Black flower and solemn smile, diamond time out of mind
> You are the day and the plasma of the word's virid spring
> Flesh you are of the first couple, the fertile belly, milk and sperm
> You are the sacred fecundity of the bright paradise gardens
> And the incoercible forest, victor over fire and thunder.[6]

In 'Prayer to Masks' Senghor sees the African race as 'the leaven that the white flour needs'. The Negro race is seen as bringing life to a world that has fallen victim to the evils of technology. It is the African who is to teach white people rhythm, joy and a natural way of life:

> For who else would teach rhythm to the world that has died of machines and cannons?
> For who else would ejaculate the cry of joy, that arouses the dead and the wise in a new dawn?
> Say, who else could return the memory of life to men with a torn hope?
> They call us cotton heads, and coffee men, and oily men,
> They call us men of death
> But we are the men of the dance whose feet only gain power when they beat the hard soil.[7]

In this we see not only a conservatism which leads the author to a romantic Rousseauesque rejection of modernity and an escape to an idyllic pre-rational past, but also a suggestion that the African as a race is endowed with certain psycho-physiological qualities lacking in other races. These qualities include the suppleness of body characteristic of the Negro, that flexibility of body and harmony of the psychic and the physiological which give the African coordination, of 'thought linked to act, ear to heart, sign to sense'. In words and rhythms that admirably reflect the content, Senghor urges white New York to let black blood flow into her blood:

> New York! I say to you: New York let black blood flow into your own blood
> That it may rub the rust from your steel joints, like an oil of life,
> That it may give to your bridges the bend of buttocks and the suppleness of creepers.
> Now return the most ancient times, the unity recovered,
> the reconciliation of the Lion the Bull and the Tree
> Thought linked to act, ear to heart, sign to sense.[8]

The white people of New York are portrayed as cold, lifeless, heartless and devoid of human feelings. Their lack of feeling is matched by their physiological inflexibility – hence they have buttocks and joints that are as rigid as bridges. This inflexibility is contrasted with the suppleness and liveliness of black people who dwell in another part of New York – Harlem:

> Harlem Harlem! Now I saw Harlem! A green breeze of corn springs up from the pavements ploughed by the naked feet of dancers
> Bottoms waves of silk and sword-blade breasts, water-lily ballets and fabulous masks. . .
>
> Listen New York! Oh listen to your male voice of brass vibrating with oboes, the anguish checked with tears falling in great clots of blood
>
> Listen to the distant beating of your nocturnal heart, rhythm and blood of the tom-tom, tom-tom blood and tom-tom.[9]

The characteristics of black people as presented by Senghor are that they are full of life, coupled with a warmth of heart that makes them fully human. They dance flexibly and gracefully because their psychology, physiology and movements are perfectly coordinated. The psychology and physiology of the black race thus represent the ideal state, whereby all creatures are able to live in peace with one another, as symbolized by 'the reconciliation of the Lion, the Bull and the Tree'.

This is a philosophy based on race, which claims that a certain race will for ever possess qualities which will make it superior; a philosophy that is both subjective and idealistic. It is the same philosophy that informs the theme of Bernard Dadie's poem 'I Thank You God', a simple but rich poem, full of subtle irony, but which nevertheless proclaims in typically subjective terms:

I thank you God for creating me black
White is a colour for special occasions
Black the colour for everyday
And I have carried the World since the dawn of time
And my laugh over the World, through the night, creates the day
I thank you God for creating me black.[10]

Abraham quite rightly defends Negritude on ideological grounds[11] but what he does not seem to see is that, in the form in which it was propounded by the Senghorian or subjective school, Negritude is an ideology of the intellectual elite. While it portrays the general political consciousness of the African people at a given historical moment it more than anything else reflects the ideology of a class that had fallen victim to acculturation and was only beginning to accept what the African masses had never rejected.

Some of this poetry consists of romantic and abstract philosophizing which bears no direct relation to economic realities. The Senghorian school of Negritude is concerned with the cultural, psychic and physiological aspects of the African and does not take into account historical conditions and levels of economic development which shape human behaviour. It takes no account of the influence of the means of production and social relations on human behaviour and culture. Black people are for ever humane, endowed with feelings, and closer to humanity than white people, who are given to cold intellectualizing. This view of humanity does not leave room for the possibility of a class of black people arising to oppress other blacks in the same manner as white people have oppressed blacks. To that extent the Senghorian school of Negritude does not accurately reflect the real conditions of existence of black people; it exaggerates and falsifies particular qualities of the Negro race to present a distorted picture in much the same way as the European has exaggerated the negative aspects of the African and consequently distorted African history.

The Realist School of Negritude – David Diop

Within the Negritude movement there is another voice which, while subscribing to the basic tenets of the movement, nevertheless sees the plight of black people from a somewhat different angle. In French-speaking Africa this voice is represented by David Diop. In Portuguese-speaking Africa those poets who wrote before the armed liberation struggle was launched are, in ideological terms, part of the Negritude tradition – poets like Agostinho Neto, Viriato da Cruz, Mindelense and Noémia de Sousa. In the works of these poets the theory that the black race possesses certain genetic qualities which make it superior to other races is no longer propounded. What is emphasized is a historical and objective fact: that black people have suffered at the hands of white people; that the African has been made the object of history and has now renounced that role; that he has become the subject of history by resisting white domination and asserting his humanity. In the works of these poets Africa and black people are presented in terms of the experiences they have had, the suffering they have endured and the new form of social consciousness they have acquired – a new awareness that they can and should make history. And, unlike the poets belonging to the school of subjective idealism, this group of writers is very much concerned about depicting the struggles of black people in concrete terms as opposed to abstract theorizing about their race. Viriato da Cruz's poem, 'Black Mother', opens with a forceful assertion of the materiality of the African experience:

Your presence, mother, is the living drama of a race
drama of flesh and blood
which life has written with the pen of centuries.

It ends with a proclamation of the new vision which arises from a new social psychology:

Through your eyes, mother
I see oceans of grief
lit by the setting sun, landscapes,
violet landscapes
dramas of Cain and Japheth
But I see as well (oh if I see –)
I see as well how the light robbed from your eyes now glows
demoniacal temptress – like Certainty
glittering steadily – like Hope in us,
your other sons making, forming, announcing
the day of humanity
THE DAY OF HUMANITY.[12]

Noémia de Sousa's poetry retains certain features of the school of subjective idealism: notions such as the mystification of Africa, the land of magic drums and rhythmic dances; and even an acceptance of the European view of Africa as a savage and primitive continent:

> Mother! my mother Africa
> of slave songs in the moonlight
> I cannot, CANNOT deny
> the black, the savage blood
> you gave me
> Because deep in me
> it is strongest of all
> in my soul, in my veins
> I live, I laugh, I endure
> through it
> MOTHER![13]

In 'Attention' Mindelense looks at the plight of black people from a historical point of view. He portrays the violence with which Europeans treated black people: he still hears the whips that cracked and sees the blood that was shed as whites drove blacks into slavery:

> I have heard of blood that ran in torrents
> And of the whip that cracked a thousand times,
> of the white man who stood guard on the slaves,
> sparks in his eyes and thunder in his voice.[14]

In Agostinho Neto's 'The Blood and the Seed' the suffering, the torture, the pain, symbolized by images of bleeding, grief and cries, become a source of hope symbolized by the seed and various images of growth:

> Our cries
> are drums heralding desire
> in the tumultuous voices, music of nations,
> our cries are hymns of love that hearts
> might flourish on the earth like seeds in the sun
> the cries of Africa
> cries of morning when the dead grew from the seas
> chained
> the blood and the seed[15]

This ·is the school to which David Diop belongs. He is indeed a Negritude poet but one whose vision is characterized by revolutionary nationalism and realism as opposed to subjective idealism. His poetry throbs with the rhythms of Africa characteristic of Negritude poetry; the colour black is celebrated while white is denigrated as the colour of the oppressor. The physical features and warmth of the Negro woman are adored and lauded as in 'Rama Kam' and 'To a Black Dancer'. In the latter poem the idealism of the Senghorian school of Negritude is quite evident. This can be demonstrated by quoting the last eight lines of the poem where philosophical abstractions reign supreme at the expense of concrete ideas:

You are dance
And the false gods burn beneath your vertical flame
You are the face of the initiate
Sacrificing folly beside the Guardian Tree
You are the idea of the All and the voice of the Ancient.
Gravely launched to attack chimeras
You are the Word that explodes
In miraculous spray on the shores of oblivion.[16]

While there is clear evidence of idealism in this and other poems, there is, on the other hand, no assertion of the superiority of the black race, and the African past is neither romanticized nor proffered as the ideal to return to. What is highlighted is the violence and oppression to which blacks have been subjected by Europeans, the struggle of Africans against white domination and their determination to emerge victorious at the end of the struggle. In 'Suffer Poor Negro', one of his early poems, we are presented with the basic facts of the Negro's physical suffering, exploitation and deprivation of the basic necessities of life. The whip 'Whistles on [his] back of sweat and blood'. The day is long 'So long for carrying the white ivory of the White Your Master'. His children are hungry and his hut is bare of his wife, who is 'sleeping on the seignorial couch'. In 'Listen Comrades' the agony and outcry of the black race through centuries of oppression is seen as a symbol of a new hope:

Listen comrades of incendiary centuries
To the flaming black outcry from Africa to the Americas
It is the sign of dawn
The fraternal sign that will come and feed the dreams of men.[17]

In 'Africa' three images of the continent of Africa are given: First, the 'Africa of proud warriors in ancestral savannas', the Africa of which the poet's grandmother sings; secondly, the humiliated Africa which has been subjected to slavery and colonial exploitation; and lastly, a new Africa which is to emerge after a bitter and protracted struggle. The whole poem is quoted here to show the contrasting images presented by the poet:

to my Mother

Africa my Africa
Africa of proud warriors in ancestral savannas
Africa of which my grandmother sings
Beside her faraway river
I never knew you
But my gaze is full of your blood
Your beautiful black blood spilt in the fields
The blood of your sweat
The sweat of your toil
The toil of slavery

The slavery of your children
Africa tell me Africa
Can this be you the back that bends
And lies flat beneath the weight of humility
This trembling red-striped back
Saying yes to the whip along the roads of noon
Then a voice answered me gravely
Impetuous son the young and hardy tree
You see there
Splendidly alone among white and faded flowers
Is Africa your Africa growing again
Growing again patiently stubbornly
With fruits that take on little by little
The bitter taste of freedom.[18]

It is important to note here that, although the poem is a kind of ode to Africa extolling the virtues of the continent in an exalted lyrical manner, it is a poem that has a more or less direct relationship with objective facts relating to the history of Africa, a continent that has had its heroes, that has gone through periods of slavery and colonization and is now seen struggling to acquire freedom. It is significant that the protagonist rejects not only the enslavement and subjugation of Africa, but also a return to the Africa of old. He starts by yearning for the Africa of proud warriors in ancestral savannas, the Africa of which his grandmother sings beside her faraway river, but the voice which answers him informs him that he does not belong to the African past. He should instead identify with a new Africa that is emerging:

Impetuous son the young and hardy tree
You see there
Splendidly alone among white and faded flowers
Is Africa your Africa growing again
Growing again patiently stubbornly
With fruits that take on little by little
The bitter taste of freedom.

Optimism is a dominant feature of Diop's poetry; however, this is not simplistic or over-insistent optimism, but a very realistic presentation of the African struggle. As the 'white and faded flowers' of colonialism wither Africa grows again. She does not receive her freedom and independence on a platter, but the poet sees her

Growing again patiently stubbornly
With fruits that take on little by little
The bitter taste of freedom.

Thus David Diop's poetry is not based on subjective philosophical abstractions, but comes out of the real conditions of human existence, out of conflicts and struggles that have a historical basis and out of what man and woman can actually do. Diop rejects a metaphysical approach to poetic composition. In 'The True Road' he rejects any Platonic conception of poetry in favour of poetry based on real life – the worker's labour, a woman's sensuousness, the love of engaged couples and so on:

> Truth beauty love are
> The worker smashing the deadly calm of their parlors
> The woman passing by sensual and serious
> The kiss that crosses the frontiers of reckoning
> And flowers of engaged couples and child in loved arms
> Everything they have lost brothers
> And that we together will unfold on the highway of the world.[19]

Conclusion – Negritude and Aesthetic Ideology

In conclusion, there are two major observations that can be made from this brief analysis of Negritude poetry. The first is that the idealist school tends towards a subjective and mystical interpretation of the African condition, while the realist school presents a revolutionary analysis of African history and the African predicament. It may be noted in this connection that, while Senghor tends to be preoccupied with cultural and philosophical issues, David Diop's poetry is concerned with history and has a very strong political content.

The second observation is that as a literary movement Negritude was remarkably successful. Whatever its weaknesses the movement was characterized by a coherent aesthetic ideology. The philosophy of Negritude as expressed in poetry is couched in a distinctive style, a style characterized by a pattern of imagery revolving around such words as 'black', 'white', 'blood', 'Negro', 'beautiful', 'hope', 'humanity', etc., and words that refer to nature and the African tradition. One of the most outstanding features of the movement is the way in which the virtues, physical attributes and struggles of black people are celebrated in some of the most passionate and lyrical verse ever written anywhere. The warmth of Africa, the sexual appeal of her women and the flexibility and suppleness of the African body are extolled in words and rhythms that recreate those qualities and attributes. This is where Senghor excels.

If the English translation of Senghor's poetry is an accurate rendering of the French original, it would seem that the Senegalese poet makes every effort to relate form to content. In 'New York', the rhythmic dance of the black people of Harlem as well as their lively life style are reflected in the very rhythm and movement of parts 2 and 3 of the poem, while the clumsiness and coldness of the white people of New York are portrayed in the rugged rhythm and the more or less matter-of-fact style of part 1. The attempt to relate sound to sense comes out even more clearly in one of Senghor's most lyrical poems, 'Night of Sine', where the silence the poet talks about, the protagonist's heart beat and that of his woman friend as well as their sexual movements are all reflected in the very rhythm of the poem. In this connection, it is evident that the last lines of the poem are not only meant to reflect the protagonist's sexual movements but also to convey the idea that the sex act ends in sleep:

> Let me breathe the smell of our dead, let me contemplate and repeat their living voice, let me learn
> To live before I sink, deeper than the diver, into the lofty depth of sleep[20]

This is performative verse which propounds a philosophy and creates a style that reflects and promotes that philosophy magnificently and effectively. In other words, the Negritude movement created an ideology, the ideology of Negritude, which was based on artistic creativity and was successfully communicated in poetic form.

Notes

1. Aimé Césaire, *Return to My Native Land* (translated by John Berger and Anna Bostock), London, Penguin Books, 1969.
2. Kinfe Abraham, *From Race to Class: Links and Parallels in African and Black American Protest Expression*, London, Grassroots Publisher, 1982, p. 1.
3. David Craig (ed.), *Marxists on Literature: An Anthology*, Harmondsworth, Penguin, 1975, p. 160.
4. See Emmanuel Ngara, *Art and Ideology in the African Novel*, London, Heinemann Educational Books, 1985, pp. 30–32.
5. Frantz Fanon, *The Wretched of the Earth*, Harmondsworth, Penguin, 1967 (Reprinted 1980), p. 170.
6. Quoted in Wole Soyinka (ed.), *Poems of Black Africa*, London, Heinemann Educational Books, 1975, p. 96.
7. Quoted in G. Moore and U. Beier (ed.), *The Penguin Book of Modern African Poetry*, Harmondsworth, Penguin, 1963 (Third edition 1984), p. 233.
8. Ibid., p. 237.
9. Ibid., p. 236
10. See Soyinka, op. cit., p. 84.
11. Abraham, op. cit., pp. 118–119.
12. Quoted in M. Dickinson (ed.), *When Bullets Begin to Flower*, Nairobi, East African Publishing House, 1972, pp. 53–56.
13. Ibid., p. 58.
14. Ibid., p. 62.
15. Ibid., p. 81.
16. David Mandessi Diop, *Hammer Blows*, London, Heinemann Educational Books, 1979, p. 13. All the poems by David Diop cited here are quoted in this collection.
17. Ibid., p. 21.
18. Ibid., p. 25.
19. Ibid., p. 7.
20. Moore and Beier, op. cit., p. 230.

4

Individualistic Idealism & Social Commitment in Christopher Okigbo

Okigbo and Western Literature and Ideology

The Nigerian civil war of the 1960s deprived Africa of one of its most promising poets when Christopher Okigbo died in defence of the Biafran cause in August 1967. Okigbo's career as a poet ended as dramatically as it had begun. He described his decision to take to poetry as a profession in the following words:

> There wasn't a stage when I decided that I definitely wished to be a poet; there was a stage when I found that I couldn't be anything else. And I think that the turning point came in December 1958, when I knew that I couldn't be anything else than a poet. It's just like somebody who receives a call in the middle of the night to religious service, in order to become a priest of a particular cult, and I didn't have any choice in the matter. I just had to obey.[1]

These words are important to an understanding of Okigbo's poetry, particularly the sequence he entitled *Labyrinths*.

Before we analyse his poetry we need to look at some of the influences that shaped his poetic vision. First, Okigbo read Classics at Ibadan and was thoroughly familiar with the literary tradition of Europe. He was also influenced by the French Symbolist movement and by the leading English-language poets of modern times – Hopkins, Yeats, Pound and Eliot. This resulted in an eclecticism which has led Chinweizu and his fellow *bolekaja* critics to accuse Okigbo – alongside Soyinka and J.P. Clark – of 'euromodernism' and 'the Hopkins disease'.[2]

While Hopkins did influence Okigbo I believe that by far the greatest single influence on him among English-language poets was T.S. Eliot. When he started writing poetry, before the goddess Idoto called him to worship her, he was completely immersed in European culture, and enthralled by the European tradition, and this is most evident in the way his poetry imitates and echoes the man who had become the leading poet and critic of the English-speaking world – T.S. Eliot. The pessimism that we find in T.S. Eliot's early poems like 'Prufrock', *The Hollow Men* and *The Waste Land*, the obscurity that characterizes these poems and the religious temperament of the later Eliot are all found in Okigbo. While in the socialist East there was hope of a new social order, the West was full of apprehension about the turn of events in Europe made worse by the wars, and bourgeois poets translated this pessimism as a universal phenomenon. Thus, in his 'The Second Coming', Yeats saw the new wave of revolutions ushered in by the victory of the Bolsheviks in Russia as 'mere anarchy' which had been 'loosed upon the world'. This was in 1920, three years after the founding of the Soviet Union. This was followed two years later by Eliot's *The Waste Land*, and five years later, in 1925, by *The Hollow Men*, in which Eliot writes:

> We are the hollow men
> We are the stuffed men
> Leaning together
> Headpiece filled with straw. Alas![3]

When at the start of his poetic career Okigbo wrote 'On the New Year' in 1958 he could not help echoing the pessimism of Eliot:

> Where then are the roots, where the solution
> To life's equation?

> The roots are nowhere
> There are no roots here
> Probe if you may
> From now until doomsday.

Anybody who has read Eliot will recognize these lines as an imitation of the following passage from 'The Burial of the Dead' in *The Waste Land*:

> What are the roots that clutch, what branches grow
> Out of this stony rubbish? Son of man,
> You cannot say, or guess, for you know only
> A heap of broken images, where the sun beats,
> And the dead tree gives no shelter, the cricket no relief,
> And the dry stone no sound of water.

In fact 'On the New Year' is shot through with echoes of T.S. Eliot. The same is true of *Four Canzones 1957–1961*, whose very title is an imitation of Eliot's *Four Quartets*. In the second of these four poems, 'Debtors' Lane', Okigbo again recreates the myth of *The Hollow Men* in Africa:

This is debtors' lane, this is
the new haven, where wrinkled faces
watch the wall clock strike each hour
in a dry cellar.

This corresponds exactly to the theme and manner of Part III of *The Hollow Men*:

This is the dead land
This is cactus land
Here the stone images
Are raised, here they receive
The supplication of a dead man's hand
Under the twinkle of a fading star.

There is nothing wrong in a poet echoing other poets but it has to be done imaginatively and Okigbo does this more successfully in his later poetry. What is amazing here is that, two years before the independence of his own country, Nigeria, and at a time when most politically conscious Africans were waiting with great expectation for the deliverance of the continent from colonial rule, Okigbo could be singing lyrics to the pessimism of Western Europe! This is a falsification of African history and of Okigbo's own experience of it. But of course he had been fed on the diet of the dominant bourgeois ideology of the West which Eliot and Yeats represented; what they said in their writings was seen by Okigbo and the African intelligentsia of his time as having a universal application, as reflecting the true state of the entire world. Okigbo knew neither the socialist world nor his own African world. It was this total assimilation into European culture that resulted in a dramatic discovery of his roots when he felt that the goddess Idoto had called him to minister to her. He then set out on a search for a poetic vision which we shall explore in *Labyrinths*.

Labyrinths and the Quest for a Poetic Vision

Labyrinths consists of four sequences of poems – *Heavensgate*, *Limits*, *Silences* and *Distances*. Each sequence comprises a number of poems, each of which is divided into parts or movements, which we shall refer to as 'sections'.

'The Passage', the first poem in the sequence *Heavensgate*, expresses the poet's complete abandonment to the goddess Idoto. It is a rite of passage in which the poet, totally enthralled by the goddess, gives himself passionately, humbly and completely to her as a prodigal son who has repented and finally decided to come home. He stands 'naked' before Idoto. He is 'lost' in her legend. So repentant is he that he utters the *De Profundis* from the depth of his heart in a manner similar to the way in which Catholics used to cry to the Virgin Mary, Queen of Heaven, in the prayer called *Salve Regina*, 'Hail Holy Queen':

Under your power wait I
  on barefoot,
watchman for the watchword
  at *Heavensgate*;

out of the depths my cry:
give ear and hearken . . .

The poem formally marks Okigbo's consecration as Idoto's priest. He is at the entrance of a new world of mystical spiritual presences, a stage which marks a transition from one way of looking at life to another, from one ideological orientation to another. It is the beginning of Okigbo's quest. An aura of romantic mysticism surrounds this entry into the poet's new world. As he sets out he invites kindred creatures to help him along:

Me to the orangery
solitude invites,
a wagtail, to tell
the tangled-wood-tale,
a sunbird, to mourn
a mother on a spray.

In 'Initiations' the actual spiritual search begins. The poem recollects Okigbo's initiation into Christianity by one Kepkanly, to music (or so it seems) by Jadum, a half-demented village minstrel, who nevertheless gives some advice, and to poetry by Upandru, a village explainer who seems to warn the poet against the pleasures of the flesh. 'Initiations' is important in at least two respects. First, it introduces one of the central symbols of the poem, the crucifix which takes the form of a 'scar of the crucifix / over the breast'. It was 'inflicted' by a 'red-hot blade'. Those images would seem to symbolize the violent imposition of Christianity on Okigbo. Secondly, the poem reveals a very independent approach to Catholicism on the part of the poet. He does not abandon Christianity – in fact he carries the cross right through to *Distances* – but he is critical of the way the Catholic Church reduces its members to non-thinking beings who cannot question authority or think for themselves, so that the adult believer becomes a 'moron'. The word 'orthocentre' would seem to indicate the dogmatic centralism of the traditional Catholic Church. Okigbo was once 'avoiding decisions' in this fashion, having accepted John the Baptist's teaching about 'life without sin', which meant 'life without life'.

Two figures are introduced in the third and fifth poems, namely, the 'watermaid' who on one level seems to be identifiable with both Idoto and the White Goddess of *Distances*; and 'Anna of the panel oblongs', who is the Christian equivalent, symbolizing either Mary, Mother of Jesus, or Mary's Mother, Anna, or both.

Thus, in 'Initiations', Okigbo seems to be dealing with the dialectic of being a Christian and remaining faithful to traditional religion, and he achieves a synthesis expressed in terms of a series of recurring symbols throughout the sequence.

With *Limits* we come to a new phase in the development of the quest. In his Introduction to *Labyrinths* Okigbo explains that 'Siren Limits' presents a protagonist 'in pursuit of the white elephant'.[4] The white elephant may be an illusory idea or conviction which becomes a burden. Okigbo again tells us in the Introduction that *Limits* was written at the end of a journey of several centuries from Nsukka to Yola in pursuit of what turned out to be an 'illusion'.[5] The sequence contains some very important pieces. In the first section of 'Siren Limits' the poet becomes 'talkative / like weaverbird'. This is no doubt because 'I have had my cleansing'. We can therefore expect to hear more secrets about the quest. In the second section a clue is given – the pilgrim poet tells us about his view of himself in relation to other poets. The other poets are all keen to burgeon rapidly and gain popularity and this results in their stunted growth. This view of other poets seems to be confirmed in Section III of *Distances*, where Okigbo passes 'the scattered line of pilgrims', including Negritude poets. They are poplars that grow rapidly, but he is a shrub whose growth is slow but firm:

> For he was a shrub among the poplars,
> Needing more roots
> More sap to grow to sunlight,
> Thirsting for sunlight,
>
> A low growth among the forest.

Eventually, however, he will overcome the suffocating effect of the poplars and become 'A green cloud above the forest'. But this growth is in fact full of hazards as we realize in Section III where a new set of images is presented. There we see the pilgrim poet moving on very dangerous terrain where there are 'Banks of reed. / Mountains of broken bottles'. Consequently he has to tread extremely carefully on velvet feet. This stealthy movement is portrayed in very beautiful and appropriate language:

> Silent the footfall,
> Soft as cat's paw,
> Sandalled in velvet in fur

The poem is constructed very much like an Eliot poem and alludes to both *Ash Wednesday* and *The Waste Land*. We are presented with a dream in which there is a crisis, resulting from two contradictory voices. On the one hand there is a voice which warns 'the mortar is not yet ready', presumably indicating that he cannot come out yet, his formation as a poet is not yet complete. On the other hand there is another voice reminiscent of the barman's voice in 'A Game of Chess' in *The Waste Land*. This latter voice urges the pilgrim poet to hurry down to a waterfront called Cable to defeat the white elephant, 'To pull by the rope / the big white elephant'. There are two sets of elephants in Okigbo's poetry, the white elephant whose defeat he celebrates in the third section of 'Lament of the Masks', and the elephant that features in *Path of Thunder*. The latter refers to Nigerian politicians, but the former, the white elephant, is a poetic vision, an illusion which the pilgrim poet is fighting to discard. The message is that he is not yet ready to defeat the white elephant.

In 'Fragments Out of the Deluge' two important flashes occur. First, in the sixth section the pilgrim poet takes on the form of a Christ figure who is rejected by his own people causing him to make the satirical comment: 'And you talk of the people: / There is none thirsty among them'. In the tenth section Okigbo deals with a theme which was of great concern to other writers of the time, the destruction of African religion by European missionaries. This harks back to his earlier reflections on Christianity, but for the first time he speaks with a public voice about a matter of general concern to the African people. However, the theme seems forced – it introduces an element of incoherence as there is no logical explanation why this movement appears here. It is out of line with what comes before and immediately after it. Be that as it may, the poetry of this section is very successful as Okigbo uses images of galloping beasts mounting a savage assault on African religion, symbolized by the sunbird. The last two stanzas read as follows:

> Their talons they drew out of their scabbard,
> Upon the tree trunks, as if on fire-clay,
> Their beaks they sharpened;
> And spread like eagles their felt-wings,
> And descended upon the twin gods of Irkalla.
>
> And the ornaments of him,
> And the beads about his tail;
> And the carapace of her
> And her shell, they divided.

The destruction is so total that in Section XI there is a voice of mourning:

> And the gods lie in state
> And the gods lie in state
> Without the long-drum.
> And the gods lie unsung,
> Veiled only with mould,
> Behind the shrinehouse

However, African religion is so resilient that in the last section of the sequence the sunbird is resurrected.

Silences marks another stage in the development of the poet's vision.

Christopher Okigbo

In the Introduction Okigbo explains that both parts of the sequence were inspired by public events: 'Lament of the Silent Sisters' by the Western Nigerian crisis of 1962 and the death of Lumumba in what was the Belgian Congo (now Zaire); and 'Lament of the Drums' by the imprisonment of Chief Obafemi Awolowo and the tragic death of the Chief's son, which coincided with his imprisonment. There is therefore a direct link between political issues and the concerns of the poem. What seems to come out is a tension between the public's view of the function of the poet and Okigbo's view. All along this private dialogue between the poet who possesses his own personal vision and the society which expects him to write about matters of public concern has been implicit, but now it is beginning to come to the surface. What Okigbo seems to be doing in this poem, therefore, is looking for an appropriate form for articulating this dialectic. He finds this medium in the lament motif. In the first poem the lament is articulated by the traditional village crier and in the second by the drum.

'Lament of the Silent Sisters' opens with an allusion to Hopkins's poem, 'The Wreck of the Deutschland', in which Hopkins recreated the drowning of five Franciscan nuns in a shipwreck. The tension between the poet's and the public's view of the functions of poetry is couched in terms of the anxiety and insecurity of the drowning nuns who are not able to cry out for help. The poet is in a similar situation as the crier says in the second section:

> So, one dips one's tongue in ocean, and begins
> To cry to the mushroom of the sky:

In the second poem the drums are also protesting. The long-drums are the spirits of the ancestors, as Okigbo explains in the Introduction. It is as if, having refused to succumb to the call to use his poetry for purposes he does not consider appropriate, he now enlists the ancestors to bear witness to the justness of his cause. In the second section of this poem the drums end by expressing an unwillingness to dance 'a dance of elephants', which probably means celebrating public events like independence that are dominated by politicians. The drums are suspicious, refusing to come out 'From the cinerary tower / To the crowded clearing'. They fear that 'The robbers will strip us of our tendons'. They fear to be captured like the children of Israel in Babylon:

> For we sense
> With dog-nose a Babylonian capture,
> The martyrdom
> Blended into that chaliced vintage;

Although they are called upon to celebrate, they only come out to mourn. In Part III the drums mourn Palinurus, who is most probably intended to stand for a fusion of Awolowo and his dead son. The drums are therefore a voice of protest against the manner in which Awolowo has been treated by fellow politicians. The bitterness of the drums is evident in Section IV:

> Long-drums dis-
> Jointed, and with bleeding tendons,
> Like tarantulas
> Emptied of their bitterest poisons

In the closing section there is an overt political comment. Instead of celebrating, the drums wail. They wail 'for the fields of crop' which 'grow not'; they wail for 'the fields of men' where children perish; they wail for the Great River, the Niger, the symbol of the Nigerian nation, because her 'pot-bellied watchers', the rich ones, despoil her. Okigbo has finally broken his silence by launching a bitter attack on the political leaders of Nigeria. He has achieved this by quoting the italicized lines from Jessie Weston's book, *From Ritual to Romance*, in which 'the Great River' refers to the Nile.[6]

The last sequence, *Distances*, celebrates the pilgrim poet's arrival at the palace of the White Goddess. There is a distinct tone of triumph and celebration in this poem, which is partly reflected by a new lyrical quality as the poet recreates the end of his search and the discovery of his vision. The goddess is no longer the mysterious Idoto whose enchantment reduces him to a humble servant. She is still 'the same voice' but transformed into the White Goddess. It seems to me that at this point Okigbo's mission as a poet is very clear to him. He has resolved his ideological and aesthetic contradictions and has arrived at his Jerusalem, a philosophy of art that is firmly based on African traditions. The voice that leads him to the Goddess 'strips the dream naked, / bares the entrails'; and he washes his feet 'in your pure head, O maid' and finally declares:

> I have fed out of the drum
> I have drunk out of the cymbal
>
> I have entered your bridal
> chamber; and lo,
>
> I am the sole witness to my homecoming

Okigbo acquires a new understanding of his first decision to become a prodigal son and worship Idoto. In this connection Okigbo's exploration is very similar to that of T.S. Eliot, whose whole career was an experiment with new forms of artistic expression and a search for a new vision. In the fourth and last poem of the *Quartets*, 'Little Gidding', which is his last major poem, Eliot has this to say:

Christopher Okigbo

With the drawing of this Love and the voice of this Calling

We shall not cease from exploration
And the end of all our exploring
Will be to arrive where we started
And know the place for the first time.

For Okigbo *Distances* represents a major turning point as we shall see. It comes at the end of a long quest for a poetic vision, for an appropriate medium of artistic expression and for a philosophy of life which is consonant with his chosen profession as a poet. *Labyrinths* is therefore an exploration in both the form and purpose of poetry. The journey is a tortuous one, both for the poet and the reader who wants to acquire more than just a superficial appreciation of Okigbo. For the poet the quest results in a positive development both in social consciousness and in artistic excellence. With regard to the latter, it is clear that his later poetry is in many ways better – it has a more graceful and enchanting rhythmic beat; it deals with issues that are of public concern and it communicates better with the reader. His development towards more natural rhythms and better communication parallels that of T.S. Eliot, and in order to get a full appreciation of Okigbo's development in aesthetic ideology we should turn to Eliot for enlightenment.

Aesthetic Ideology and Political Consciousness

Okigbo's early poetry, including most of the sequences in *Labyrinths*, is completely in agreement with Eliot's dictum on the relationship between tradition and the individual poet. Eliot emphasizes the importance of what he calls 'the historical sense'. The poet must be aware of his ancestors, of his tradition: he must incorporate the achievements of his predecessors in his own works but be aware of his own time and place so that his work reflects a consciousness of both his own time, his own culture, and that of his ancestors:

> Tradition is a matter of much wider significance. It cannot be inherited, and if you want it you must obtain it by great labour. It involves, in the first place, the historical sense, which we may call nearly indispensable to anyone who would continue to be a poet beyond his twenty-fifth year; and the historical sense involves a perception, not only of the pastness of the past, but of its presence; the historical sense compels a man to write not merely with his own generation in his bones, but with a feeling that the whole of the literature of Europe from Homer and within it the whole of the literature of his own country has a simultaneous existence and composes a simultaneous order. This historical sense . . . is what makes a writer traditional. And it is at the same time what makes a writer most acutely conscious of his place in time, of his own contemporaneity.[7]

Eliot is of course saying this with specific reference to European poets. But Okigbo and his contemporaries were deracinated Africans.

They were fed upon a diet of western bourgeois culture and ideology and were so completely immersed in it that they could easily see themselves obeying T.S. Eliot to the letter. However, Eliot also jolts the likes of Okigbo. The historical sense makes a writer 'most acutely conscious of his place in time, of his own contemporaneity'. Thus Okigbo has a challenge – he cannot follow the European tradition without being conscious of his own African tradition and contemporaneity. What he does in *Labyrinths*, therefore, is to explore this dialectic between his own traditional culture and the western tradition, with what success we shall see below. For now we shall note that in order to achieve this synthesis of the past and the present, the western and the African, Okigbo employs what Eliot called the mythical method, which involves abandoning a logical composition and using myth and indirect references to relate one part of a poem to another. This enabled Eliot to manipulate parallels between contemporaneity and antiquity.

The mythical method is most clearly exemplified by T.S. Eliot's *The Waste Land*, which has no logical structure. The method is at work in Okigbo's 'On the New Year' and *Four Canzones*. It is still present as late as *Silences* where the poet associates Obafemi Awolowo's son with Palinurus, a character taken from Roman literature, and where there is an allusion to Tamuz, a god of Egyptian origin who caused the rise and fall of the Nile. The idea is to enable the reader to appreciate the present by associating it with what he or she knows about the past. The same principle is at work in 'Lament of the Silent Sisters'. For the reader to fully appreciate the force of the first section he or she should really be familiar with Hopkins. Consider, for example, how Hopkins dramatizes the vision of the nun who sees glimpses of Christ through the storm in stanza 28 of 'The Wreck of the Deutschland':

But how shall I . . . make me room there:
Reach me a . . . Fancy, come faster –
Strike you the sight of it? look at it loom there,
Thing that she . . . there then! the Master,
Ipse, the only one, Christ, King, Head:
He was to cure the extremity where he had cast her:
Do, deal, lord it with living and dead;
Let him ride, her pride, in his triumph, despatch and have done
   with his doom there.[8]

The dramatic situation of the storm is imaginatively recreated in this stanza. The broken sentences correspond to the nun's interrupted vision of Christ: the excited tone re–enacts the experience of the nun fighting with the storm while receiving these glimpses. And then in the fourth line Christ suddenly appears in full. Okigbo recreates the same sort of dramatic situation in 'Lament of the Silent Sisters' although the tone and manner are different. The tone is not one of excitement but frustration. The crier wants to speak but cannot speak. His voice is not strong enough in the thunder:

Christopher Okigbo

IS THERE . . . Is certainly there . . .
For as in sea-fever globules of fresh anguish
immense golden eggs empty of albumen
sink into our balcony . . .

How does one say NO in thunder . . .

Instead of ending with the vision of the Franciscan nun, instead of finding fulfilment in the thunder, instead of rising above the ocean, the crier 'dips [his] tongue in ocean, and begins / To cry to the mushroom of the sky'. So Okigbo uses Hopkins's technique to suit his own theme. In 'The Passage' there is a consistent fusion of Christian and traditional African symbolism and this, as explained elsewhere in this chapter, persists right through to *Distances*, where a major change begins to occur. The question that arises is: how successfully does Okigbo use the mythical method and Eliot's concept of the historical sense to portray the African condition? Obviously there is now a development in the manner in which Okigbo uses material from European culture, in that he no longer simply refers to the European tradition but also brings in elements from his African background. However, his method still leaves much to be desired.

The reason for the inadequacy of Okigbo's new aesthetic ideology is that the mythical method as used by him in the greater part of *Labyrinths* is based on an inadequate authorial ideology. When he was writing *Labyrinths* Okigbo had not yet sufficiently developed in political consciousness to see any contradiction between a western-oriented consciousness and an Africa-centred consciousness. The acceptance of Idoto was not the result of a negative reaction to the dominance of western culture and ideology. What he thought he had achieved was that he was now writing not only with the European tradition in mind but also with an awareness of his own cultural background. By accepting the values that go with the worship of Idoto he believed he had brought about a natural synthesis between the two cultures to which he thought he belonged – what he called 'the indigenous' and 'the modern'.[9] But Okigbo did not seem to see the distinction between 'the modern' and 'the western'. His allusions to Eliot, Hopkins and the Classics are in reality an expression not of a 'modern' sensibility, but a European consciousness. What Eliot advocates in his theory of the historical sense is the necessity for the European poet to preserve European culture and to immortalize European writers. And what he achieved in *The Waste Land* was to do just that. At a time when westerners thought that their whole cultural tradition was in danger of dissipating Eliot appeared on the literary scene and created a poem in which the values of that tradition were asserted. This is why the Fisher King says at the end, 'These fragments I have shored against my ruins'. He has managed to put together the remaining bits and pieces of his culture in order to preserve it.

Contrasting Responses to Colonialism

Eliot was a spokesperson for Europe. He had a strong nationalistic consciousness and a feeling for Europe which led him to leave America and return to England where his ancestors came from. Now, when an African poet adopts Eliot's method and modifies it by including material from his African tradition without a clear understanding of the ideological imperatives that led Eliot to adopt that method, he gets trapped in the web of European buorgeois ideology and fails to speak to his people. In order to use the mythical method creatively in a manner that promotes an African consciousness, the African poet must acquire a certain degree of political consciousness, which enables him to stand European values on their head. This requirement is lacking in Okigbo. He is hardly aware of the problems of cultural imperialism and so when in Section X of *Limits* he launches a surprising attack on Europeans for destroying African traditional religion he sounds unconvincing, as this attitude is not reflected elsewhere. His earlier criticism of the Catholic Church is not based on what is perceived as its European orientation but on its dogmatic centralism, which affects both Africans and westerners. In this Okigbo is not speaking as an African Catholic, but simply as an independent-minded Christian intellectual. He could be European, American or Japanese. And unless Idoto is conceived of in terms of a definite Africa-centred consciousness she could be a traditional goddess from any culture, Greek, Chinese or Saxon. Judged as a separate poem, therefore, Section X of *Limits* has much to offer, but, taken as part of Okigbo's poetic vision at that point of his development, it rings hollow.

In *Distances*, however, there is an important shift. To get a full appreciation of the principle on which the poem works, it is useful to be aware of the fact that the poem uses as its setting the operating table in a theatre, the effects of anaesthesia on a patient and how the patient comes round after an operation. In his Introduction Okigbo says 'Distances was written after my first experience of surgery under general anaesthesia'. He also explains that the homecoming referred to is homecoming in 'its spiritual and psychic aspect'. And he goes on to add, 'The self that suffers, that experiences, ultimately finds fulfilment in a form of psychic union with the supreme spirit that is both destructive and creative.'[10]

In terms of Okigbo's new artistic vision which becomes evident in *Late Poems* the homecoming can be seen from two perspectives. First we see that from now on the excessive reliance on Eliot's mythical method is eschewed. The white elephant has finally been pulled by the rope and conquered. This is the destructive aspect of the new vision. Secondly, his remaining poems are based on a different aesthetic ideology. They are quite plain; they have a lyrical quality and some of them are clearly meant to be read to the accompaniment of drums and rattles. Furthermore, Okigbo seems to have resolved his dilemma on

the function of the poet in society. After *Distances* the private voice of
the poet is replaced by a voice that speaks for the community. In *Path
of Thunder* he plunges into themes of social concern. He has accepted
that poetry has a social function; he has cast away the garb of individ-
ualism. This is the creative aspect of his new vision. He has indeed
hunted and killed the white elephant and it is time for him to descant
his praise-names in a triumphant voice in 'Lament of the Masks':

> THEY THOUGHT you would stop pursuing the white elephant
> They thought you would stop pursuing the white elephant
> But you pursued the white elephant without turning back –
> You who chained the white elephant with your magic flute
> You who trapped the white elephant like a common rabbit
> You who sent the white elephant trembling into your net –
> And stripped him of his horns, and made them your own
> You who fashioned his horns into ivory trumpets –

From Romantic Idealism to Critical Realism

In the previous section we focused on the problem of political
consciousness in Okigbo's artistic vision. To get a full appreciation of
his aesthetic ideology we should understand that his political
immaturity was coupled with an individualistic idealism which
resulted in a very strong element of romanticism. Okigbo was an
individual searching after ideas and religious experiences. The spiritual
world dominated his artistic vision to the extent of negating the
material world around him. Instead of basing his conception of the
function of poetry on social reality, the real relations between people in
society, he turned away from reality into the world of the spirit and the
imagination. This gave rise to a romanticism which associated artistic
creativity with imaginary things like watermaids and goddesses.

Okigbo is a typical idealist – the very opposite of Okot p'Bitek. The
latter was concerned about the material world. His search for African
forms was motivated by a desire to comment on the real conditions of
existence of the African people, on how the African petty bourgeoisie
related to African culture and that of western bourgeois society.
Okigbo, on the other hand, was first preoccupied with finding the
forms and functions of poetry through a spiritual search and this is
what happens in *Labyrinths*. Such an approach can lead to an idealistic
mysticism where the material world is completely rejected and the individual searcher becomes utterly possessed by an other-worldliness
which ignores and defies the world of flesh and blood. As a result of
this extreme form of idealism early Christian hermits turned away from
society and lived secluded lives. Okigbo gives the impression of a poet
on the verge of becoming a mystic in 'The Passage'. His total abandonment to Idoto is evidence of this. There is a mystical aura that
surrounds this most enchanting opening of the poem. Then, as one

reads on, one notices a fascination with such symbols as 'the watermaid', 'the wagtail' and 'the sunbird'.

The crucifix has a peculiar mystical aura about it. It is 'scar of the crucifix' which is 'by red blade inflicted / by red-hot blade'. His initiation into Christianity becomes 'Mystery which I initiate / received newly naked'. Of course, another poet could use the same symbols in quite a different manner, but Okigbo becomes a Romantic poet; he invests his symbols with a certain aura of mysticism, creating a dreamlike atmosphere. Consider, for example, how the watermaid is depicted in 'Watermaid':

BRIGHT
with the armpit-dazzle of a lioness,
she answers,

Wearing white light about her;

and the waves escort her,
my lioness
crowned with moonlight.

In *Labyrinths* we see a poet who is preoccupied with his own personal relationship to Christianity, traditional religion and poetry. It is a private poetry in which the poet shuns society and ministers unto a private god, not as a link between human beings and God, not as a go-between, but as a priest who represents none other than himself. That priest is neither a priest of the Christian Church nor that of traditional Igbo society. In Igbo society Ezeulu is a Chief Priest who is expected to mediate for the people. In the Catholic Church to which Okigbo belonged the priest offers the sacrifice of the Mass on behalf of humanity. On whose behalf does Okigbo perform his rituals?

We will understand the Okigbo of *Labyrinths* if we see him as an example of that writer in modern capitalist society who has withdrawn from society and subscribes to the philosophy of art for art's sake. That artist who begins to appear with the rise of Romanticism is a product of the development of private property and believes in turning art into a private affair. In Africa the philosophy of art for art's sake has been rejected by both writers and critics and the tension that we see running through *Labyrinths* is partly a result of Okigbo the poet engaging in a dialogue with the writers and critics who expect his art to be more relevant to the needs and problems of Africa.

However, solitary contemplation can lead to wisdom, and this is what happens in Okigbo. In *Labyrinths* we see him gradually developing from a fanatical worshipper of Idoto and an unthinking Christian to someone who possesses a critical mind. In 'Siren Limits' he becomes 'talkative / like weaverbird'. His relations with the watermaid or lioness are quite different now. And when he enters the palace of the White Goddess in *Distances* he no longer has the supplicating humility

Christopher Okigbo

of the prodigal son that we see in *Heavensgate*. He is master, almost the hero that the Goddess has been waiting for. 'I wash my feet in your pure head, O maid', he says, and, as she receives him with a smile, he seeks 'among your variegated teeth, / the tuberose of my putrescent laughter'. With this new-found happiness he triumphantly declares:

> I have entered your bridal
> chamber; and lo,
>
> I am the sole witness to my homecoming.

The aura of mysticism is dispelled. It is as if through the quest the pilgrim poet discovers that Idoto is of this world after all and not of some faraway romantic world. Poetry belongs in the day-to-day material world, in other words, not some hidden spiritual world. From now on his poetry changes its orientation. His poetry becomes a poetry of social concern. Hence in *Path of Thunder* his poems are very much about the Nigeria that everybody knew. Okigbo has accepted the social function of poetry. He has adopted critical realism as an aesthetic ideology and eschewed the philosophy of art for art's sake. He has indeed come home.

It is a great pity that Okigbo died just as he had risen to maturity. The fact that he died fighting for a national cause is sufficient evidence of his new image of a poet who is involved in the issues of the day. Whether or not he was right to support the Biafran cause is a moot point. Suffice it here to note that he was now a committed writer, as his *Late Poems* show. Had he survived the war, he might have lived to become a great revolutionary poet.

Notes

1. Quoted in Christopher Okigbo, *Collected Poems*, London, William Heinemann, 1986, p. xii. All quotations from Okigbo are taken from this volume.
2. See Chinweizu, Jemie O. and Madubuike, I., *Toward the Decolonization of African Literature*, Volume 1, Washington D.C., Howard University Press, 1983, p. 163 ff.
3. T.S. Eliot, *Collected Poems, 1909–1962*, London, Faber and Faber, 1963. All references are to this edition.
4. Okigbo, op. cit., p. xxiii.
5. Ibid., p. xxiv.
6. J. Weston, *From Ritual to Romance*, New York, Peter Smith, 1941. For a comment on T.S. Eliot's use of the words from Weston's book see E.A. Ngara, 'The Significance of Time and Motion in the Poetry of T.S. Eliot', University of London, M.Phil. thesis, 1973, pp. 77–78.
7. T.S. Eliot, 'Tradition and the Individual Talent', in Frank Kermode (ed.), *Selected Prose of T.S. Eliot*, London, Faber and Faber, 1975, p. 38.
8. W.H. Gardner (ed.), *Poems and Prose of Gerard Manley Hopkins*, Harmondsworth, Penguin, 1963, p. 21.
9. See Dennis Duerden and Cosmo Pieterse (eds.), *African Writers Talking*, London, Heinemann, 1972, p. 144.
10. Okigbo, op. cit., p. xxi. My italics.

5

Realistic Traditionalism
in the Poetry
of Gabriel Okara

Introduction

Gabriel Okara is one of the oldest contemporary writers from English-speaking Africa. He started writing poetry in the early 1950s, so that some of his poems were written before the nationalist campaign for independence in his country had reached its peak, while some were written as late as 1976, sixteen years after Nigeria had attained independence. The poetry that we will discuss in this chapter therefore spans more than two decades of his life, but the focus will be on the earlier period.

Okara estabished an international reputation with the publication of his famous novel, *The Voice*, but he is also acclaimed as one of the most outstanding poets of the first generation of modern African writers. Much of his poetry is reported to have been lost, and what has survived is published in *The Fisherman's Invocation*.[1] Some of the poems in the collection evidently fall outside the central theme that runs through the major part of the volume, which is concerned with exploring the dialectic between tradition and modern influences, including the influence of technology and western civilization. Among the major poems that fall outside this central concern are 'The Revolt of the Gods', 'Franvenkirche' and, in a sense, 'The Snowflakes Sail Gently Down'. In the first-mentioned poem, written in 1969, Okara is as far from his central theme as can be. In this rather unsuccessful poem he dramatizes the idea that gods are in reality creations of human beings who create these figments in their minds and then turn round to worship them. The lighthearted tone of this poem contrasts rather sharply with the style of 'Franvenkirche', which Okara wrote in memory of his visit to Our Lady's Cathedral in Munich, West Germany. This monument fascinates Okara and gives him a feeling that makes his hands one 'with those that set brick upon brick / to build this memorial'. These lines strike the present writer, who witnessed Okara being fascinated in the same way by Great Zimbabwe in 1983. On reaching that part of the lower enclosure of Great Zimbabwe which pierces the sky in the form of a temple, Okara touched it with great reverence, saying, 'Let my hands touch where our ancestors touched.' The incident at Great Zimbabwe and the poem on the Munich cathedral reveal something of Okara's religious turn of mind.

In 'The Snowflakes Sail Gently Down' Okara creates a poem that focuses on one of his most frequently used motifs – the dream. The motif is used in such poems as 'Rural Path', 'Silent Girl', 'To a Star' and 'The Fisherman's Invocation'. In 'The Snowflakes', the poet sees snowflakes coming gently down as he sleeps and succeeds in creating a dreamlike atmosphere. But this poem points obliquely to the poet's central theme – that of his roots, of his culture on the one hand, and modernity on the other, the two being seen in binary opposition at first. It is to Okara's treatment of this dialectic between tradition and modernity that we shall now turn, and it is in respect of his handling of this theme that we shall probe into his authorial ideology, explore the poetic forms which give expression to his aesthetic ideology and evaluate his ability to communicate with the reader.

The Contradiction between Tradition and Modernity

A good starting point in our analysis is 'Piano and Drums', in which the contrast between the old and the new culture is shown in their apparently contradictory influences on the protagonist. The contradiction is expressed in terms of the very different ways in which the rhythmic drums and the music of the piano affect him. The drum is a symbol of tradition and it is associated with natural images – 'the mystic rhythm', 'the panther ready to pounce', 'the leopard snarling' and 'the naked warmth of hurrying feet'. The drum is also associated with life. Everything is galvanized into action by its sound. The protagonist himself is turned into a frenzy of activity, almost wild, like Rousseau's noble savage:

And my blood ripples, turns torrent,
topples the years and at once I'm
in my mother's lap a suckling;
at once I'm walking simple
paths with no innovations,
rugged, fashioned with the naked
warmth of hurrying feet and groping heart
in green leaves and wild flowers pulsing.

The wailing piano, on the other hand, only manages to produce discordant and what appear to be futile sounds. It speaks of 'complex ways', in 'tear-furrowed concerto'. Instead of making him feel at home with his environment it takes him to 'far-away lands' and 'new horizons' speaking in such strange sounds as 'diminuendo', 'counterpoint' and 'crescendo'. So confused is the piano itself with its own complex system that 'it ends in the middle / of a phrase at a daggerpoint'.

The tension between the past and the present cum future, between tradition and modernity, is at its worst in this poem. The poet is 'lost', he keeps 'wandering' not knowing which rhythm to follow – that of the jungle drums or that of the piano's 'concerto'. The poet or protagonist of course stands not only for himself, but for his generation, his class, which finds itself facing this dilemma of a society in transition. The class's confusion and lack of a sense of direction is symbolized by 'the morning mist' in which it is lost in an age which is 'at a riverside', namely at a crossroads.

The conflict persists in such poems as 'Were I to Choose', 'Spirit of the Wind', 'The Mystic Drum' and 'You Laughed and Laughed and Laughed'. In the last-mentioned poem there is no hint of any kind of synthesis between tradition and modernity. Okara is firmly on the side of tradition. The contradiction between the two is expressed in terms of the incongruity between the traditionalism of the poet–protagonist and the contrary views and outlook of another person who scorns tradition and takes pride in modern technology and new ideas. Here modernity is represented by imagery of the 'motor car' and 'ice-blocks'. When the traditionalist sings, his song is so unpleasant to the modern man that it strikes the latter as a 'motor car misfiring / stopping with a choking cough'. He is not in touch with mother earth and with nature because he shuts himself in this machine – the motor car – which is mechanical and prevents him from growing close to nature. His laughter is consequently unnatural and as cold as ice-blocks and freezes the one who laughs:

> You laughed and laughed and laughed
> But your laughter was ice-block
> laughter and it froze your inside froze
> your voice froze your ears
> froze your eyes and froze your tongue.

The protagonist on the other hand is his natural self. He does not use a car as a means of transport but walks on his bare feet. The rhythm of his dance is that of talking drums, and he opens not a car, but his 'mystic inside', and when he laughs he laughs a natural laughter which, far from destroying him or his rival, positively affects and transforms the latter. It warms the man of modern ways, and it illuminates him by its fire of life:

My laughter is the fire
of the eye of the sky, the fire
of the earth, the fire of the air,
the fire of the seas and the
rivers fishes animals trees
and it thawed your inside,
thawed your voice, thawed your
ears, thawed your eyes and
thawed your tongue.

Because the laughter of the protagonist issues from a life-giving force, it warms and invigorates every sense, every organ and every tissue of the other man so that awakening to this new life he is filled with amazement and asks for an explanation:

So a meek wonder held
your shadow and you whispered:
'Why so?'
And I answered:
'Because my fathers and I
are owned by the living
warmth of the earth
through our naked feet.'

In this poem Okara can be accused of being downright reactionary. He sees no compromise between tradition on the one hand and technology and modern or western influences on the other, and he seems to be advocating a Rousseauesque return to the past. It is as if walking on foot is inherently virtuous and using a car inherently bad and evil. There is no indication of the poet's attempt to explore the conditions under which this or that means of transport is either salutary or likely to dehumanize one.

There is a strong element of romanticism in Okara's traditionalism. This romanticism comes out in the ubiquitous images of nature that occur in 'You Laughed' and other poems. Throughout this collection of poems there are references to the earth, the sky, fire, the sea, rivers, waves, fish and other natural objects. In this set of images we can see a combination of romanticism and traditionalism – a refusal to come to terms with the world of modern technology. The drum is also a key symbol. Okara is anxious to be guided by the rhythm of the drum, and following the rhythm of the drum symbolizes obedience to nature, being guided by tradition. He or she who refuses to obey the drum is only heading for destruction. This seems to be the message of 'The Mystic Drum' where everything else follows the beat of the drum – people, fishes, the dead, trees, the sun and the moon – everything except she who stands behind a tree 'with leaves around her waist', for 'she only smiled with a shake of her head'. She refuses to accept the rhythm of the drum and consequently she gets destroyed.

When the mystic drum stops beating everything else finds its place but not the girl:

> And behind the tree she stood
> with roots sprouting from her
> feet and leaves growing on her head
> and smoke issuing from her nose
> and her lips parted in her smile
> turned cavity belching darkness.

'Piano and Drums', 'You Laughed and Laughed and Laughed', 'Once Upon a Time' and other poems are concerned with matters of a social nature. They allude to the contradictory forces that put Okara and other members of the African intelligentsia of his time on the horns of a dilemma. But some of the other poems seem to be concerned more with spiritual matters. 'The Call of the River Nun' and 'Spirit of the Wind' can be included in this category. 'The Call of the River Nun' has a distinctly religious flavour. There is, in the first place, the use of the word 'nun', which has an obvious religious connotation in the context of Christianity. On the other hand 'the river nun' could be a mermaid. There are several references to mermaids in 'The Fisherman's Invocation'. Okara may be using the word with both meanings in mind. With regard to the Christian sense of the word, there is in fact an allusion to Gerard Manley Hopkins's poem 'The Wreck of the Deutschland', which deals with the drowning of nuns, one of whom calls out like Okara's nun.

Whatever meaning the reader attaches to the word 'nun' – and both are perfectly acceptable – Okara's poem ends as a prayer. The call of the river nun is transformed into the call of the protagonist's 'river':

> My river's calling too!
> Its ceaseless flow impels
> my found'ring canoe down
> its inevitable course.

In the final stanza there is an anguished call to the poet's God, to his 'incomprehensible God'. This spiritual anguish is akin to the inner turmoil that is depicted in 'Spirit of the Wind', where the poet contrasts the freedom with which the storks move 'beyond the god's confining / hands' and his own imprisonment, which gives him the sense of his 'spirit', his 'stork', being 'caged':

> But willed by the gods
> I'm sitting on this rock
> watching them come and go
> from sunrise to sundown, with the spirit
> urging within.

There is unrest in him, a feeling of being spiritually shackled as he struggles to break free. This turbulence that Okara expresses is similar to the tension that characterizes what he sees as the relations between old and new values in his society. So whether he is treating a spiritual or social theme Okara tends to see a violent clash between two principles and he becomes the focus of that violent clash – he and his fellow intellectuals, in whom the antagonistic forces meet. But is there a possible resolution to the conflict? To answer this question we need to turn to 'The Fisherman's Invocation'.

'The Fisherman's Invocation' and Okara's Authorial Ideology

The ideological contradictions that oppress Okara and members of his class are resolved in the title poem, 'The Fisherman's Invocation', which is also the longest poem Okara has published. That the poem gives Okara's first collection its title is significant – it is an indication of the importance the poet attaches to the poem, and quite rightly so, because, in my view, 'The Fisherman's Invocation' marks the high point of Okara's achievement as a poet. Indeed some of the shorter poems, for example 'The Call of the River Nun', 'Piano and Drums' and 'The Snowflakes Sail Gently Down', are among the finest poems in African literature but their literary worth can only be fully appreciated when they are placed side by side with 'The Fisherman's Invocation'. It is, of course, a common tendency among students and readers of literature to go for shorter poems in preference to longer ones, and this puts 'The Fisherman's Invocation' at a disadvantage. Professors of literature are likely to teach Okara's shorter poems and to neglect what is in a sense the central poem in the Heinemann collection. In this section we shall explore very briefly some of its merits. The poem was probably meant in part to celebrate the birth or independence of Nigeria, but it fits very well into the poet's general theme of tradition and modernity.

One of the features which immediately strike the reader is that, like some of the poems discussed earlier, 'The Fisherman's Invocation' abounds in nature imagery. There are constant references to water, the sun, the moon, the earth and so on. Also running throughout are images referring to fishing – canoes, paddles, nets and water. Another important category is that of fertility imagery which has sexual connotations. There are, however, two dominant images – the Back and the Front symbolizing the past and the future, or tradition and modernity respectively. The two are not depicted as being in binary opposition but in dialectical interaction with each other. In this connection the theme of the poem can be summarized as the reconciliation of these two apparently contradictory forces. For Okara this is the only way for the African intelligentsia, placed on the horns of a dilemma by the contradictory demands and pressures of tradition and modernity.

Okara's argument is advanced forcefully in the opening movement of the poem where fishing is used as the dominant motif. The fisherman and his companion are fishing from a canoe. The canoe is that which ferries one across or along the course of life; it is the guiding principle of life without which one cannot survive the pressures of history; it is that which provides one with moral principles and social values. The canoe, in other words, is equivalent to a guiding ideology. The net is the means by which the necessary connection between the past, the present and the future can be effected. The canoe must move forward, but to do so it must draw sustenance from somewhere with the assistance of the net. Now the net brings nothing from the right side, nothing from the left side, but something from the Back:

> It's only the Back caught
> in the meshes of Today
> and I see past moons past suns
> past nights and past gods reflected
> by the Back trying to slip
> through the Meshes like a fish.

But the Back is not easy to catch and bring up into the canoe. It comes after a long, careful and persevering search; it is heavy and can easily slip through the net:

> Draw gently
> draw carefully
> don't let it slip
> draw it up into
> the canoe and let's hold
> it in our palms
> the Back, the gods,
> even for only
> one still moment
> one still moment
> one teaching moment.

Without the necessary link between the Front and the Back there will be no life; the Child-Front will be only a still-born. For the Front, the future, the new way of life, to be born healthy and alive there has to be a ritual, a fertility dance, a coming together of male and female. This ritual takes place during the invocation in the second movement. Here the sun is the male principle, the earth is the female principle and the moon the midwife. The earth is 'the womb of wombs' and the sun 'sperm of sperm', so the midwife moon must rub 'down the back of the Back' while 'the sun play(s) his play'. The reconciliation of tradition and modernity which is the result of this ritual dance is further facilitated by an amazing synchrony of traditional and modern musical instruments – the former with their deep 'boom' and the latter with their 'clatter':

And let O let the deep drums
of deep waters boom and mingle
with deep drums of deep Gods
in their play in your inside

Let them mingle O mingle with the clatter
of the drums of Today
for the coming, safe coming of the Front

This synchronizing of old and new instruments, the reconciliation of
piano and drum, has striking poetic and conceptual power. The child
too is no ordinary child. His birth, like that of an epic hero such as
Sundiata, is accompanied by the rumble and booming of thunder.
Okara's poetry takes on an epic dimension as the birth pangs of the
earth shake the heavens:

Rumble thunder God rumble.
Stride down to the edge
of the world and rumble
until your booming voice
encircles the earth
booming until the earth
trembles in agony of birth

As in the second movement so in the fourth movement Okara creates
performative verse. The fourth movement celebrates the birth of a
new, healthy baby, made significant by the coming together of traditional and new values. The rhythmic beat is the result of repetition
within carefully constructed sentences, which follow English stress
patterns while recreating an African drumbeat. Consider the following
three stanzas, for example:

Let's dance let's sing
Let's sing and dance
for the great child-Front
has come is coming

Let your feet be
knowing-something feet
and let your voice be
knowing-something voice

Let's dance let's sing
let's sing and dance
for the great child-Front
has come is coming

This contrasts sharply with the rhythm of the final movement, which is
no longer celebratory since the child-Front is now lying quietly on laps,
'feeding from measureless breasts of the Back'. A new type of African
has been born into a new environment, nourished by tradition but no

longer vexed by its conflict with modern culture. To symbolize the peace that surrounds the new baby after the violence and turmoil that accompanied his birth, Okara creates rhythms which are deliberate and slow:

> The celebration is now ended
> the drums lie quiet, silent, waiting.
> And the dancers disperse, walking
> with feet that have known many dances
> waiting for the next; walking
> with their hearts climbing up their feet
> to their places and the palmwine descending
> from their heads to settle in their bellies
> and their bodies turn cold. For the spirit
> of the dance has left and their faces become naked

Summation – Ideology and Communication in Okara

It would appear from what has survived of his poetry that Okara saw a high degree of tension in the cultural and social life of his class, arising from what were perceived as two contradictory forces, tradition and modernity. Okara saw himself and other members of the educated elite being tempted to abandon tradition in favour of modern influences and was filled with trepidation at the prospect of this happening. He felt that Africans would fall into a trap, by choosing a way of life built on shifting sands which would freeze them like the character in 'You Laughed and Laughed and Laughed'. The answer to the problem, as indicated in our analysis of 'The Fisherman's Invocation', is to effect a reconciliation, to bring the two sets of values together by ensuring that the new values have a strong link with tradition. Okara advocates neither a total rejection of modern civilization, nor a complete return to the past. His authorial ideology can therefore be characterized as *realistic traditionalism*. Okara is obviously a writer who values traditional cultural values but who also realizes that it is futile in this day and age to ignore the concrete reality of modern technology and civilization, or what is often referred to as 'western civilization'.

This account of Okara's authorial ideology is obviously a simplified one and can be accused of reductionism. There are indeed other currents that should be taken into account, such as the fact that the poet's development in ideological consciousness was a process, and the crystallization of ideology that appears in 'The Fisherman's Invocation' is the result of that process; such as the religious undercurrents and the mysticism referred to earlier in this chapter. We are, however, concerned with what may be identified as the dominant feature of Okara's world outlook, which shapes his poetic vision, and this is what we have referred to as realistic traditionalism. While there is a strong element of mysticism in Okara, his poetry is devoid of the subjective

Gabriel Okara

idealism of Senghor. There is no suggestion that the African has certain qualities and talents that other races do not have. Such symbols as 'the mystic drum', 'the sun', 'the Back' are only used as aesthetic motifs that express the poet's vision of tradition as a life-giving force.

Nor is the dialectic between tradition and modern influences couched in political terms in Okara. There is no overt reference to neo-colonialism or cultural imperialism, and, unlike Ngugi, Okara does not relate the problem of culture to the economic sphere. His poetry is in that sense apolitical and would seem to indicate the need for further development in consciousness on the part of the writer.

On the other hand, Okara the poet is guided by a consciously formulated aesthetic ideology. His poetry reveals certain patterns – the use of images of nature, and of things associated with the African traditional mode of life, the use of simple words, the creation of rhythms patterned on the drumbeat, the use of Ijaw modes of expression and so on. All this is clearly linked to his authorial ideology, and in those few poems where images referring to modern technology are employed it is quite clear that they are used to show the contrast in values that the poet is anxious to articulate. This is true of 'Piano and Drums' and 'You Laughed and Laughed and Laughed'. Here I wish to express my disagreement with the view that is now commonly held by critics of African poetry that Okara is not a traditionalist.

In *Tasks and Masks* Lewis Nkosi sees African poets falling into two groups. The first is the group of poets who are influenced by the modernist movement, namely, Okigbo, Soyinka and Clark. The second is the group of poets who have 'fought to recover the idiom of oral African poetry and to make it the basis of a new manipulation of the English language'.[2] In this group Nkosi includes Kofi Awoonor, Okot p'Bitek and Mazisi Kunene. Echoing Nkosi, Chinweizu and his co-authors discern three major 'tendencies' in African poetry in English: the euromodernists (Soyinka, Clark and Okigbo); the traditionalists (Kunene, Awoonor and p'Bitek); and 'a miscellany of individual voices of the middle ground who, unlike the euromodernists, share no strongly distinguishing characteristics'.[3] Okara is then lumped with Lenrie Peters and Dennis Brutus in this group. From our analysis of Okara in this chapter we can only say that these critics have not carefully studied his poetry.

The recourse to images referring to nature and tradition gives Okara's poetry an aura of simplicity, rather like Blake's *Songs of Innocence* and *Songs of Experience*. This simplicity conceals a complexity of thought and poetic structure which at times makes Okara's poetry quite difficult to interpret, although it remains immensely readable.

A close examination of Okara's poetry reveals that there is no emotion in the manner in which it gives expression to the ideological imperatives discussed in this chapter. There is no attempt to sentimentalize the problem, yet the genuineness with which the poet articulates it and the lyrical quality of the verse speak of deep feeling. The reader's own ideology may be quite at variance with the poet's, yet Okara says what he has to say so naturally and often with such grace and lyricism that the reader cannot but derive pleasure from the experience of reading the poetry.

Much of the pleasure comes from a combination of rhythm and the melodious chiming of sounds. This is even true of such a slow-moving poem as 'The Snowflakes Sail Gently Down':

> The snowflakes sail gently
> down from the misty eye of the sky
> and fall lightly on the
> winter-weary elms . . .

This lyrical quality results from a judicious use of poetic devices such as parallelism, repetition and linking, all of which are fully utilized in 'The Fisherman's Invocation'. In the following lines, for example, parallelism consists in repeating elements at the beginning and the end while the invariant elements occur in the middle:

> You are seeing the sun in my hands
> You are seeing Gods in my hands
> You are seeing the Back in my hands
> You are seeing the Front in my hands

In the following lines the device of linking – where a word used in one line is repeated in the next – is effectively employed together with free verbal repetition to produce an incantatory effect:

> And let O let the deep drums
> of deep waters boom and mingle
> with deep drums of deep Gods
> in their play in your inside.

A device Okara uses particularly effectively is dramatization. This is seen in many of the major pieces, including 'The Call of the River Nun', 'You Laughed and Laughed and Laughed', 'The Mystic Drum' and 'The Revolt of the Gods'. In these poems the poet creates dramatic situations in which there is some activity or dialogue or both. The device is particularly effective in 'The Fisherman's Invocation', in which we are presented with two principal actors – the protagonist or the fisherman and the other person, who is not clearly identified. The two are involved in both an activity and a communicative act. These are the casting of a net, the paddling of a canoe, an invocation, a dance and a concluding ceremony. By the time we are told in the last movement that the celebration for the Child-Front is over, we too have gone through the experience of dancing and have witnessed the birth of the

Child-Front. Okara has created an objective correlative, a set of events and objects which together form a vivid picture of the reconciliation of tradition and modernity.

Notes

1. *The Fisherman's Invocation*, London, Heinemann African Writers Series, 1978.
2. *Tasks and Masks, Themes and Styles of African Literature*, Harlow, Essex, Longman, 1981, p. 148.
3. See Chinweizu, Jemie O. and Madubuike, I., *Toward the Decolonization of African Literature*, Volume 1, Washington DC, Howard University Press, 1983, p. 163.

6

Cultural Nationalism
& Form
in Okot p'Bitek

Okot p'Bitek's Two Voices

Okot p'Bitek is one of the most widely acclaimed African poets. He has been lauded for his successful use of oral forms in his English-language poems. Okot published several major pieces before he died, and, except for *Horn of My Love*, all of them are called 'songs' – *Song of Lawino, Song of Ocol, Song of Prisoner* and *Song of Malaya*. Perhaps the most successful of these are *Song of Lawino*[1] and *Song of Prisoner*[2]. The former is not only the most well-known of his poems but also epitomizes two significant features of the Ugandan poet's work – a serious concern with African culture on the one hand, and, on the other, a lighthearted style. *Song of Prisoner* is more serious in tone and captures with greater power and beauty something of the tragic aspect of African independence, including what the poet sees as the loss of freedom for the majority of African citizens and the political fortunes of bloodthirsty tyrants on the continent. The anger of those who have lost their freedom is expressed very effectively in the last lines of Section 5 of *Song of Prisoner*:

I want to drink
Human blood
To cool my heart,
I want to eat
Human liver
To quench my boiling thirst,
I want to smear
Human fat on my belly
And on my forehead.

Mix chyme
With goat blood
And I will drink it,
My inside is full of fire
I must drink
Human blood
To cool me down –.

In the closing lines of the poem there is not only anger but also a devastating sense of frustration and hopelessness which underlies the escapism of the protagonist:

Open the door,
Man,
I want to dance
All the dances of the world,
I want to sleep with
All the young dancers.

I want to dance
And forget my smallness,
Let me dance and forget
For a small while
That I am a wretch,
The reject of my Country,
A broken branch of a Tree
Torn down by the whirlwind
Of Uhuru.

The reader is left in no doubt as to the magnitude of the problem the poet is addressing. The gravity of the subject matter comes out in the serious tenor of discourse that characterizes the poem. The tone of these two passages contrasts sharply with that of the last lines of Section 12 of *Song of Lawino*, which deals with a very serious subject – the negative effects of neo-colonial education on the educated African elite – but in a very lighthearted manner:

Bile burns my inside!
I feel like vomiting!
For all our young men
Were finished in the forest,
Their manhood was finished
In the class-rooms,
Their testicles
Were smashed
With large books!

This lightheartedness, with which Okot p'Bitek is often associated, is even more pronounced in *Song of Malaya*, a poem written in a flippant tone, very much in the manner of David Maillu's *After 4.30*.

We can summarize the foregoing by saying that Okot p'Bitek speaks with two voices – a serious voice and a lighthearted one. There is, however, something common to all his 'songs', and that is the use of traditional modes of expression and African imagery. The imagery is typical of the mode of production and thought processes of a pre-capitalist, peasant society. Okot's imagery is similar to that of Gabriel Okara, but the binary opposition between nature imagery and metaphors derived from modern technology is not as strong in the Ugandan poet as it is in the Nigerian. Even in passages where he is depicting modern life Okot p'Bitek tends to make use of images taken from a traditional set-up. For example, when portraying the new class struggle in independent Africa, in Section 8 of *Song of Prisoner*, he employs the image of fighting bulls:

Two bulls wrestle
With their horns,
The horn of the ruling bull
Breaks
And he tumbles down
The smooth breast
Of the hill
And plunges
Into the River.

The English and Acoli Versions of *Song of Lawino*

This brief introduction to Okot p'Bitek provides a perspective for our analysis of his most popular poem, *Song of Lawino*, on which this chapter is based. The poem is unique in that it was written in both the poet's mother tongue, Acoli, and as an English translation of the Acoli original. In assessing the poet's achievement in *Song of Lawino* we have to reckon with the fact that we are dealing with a translation, which can only partially capture the poetic qualities, nuances and effectiveness of the Acoli original, *Wer pa Lawino*. Yet *Song of Lawino* is not just a literal translation of *Wer pa Lawino*. It is a poem in its own right, composed and published as such. Whatever strengths and weaknesses the Acoli poem may have cannot be used to judge the merits or demerits of *Song of Lawino*, although an awareness of the merits of the Acoli original is likely to shed some light on the problems of translation. This is the value of Heron's book on Okot p'Bitek. His comparison of the Acoli and English versions of *Song of Lawino* is both interesting and illuminating.[3]

In this connection I should hasten to add that Heron's book gives an exhaustive account of Okot p'Bitek's use of oral traditions. What we are chiefly concerned with in this chapter are the ideological imperatives that motivated Okot to use oral forms, and the effectiveness with which these are integrated into English.

Okot p'Bitek
Culture, Politics and Ideology in *Song of Lawino*

Song of Lawino is a very rich poem, addressing important issues affecting post-independence Africa. Briefly, the poem is a satirical comment on the neo-colonial mentality of the African petty bourgeoisie – the intellectuals and political leaders of Africa. The target of Lawino's criticism, Ocol, is a representative of this class. He is both an intellectual and a politician, an embodiment of the disease Lawino diagnoses in her song, satirizing the ills of African leaders described elsewhere by Okot in an essay entitled 'Indigenous Social Ills', in which he refers to them as 'culturally barren ladies and gentlemen'.[4]

While Okot is primarily concerned with culture and only marginally with the economic development of Africa, it would not be quite right to suggest that his poems ignore economic problems. In Section 11 of her song, Lawino criticizes Ocol and the African political elite for political ineptitude and economic mismanagement. She lashes out at corruption, pointing out that many politicians joined the campaign for independence for material gain:

Someone said
Independence falls like a bull buffalo
And the hunters
Rush to it with drawn knives,
Sharp shining knives
For carving the carcass.
And if your chest
Is small, bony and weak
They push you off,
And if your knife is blunt
You get the dung on your elbow,
You come home empty-handed
And the dogs bark at you!

Using political power for personal wealth is a common feature of the petty bourgeoisie in developing countries, for in these countries there is no true national bourgeoisie, as in the U.S.A. or Europe, which derives its economic power from ownership of the means of production. Because it is not directly involved in the production of wealth, the African petty bourgeoisie is parasitic. Political power is the only means by which the political elite can acquire substantial wealth. Lawino speaks in Fanonian terms when she says:

The stomach seems to be
A powerful force
For joining political parties,
Especially when the purse
In the trouser pocket
Carries only the coins
With holes in their middle,

And no purple notes
Have ever been folded in it . . .

Lawino is not blind to the fact that, while politicians are fighting to
enrich their own pockets and inter-party strife rages, the common
people suffer, for they bear the brunt of the economic problems
wrought by the ineptitude of the political elite:

And while the pythons of sickness
Swallow the children
And the buffaloes of poverty
Knock the people down
And ignorance stands there
Like an elephant,
The war leaders
Are tightly locked in bloody feuds,
Eating each other's liver . . .

This view of the African petty bourgeoisie in control of political
power is corroborated by Ocol in *Song of Ocol*. First, he is so
thoroughly colonized that he hates himself for being black:

Africa
This rich granary
Of taboos, customs,
Traditions . . .

Mother, mother,
Why,
Why was I born
Black?

Accordingly, he and his fellow members of the elite want to destroy all
things African, anything that reminds them of their African past.
Instead, they will erect monuments to the architects of African
colonialism – Bismarck, David Livingstone, Leopold of Belgium and
others:

To the gallows
With all the Professors
Of Anthropology
And teachers of African History,
A bonfire
We'll make of their works,
We'll destroy all the anthologies
Of African literature
And close down
All the schools
Of African Studies.

Secondly, Ocol lends weight to Lawino's view that the misdemeanours
of African politicians lead to the impoverishment of the workers and

peasants. He has the cheek to deny responsibility for the poverty of the peasants, for rampant unemployment, for prostitution and other ills that have come with independence. But it is clear that Okot intends the denial to provide evidence for Lawino's claim. The denial is not convincing:

> Do you blame me
> Because your sickly children
> Sleep on the earth
> Sharing the filthy floor
> With sheep and goats?
> Who says
> I am responsible
> For the poverty of the peasantry?
> Am I the cause of unemployment
> And landlessness?
> Did you ever see me
> Touring the countryside
> Recruiting people's daughters
> Into prostitution?

There is of course an element of exaggeration, simplification and even unfairness in all this. We know, for instance, that many African leaders will not openly decry African customs and traditions, but pay lip service to African culture by creating such bogus philosophies as 'authenticity', empty slogans to befog the people and turn their attention away from real economic and social problems. Alternatively, as in some countries, they can perpetuate an oppressive feudal structure in the name of African tradition. We also know that there are exceptions to the portrait of the African political elite that Okot p'Bitek paints for us. Individuals like Julius Nyerere, Robert Mugabe and Samora Machel, despite their mistakes, genuinely worked for the good of the people in their individual capacities as leaders. In any case we are not blind to the fact that the economic and political destabilization of socialist countries like Mozambique, Angola and Zimbabwe is caused by external forces that do not wish to see genuinely patriotic leaders maintaining political control. However, Okot p'Bitek's poems have identified a serious problem of the African petty bourgeoisie. *Song of Lawino* and *Song of Ocol* are in fact footnotes to the warning given by that prophet of the African predicament, Frantz Fanon, who even before a significant number of African nations achieved their independence prophesied the ideological poverty and economic greed of the African ruling class. The following is as good a passage as any to vindicate this claim:

> A bourgeoisie similar to that which developed in Europe is able to elaborate an ideology and at the same time strengthen its own power. Such a bourgeoisie, dynamic, educated and secular, has fully succeeded in its undertaking of

the accumulation of capital and has given to the nation a minimum of prosperity. In under-developed countries, we have seen that no true bourgeoisie exists; there is only a sort of little greedy caste, avid and voracious, with the mind of a huckster, only too glad to accept the dividends that the former colonial power hands out to it. This get-rich-quick middle class shows itself incapable of great ideas or of inventiveness. It remembers what it has read in European textbooks and imperceptibly it becomes not even the replica of Europe, but its caricature.[5]

Unlike Fanon, however, Okot tends to highlight the cultural element and underplay the economic so that the dominant feature of his authorial ideology can be characterized as cultural nationalism, expressed with feeling and conviction. His is a voice of protest, directed not so much at cultural imperialism as at the African political and intellectual elite that has allowed itself to become the vehicle of neo-colonial culture. In a manner which shows his inability to link the behaviour of African leaders to the designs of the international bourgeoisie Okot p'Bitek declares: 'I believe that most of our social ills are indigenous, that the primary sources of our problems are native. They are rooted in the social set-up.'[6] This is a clear indication of a limited authorial ideology, of the poet's failure to understand that, while the local political elite contributes to the social and political problems of developing nations, there are other forces, such as imperialism and the international economic order, which play a major role in the political and economic destabilization of these countries.

Be that as it may, *Song of Lawino* is more than an attack on the colonial mentality of the African petty bourgeoisie. It is also a mine of information on Acoli culture. Lawino is a *fundi*[7], she is an expert on Acoli traditions; she compares Acoli culture with western culture; she holds forth on Acoli concepts of time, the significance of Acoli names and Acoli philosophy. Her song contains valuable information for sociologists, anthropologists and students of politics and oral traditions alike. We learn all these things while we are being entertained by her verbal skill, intellectual acumen and wonderful sense of humour. In the next section we shall attempt to account for the manner in which Okot p'Bitek articulates his vision and to comment on how successfully he achieves his goal. In the meantime, we should not overlook that the strong nationalistic sentiments of *Song of Lawino* are toned down in *Song of Prisoner*, where the protagonist shows an appreciation of a wide variety of cultures, both African and non-African. In his frustration and misery the protagonist (the prisoner) yearns for the rumba and cha-cha-cha dances as well as the sword dances of the Russians, the beer songs of Germany, the bamboo dance of the Chinese, the rice dance of the Japanese, and so on (pp. 106–108). This seems to indicate that Okot acquired a broader view of culture later in life.

Okot p'Bitek

Form and Communication in *Song of Lawino*

The power of *Song of Lawino* is due in large measure to the author's successful portrayal of an authentic spokesperson, an uneducated woman who has become highly aware of the necessity for her race to preserve its own culture and identity. She is a vivid and memorable character. At first she may appear lighthearted and flippant, but in fact she advances a sound and serious argument. Unlike the Negritude poets she does not overtly claim that African culture is superior to European culture. Her central argument is summed up at the end of Section 2:

> Listen Ocol, my old friend,
> The ways of your ancestors
> Are good,
> Their customs are solid
> And not hollow
> They are not thin, not easily breakable
> They cannot be blown away
> By the winds
> Because their roots reach deep into the soil.
>
> I do not understand
> The ways of foreigners
> But I do not despise their customs.
> Why should you despise yours?

To enable Lawino to advance her argument forcefully Okot gives her the gift of wit and employs Acoli poetic forms to produce a pungent work of satire. She first displays her wit forcefully at the beginning of Section 2, where she makes a mockery of modern notions of beauty, including the use of make-up and cosmetics, by comparing her rival, Clementine, the girl of modern ways, to what in traditional Acoli society must be regarded as the ugliest and most weird of all creatures. That which is considered most beautiful by admirers of European culture is made to appear absurd and grotesque. We shall quote a long passage to show how she builds up her argument:

> Ocol is no longer in love with the old type;
> He is in love with a modern girl,
> The name of the beautiful one
> Is Clementine.
>
> Brother, when you see Clementine!
> The beautiful one aspires
> To look like a white woman;
>
> Her lips are red-hot
> Like glowing charcoal,
> She resembles the wild cat
> That has dipped its mouth in blood,

67

Her mouth is like raw yaws
It looks like an open ulcer,
Like the mouth of a fiend!
Tina dusts powder on her face
And it looks so pale;
She resembles the wizard
Getting ready for the midnight dance

She dusts the ash-dirt all over her face
And when little sweat
Begins to appear on her body
She looks like the guinea fowl!

We note here that the attack starts as a fairly straightforward factual account of Lawino's husband's preference for a modern girl. Then in the next stanza the tone changes dramatically to a contemptuous one: 'Brother, when you see Clementine!'. Then the criticism gathers momentum and builds up to a crescendo as we get horrible image after horrible image, in the process of which Clementine is disfigured and transformed from 'the beautiful one' into a veritable 'guinea fowl'. But that is not the end. Before Lawino is done she must demonstrate to us how she is revolted by this monster of a woman and by the soap the monster uses until she, Lawino, is possessed by strange ghosts which make it necessary for a whole ritual to be performed before she can recover:

The smell of carbolic soap
Makes me sick,
And the smell of powder
Provokes the ghosts in my head;
It is then necessary to fetch a goat
From my mother's brother.
The sacrifice over
The ghost-dance drum must sound
The ghost be laid
And my peace restored.

This dramatic reversal of values is not limited to cosmetics and make-up. It is only a prelude to a more generalized attack on European social and cultural values which go against traditional codes of behaviour. Imported forms of dancing, for example, result in immoral behaviour when each man dances with a woman who is not his wife. Apart from being immoral, their kissing and dancing are seen as grotesquely ugly!

You kiss her on the cheek
As white people do,
You kiss her open-sore lips
As white people do,
You suck slimy saliva

From each other's mouths
As white people do.

And the lips of the men become bloody
With blood dripping from the red-hot lips;
Their teeth look
As if they have been boxed in the mouth.

Lawino is not only witty, she is versatile, conjuring up all kinds of images to bring her point home. This talent is coupled with a sense of humour and an ability to admit her weaknesses in a clever way, as in the following passage from Section 2, in which she cunningly confesses that she is jealous of the woman she ostensibly despises:

Forgive me, brother,
Do not think I am insulting
The woman with whom I share my husband!
Do not think my tongue
Is being sharpened by jealousy.
It is the sight of Tina
That provokes sympathy from my heart.

Then the truth comes out:

I do not deny
I am a little jealous
It is no good lying,
We all suffer from a little jealousy.
It catches you unawares
Like the ghosts that bring fevers;
It surprises people
Like earth tremors:
But when you see the beautiful woman
With whom I share my husband
You feel a little pity for her!

We also see her wit at work when she gives an account of the differences between European and African traditions and values. Ostensibly, her argument is that European culture is good for Europeans and African culture good for Africans, but in an apparently objective comparison she uses subtle animal imagery to portray a negative picture of things European and a positive picture of African values. This is particularly striking in Section 5, where the dominant motif is the comparison of the 'graceful giraffe', which symbolizes the beauty of the African woman, and the 'monkey', which stands for the ugliness of white women and those who ape whites by wearing white people's wigs:

I am proud of the hair
With which I was born
And as no white woman

Wishes to do her hair
Like mine,
Because she is proud
Of the hair with which she was born,
I have no wish
To look like a white woman

No leopard
Would change into a hyena
And the crested crane
Would hate to be changed
Into the bald-headed,
Dung-eating vulture,
The long-necked and graceful giraffe
Cannot become a monkey

In addition to investing Lawino with a witty mind, a sense of humour and a capacity for dramatization, Okot p'Bitek has the ability to make use of traditional tropes and modes of expression in a manner which enriches his poetry and lends it a peculiar freshness. Comparing the modern technological concepts of time with Acoli concepts Lawino describes the Acoli idea of late morning in the following terms:

When the sun has grown up
And the poisoned tips
Of its arrows painfully bite
The backs of the men hoeing
And of the women weeding or harvesting
This is when
You take drinking water
To the workers.

The devices that are most frequently and most effectively used are apostrophe and lampoon.[8] Apostrophe is the device by which the protagonist or persona directly addresses the interlocutor or the imagined audience. For example, Lawino frequently addresses her husband using such expressions as 'Listen, my husband', 'My husband, Ocol', 'Ocol, my friend'. Apostrophe is also frequently used simultaneously with the satirical mode of the lampoon. Lawino addresses her husband directly in the second person and at the same time speaks in a manner which reduces him to the level of a fool. In Section 12 she lampoons Ocol by telling him directly how stupid he is to ape and be subservient to white people. Lawino pleads with her husband, but in a manner that ridicules him:

Listen, my husband,
Hear my cry!
You may not know this
You may not feel so,
But you behave like

A dog of the white man!
A good dog pleases its master,
It barks at night
And hunts in the salt lick
It chases away wild cats
That come to steal the chicken!
And when the master calls
It folds its tail between the legs.

The dogs of white men
Are well trained
And they understand English!
When the master is eating
They lie by the door
And keep guard
While waiting for left-overs.

But oh! Ocol
You are my master and husband,
You are the father of these children
You are a man,
You are you!

Do you not feel ashamed
Behaving like another man's dog
Before your own wife and children?

Section 12, from which the above quotation is taken, constitutes the climax of Lawino's argument and demostrates Okot p'Bitek's use of apostrophe. The section falls into three major subsections if we go by Lawino's subject matter and her audience. In the first subsection Lawino addresses her clansmen. The subject matter is her husband's 'dark forest of books':

Listen, my clansmen,
I cry over my husband
Whose head is lost.
Ocol has lost his head
In the forest of books.

This, as we shall see, is at the heart of her argument. In the second sub-section she addresses Ocol in the words quoted above and does not mention books at all. Then she ends the section by going back to address the clansmen and returning to the subject of books. In the last section, Section 13, her whole approach, manner and tone of voice change: she tones down the bitterness in her voice and instead of lampooning her husband she cajoles him, coaxes him like a loving wife, even advising him to buy clothes, beads and perfumes 'for the woman / With whom I share you'. She assumes the role of both a teacher and a loving wife. In Section 13 she does not address her clansmen at all. In Section 12, however, her clansmen occupy the centre of the stage in her address. They are her primary audience as she expounds her views on the danger of books. Using apostrophe and other traditional tropes Lawino deals a deadly blow to the educated elite that has imbibed western bourgeois culture through exposure to books written in the West. Whereas books are ordinarily regarded as a source of knowledge and enlightenment, Lawino likens the large volumes of books in her husband's study to a dark and deadly forest:

My husband's house
Is a mighty forest of books,
Dark it is and very damp,
The steam rising from the ground
Hot thick and poisonous
Mingles with the corrosive dew
And the rain drops
That have collected in the leaves

This mighty forest is indeed a deadly one for the books 'choke you / if you stay there long'. So poisonous are they that 'the boiling darkness / Bursts your eye balls' and blocks your sense of hearing as well. So the description goes on in a manner which can make readers and critics of Okot p'Bitek miss the centrality of this section to Lawino's argument. She sounds naive or even flippant, but in actual fact Okot is using a very sophisticated device. In what is only superficially a naive comparison, Lawino goes on to associate death with the books in her husband's house because, as she says, the books were written by dead white men and women. So she claims that the 'ghosts' of the dead men and women who wrote these books have 'captured' her husband and will capture and destroy anybody who stays too long in the house:

If you stay
In my husband's house long,
The ghosts of the dead men
That people this dark forest,
The ghosts of the many white men
And white women
That scream whenever you touch any book,
The deadly vengeance ghosts
Of the writers
Will capture your head,
And like my husband
You will become
A walking corpse.

This is a simple but effective way of explaining how African intellectuals who are educated in western-type schools become helpless victims of neo-colonialism in the same way as people who entered a dangerous forest in traditional society fell prey to the ghosts of dead

people. We notice here that what the ghosts in Ocol's dark forest of
books are keen to capture is the 'head' of the victim, which means the
mind. Okot p'Bitek is analysing the malady of a social class of which
Ocol is a representative. This class has been emptied of all its African
cultural values by imbibing western culture. It is because of her sense of
the devastating effects of this alien culture on her husband that, using
apostrophe in a most dramatic way, Lawino calls upon all her
clansmen to come and mourn her 'dead' husband:

> O, my clansmen
> Let us all cry together!
> Come,
> Let us mourn the death of my husband,
> The death of a Prince
> The Ash that was produced
> By a great Fire!
> O, this homestead is utterly dead,
> Close the gates
> With *lacari* thorns,
> For the Prince
> The heir to the Stool is lost!

But at this juncture Lawino comes into the open and makes it clear that
she is not only concerned about her husband. Her concern is for the
entire social class to which Ocol belongs. To draw her argument to a
close she employs the traditional conceit of young men losing their
manhood in the forest. This time it is the dark forest of books that has
done the deed:

> For all our young men
> Were finished in the forest,
> Their manhood was finished
> In the class-rooms,
> Their testicles
> Were smashed
> With large books!

In this way, through the use of apostrophe, lampoon, Acoli expressions and other devices both oral and modern, Okot creates a
memorable satirical touchstone in *Song of Lawino* for the rest of
African poetry.

Conclusion

We must not, however, exaggerate Okot p'Bitek's success, for *Song of
Lawino* is not without shortcomings. One of these is that it is uneven,
parts of it being dull and flat. For example, parts of Section 4, where
Lawino boasts about having been the leader of girls in her younger
days, are quite tedious. The weakness of the poem in this regard

becomes even more apparent when it is compared with *Song of Prisoner*, whose density of texture is sustained throughout and whose language is packed with emotion and feeling.

Some of the traditional modes of expression Okot employs in *Song of Lawino* do not come off – at least for those readers who do not understand Acoli. In this connection, the proverb which says 'the pumpkin in the old homestead should not be uprooted' occurs frequently, and is clearly meant to play a key role in conveying Lawino's message. But to the author of this book, to whom Acoli is a strange language, the proverb conveys little or no meaning. This is also true of some of Okot's imagery. Consider, for instance, the following lines from Section 2 where Lawino introduces the conceit of Clementine as the woman with whom she shares her husband:

Her body resembles
The ugly coat of the hyena;
Her neck and arms
Have real human skins
She looks as if she has been struck
By lighting;

Or burnt like the Kongoni
In a fire hunt.

This is far from being as effective as the description of Clementine which occurs at the beginning of the same section and which was quoted earlier in the chapter.

There are also some inconsistencies and contradictions in *Song of Lawino*. As a character, Lawino sometimes gets out of hand and Okot is not able to control her and shape her plausibly. What Lawino says in Section 11 is out of character. Her analysis of the behaviour of politicians in Uganda is so sophisticated that one wonders whether she is the same woman who is at one time amazed at the ticking of Ocol's clock (Section 7). In Section 11 Lawino does not strike the reader as a simple woman commenting in a simple way about political rivalry. Naturally, I am not suggesting that peasants cannot be political analysts. They can in fact be more revolutionary than the intelligentsia; but the problem here is that Okot presents us with a seemingly simple peasant woman and then turns her into a political scientist without creating the circumstances that give rise to such a transformation.

From the point of view of the flow of the verse, *Song of Lawino* is not particularly well constructed. The poetry is much too rugged and devoid of lyrical qualities. Okot p'Bitek was not entirely successful in employing such devices as alliteration and repetition which could have made his poetry more pleasant to the ear. There are, however, instances of the effective use of such devices, especially in *Song of Prisoner*. In *Song of Lawino* too, one can cite Section 11, where repetition and parallelism help to quicken the pace of the verse, as in the following passage:

> The women yodel
> And make ululation!
> They yodel and make ululation
> Not because they understand,
> They yodel so that their voices may be heard
> So that their secret lovers may hear them,
> They shout and make ululations
> Because they are tired
> Tired of the useless talk
> Tired of the insults
> And the lies of
> The speakers.

All said and done, however, we can justifiably say that Okot p'Bitek's achievement in *Song of Lawino* is unparalleled in African poetry to date. Using traditional modes of expression and tropes he created a powerful and memorable poem in the medium of English. His achievement becomes more significant if we take into account the fact that he communicates even more effectively in the Acoli language, the language of the peasant community that gave him the inspiration to champion the cause of African culture. In this poem Okot successfully resolved the problem of the contradiction between the writer's medium and his audience. He cannot be accused of elitism because he speaks directly to the Acoli masses in their own language and is at the same time able to communicate with all those who understand English the world over. Okot p'Bitek's art is an example of that rare phenomenon: popular art which appeals to the highly educated while being intelligible to the common man and woman in the street.

Notes

1. This chapter is based on the combined edition *Song of Lawino* and *Song of Ocol*, Nairobi, East African Publishing House, 1972. There is now a Heinemann edition of the same volume. The two poems were first published in 1966 and 1967 respectively.
2. All the references to *Song of Prisoner* and *Song of Malaya* in this chapter are from Okot p'Bitek, *Two Songs*, Nairobi, East African Publishing House, 1971.
3. G.A. Heron, *The Poetry of Okot p'Bitek*, London, Heinemann Educational Books, 1976.

4.   See Okot p'Bitek, *Africa's Cultural Revolution*, Nairobi, Macmillan, 1973, p. 13.
5.   Frantz Fanon, *The Wretched of the Earth*, Harmondsworth, Penguin, 1967, p. 141.
6.   See *Africa's Cultural Revolution*, pp. 6–7.
7.   A Hindi word current in East Africa, meaning 'maker' or 'expert'.
8.   See Heron, op. cit., Chapter 2.

7

Afrocentric Consciousness
& Dialectical Thought
in Mazisi Kunene

Kunene and Zulu Literature and Culture

Of all the poets discussed in Part II of this book Kunene is probably the one who best exemplifies an authorial ideology that is based on a well-conceived Afrocentric philosophy. His poetry not only shows an Africa-centred consciousness; it is also based on a profound under-standing of the culture and cosmology of an African nation – the Zulu. For Kunene, the use of traditional material involved a careful study of the Zulu literary tradition, Zulu literary forms and the effects of colonialism and Christianity on Zulu literature. As a consequence, he became acutely aware of the fact that when modern Zulu poets tried to write poetry in Zulu after being brought up on a tradition of English poetry they faced 'immeasurable problems' in both content and form. Modern Zulu poets found themselves imitating nineteenth-century English poets like Keats, Shelley and Wordsworth, with disastrous consequences.[1] Kunene's own poetry is based on Zulu literary forms and Zulu thought, as he explains in the Introduction to *Zulu Poems*.[2]

In focusing on Zulu traditions, however, Kunene does not degene-rate into narrow-mindedness and ethnicity. He does not write as a Zulu who is unaware of Africa. He uses the Zulu tradition and Zulu cosmology to assert his Africanness. Zulu literature is therefore given as an example of an African literary tradition. The philosophy that Zulu literature expresses is seen as an African philosophy which differs from a European world view. Explaining some of the characteristics of traditional African literature, Kunene has this to say:

Contrasting Responses to Colonialism

Zulu literature, like most African literatures, is communal. This has fundamental stylistic and philosophical implications. The communal organisation
in Africa is not just a matter of individuals clinging together to eke out an
existence, as some have claimed, nor is it comparable (except very superficially) to the rural communities in Europe. It is a communal organisation
which has evolved its own ethic, its own philosophical system, its own forms
of projecting and interpreting its realities and experiences.[3]

However, Kunene is sometimes in danger of falling into the trap of
overgeneralization in his assertion of Zulu thought as representative of
African thought, for there are differences from one African culture to
another in concepts of time, in morality and other aspects. There is
unity and diversity in Africa and the writer should not lose sight of this.

In *Zulu Poems*, Kunene uses traditional modes of thinking and
expression without advocating a return to the past, nor does he
necessarily glorify the past like the Senghorian school of Negritude. On
the contrary, Kunene's writing at this stage is characterized by
dialectical thinking. His poetry depicts a world which is constantly
moving forward to a higher state, and this partly accounts for the
strong element of optimism that runs through the poems on resistance
to apartheid. However, the picture changes somewhat in *The
Ancestors & the Sacred Mountain*, as we shall see.

Kunene writes in Zulu and translates into English. As explained in
the chapter on Okot P'Bitek, this resolves the problem of writer and
audience which bedevils other African writers. Needless to say,
translation also presents its own problems and this is one of the issues
we will address in our examination of his poetry.

To date, Mazisi Kunene has published four volumes of poetry in
English: *Zulu Poems*,[4] which came out in 1970, two epics, *Emperor
Shaka the Great: A Zulu Epic*[5] and *Anthem of the Decades: A Zulu
Epic*,[6] and a second collection of short poems, *The Ancestors & the
Sacred Mountain*.[7]

It is not our intention to discuss all four books in this chapter. The
two epics are analysed and summarized in Ken Goodwin's *Understanding African Poetry*, whose chapter on Kunene is undoubtedly one
of his best.[8] *The Ancestors & the Sacred Mountain* was published in the
1980s and, like the epics, it falls outside the period under consideration
in this section of the book where we are concerned with poetry written
not later than the early 1970s. Consequently, this chapter will focus on
Zulu Poems, a volume which not only marked Kunene's début into
African poetry of English expression but is an important point of
reference in any discussion of the poet's later development. However,
in order to give a complete picture of his handling of shorter, non-epic
forms of poetry and to determine whether there has been a shift in his
authorial and aesthetic ideology, we shall refer briefly to *The

Ancestors & the Sacred Mountain in the appropriate sections of the chapter.

Traditional World View and Dialectical Thought in Kunene's Poetry

There are numerous poems in *Zulu Poems* which not only in their idiom but also in their very subject matter exemplify Kunene's interest in Zulu philosophy and culture. These include 'In Praise of the Earth', 'Stages of Existence', 'The Bond' and 'Three Worlds', to mention but a few. In these poems Kunene the poet explores the cosmology of the Zulu people, their attitude to moral issues, social relations, death and other issues. But in exploring Zulu beliefs and cosmology he is not content merely to give us an artistic picture of what Zulus thought and believed. He uses Zulu traditional thought to articulate his own philosophy of life, his own view of the world. Zulu traditional literature and thought are therefore used to illuminate the present and the future. In *Zulu Poems* there is no advocacy of a return to the past, no sentimentalization or idealization of the past. An interesting example of how Kunene utilizes traditional material to project his own philosophy in *Zulu Poems* is 'Anthem of Decades', an extract from the epic *Anthem of the Decades* which dramatizes the Zulu creation myth. The extract presents an apocalyptic and dramatized account of the creation of animals and human beings. In the beginning, the earth was surrounded by darkness and silence before the creator filled the planet 'with the commotion of beasts'. Then the earth is depicted as a pregnant woman who gave birth to all manner of creatures:

> The belly of the earth split open
> Releasing animals that crawl on the earth
> And others that fly with their wings
> And others that drum their hoofs on the ground.
> The lion roared thundering the first fear.
> Other beasts less ferocious stared
> Until, aware of the satisfying taste of blood,
> Joined in the general carnage.
> So the lesson was learnt. Life must continue
> And good things must feed the ruthlessness of appetites.

Before one goes very far it becomes clear that, while his aim is to recreate the Zulu myth on the origins of life, Kunene is also influenced by John Milton's *Paradise Lost* or the Bible creation story in the Book of Genesis or both. The parallels and echoes are too strong to be purely fortuitous. Just as in *Paradise Lost* there is a debate among the angels in heaven, there is also a debate in Kunene; just as there are good and bad angels in Milton there are progressive and conservative messengers in

Kunene. There is Sodume, who represents the progressive forces that together with the creator's daughter, Nomkhubulwane, favour the creation of human beings, while Somwazi represents the conservative faction that fears the new creature. In the Bible story 'man' is created last of all, and the same is true of Kunene's story. The debate among the celestial beings is about whether or not human beings should be created. Kunene admits in the Introduction that not everything in 'Anthem of Decades' is taken from the Zulu creation myth. 'I have used the story of the origin of life', he says, 'and added my own detailed descriptions according to the dictates of Zulu culture.'[9] The important thing, however, is that, while he may have been influenced by the Christian creation story, Kunene has been careful not to introduce into his poem elements that are obviously alien to Zulu culture. The idea of good and evil, for example, does not appear as such: 'I have not however presented Somwazi as the devil since such a concept does not exist in traditional Zulu thought. He is the opposing force which has good and valid questions to put.'[10] At the end of the day, Nomkhubulwane and Sodume carry the day and the progressives win. 'I and others who love the extension of life', declares Sodume, 'say let men stand supreme over the earth.'

What is more important for us here is Kunene's translation of this myth to fit into modern thinking. As already indicated, Kunene's thinking is characterized by dialectical materialism, which sees the world as being in a constant state of motion, progressing from lower to higher levels of existence. His world is not a static one. This is the very basis of Nomkhubulwane's argument in the whole debate on the creation of human beings:

> Those who oppose the hand of creation
> Do so believing that what is, is complete.
> But they do not understand, creation must always create
> Its essence is its change.
> From it abundance splits itself to make abundance.
> Whoever loves its greatness does not question it
> Since to question is to weave strange tangles.
> Its greatness is its expense as always.

This philosophy permeates Kunene's thinking at this stage of his career, as we shall see. Coupled with this progressive outlook is an optimism which believes that progressive forces will ultimately triumph. In brief, therefore, we can summarize Kunene's authorial ideology in *Zulu Poems* as that of an Afrocentric, optimistic and dialectical thinker who uses Zulu culture and traditional thought to give expression to his own vision. This is best exemplified by those poems that deal with what may be called 'themes of resistance'. I use this term to distinguish these poems based on an abstract conception of the South African situation from those that deal more directly with the present stage of the concrete struggle in South Africa. Of course, some poems belong to both categories and this is shown by the fact that some of the poems in *Zulu Poems* appear in Feinberg's *Poets to the People*,[11] which features in Part III of this volume.

Poems on themes of resistance fall into three categories. First, there are poems which record Kunene's response to European culture and ideology; secondly there is a group which treats the theme of resistance to oppression in South Africa in an indirect, almost allegorical way, using the traditional idiom; and finally there are those that portray the theme of resistance more directly, in what I call 'the modern idiom'.

The first category consists of very few poems, the best ones being 'Europe' and 'The Civilisation of Iron'. In both of these poems there seems to be a major problem of translation in that some of the images blur the meaning and bring about an apparent inconsistency in the treatment of the theme. But the central message is clear – the hard-heartedness and complete lack of warmth of Europe. Thus 'Europe' opens with this declaration:

> Europe, your foundations
> Are laid on a rough stone.
> Your heart is like cobwebs
> That are dry in the desert.

It is this hard-heartedness which led Europe to choose 'the bridegroom of steel'. In 'The Civilisation of Iron', steel is similarly associated with cold and violent cruelty:

> I saw them
> In their long processions
> Rushing to worship images of steel:
> They crushed the intestines of children
> Until their tongues fell out.
> I saw iron with sharp hands
> Embracing infants into the flames.
> They wandered on the roads
> Preaching the religion of iron,
> Pregnant with those of blood and milk.

In 'Europe' the poet articulates his ideological opposition to this in clear terms. As in the case of other members of the African intelligentsia he went through a period in which European values were accepted without question, but that period is over now:

> Once I believed the tales.
> Once I believed you had breasts
> Over-flowing with milk

While these two poems were consistent with the poet's Africa-centred consciousness they reveal a manner of thinking which is not typical of

Kunene. They smack of Negritude and it is probable that Kunene wrote them under its influence. The images of steel and iron have a peculiarly Senghorian ring about them. They remind one of Senghor's 'New York'. To see the real Kunene at work we should move on to the second and third groups of poems we have identified.

The poems in which Kunene employs what I have called 'the traditional idiom' operate on two levels, giving two layers of meanings. On one level they portray a traditional world view. On another level the poems convey a deeper meaning which makes them relevant to the contemporary situation in South Africa. I include in this category such poems as 'Thoughts at the Gathering of the Storm', 'Peace', 'Stages of Existence', 'A Great Generation', 'The Spectacle of Youth' and many others which work on this principle.

In 'Thoughts at the Gathering of the Storm' clouds are conceived of as fumes from the pipe of 'the great smoker' in the skies, which at the various stages of their movement blot out the rays of the sun, then wipe out 'the centre of the sun' and finally let out 'tears' of rain. The image of the great smoker is a particularly effective one:

> The great smoker smokes wild hemp in the skies.
> The smoke clouds move patiently
> Giving life to a million images.

In the third stanza we move away from the description of the storm to a mood of contemplation of its significance. Using the first person plural, the protagonist reflects on the idea of the end of the world, which in turn brings thoughts about tomorrow being followed by another tomorrow, meaning that time does not remain static – it moves on. This realization is followed by another puff from the great smoker, who is no longer just a smoker but 'the smoker of time':

> We do not know when the world will end.
> So we stand on an ant hill
> Eulogising a thousand years
> Saying tomorrow, there will be tomorrow
> Suspended with our shadows on the clouds.
> It is then that the great smoker of time
> Will smoke again, in the abyss of the south.

The last two lines, following on 'Saying tomorrow, there will be tomorrow', bring about a second layer of meaning. The great smoker smokes again 'in the abyss of the south'. By association this refers to the inevitability of change in South Africa. When the great smoker of time smokes in the south there will be another tomorrow there.

In 'Stages of Existence' we move away from smoke and clouds to the rainbow. The protagonist uses the rainbow to tie the earth so that it gives birth. Two sets of images contend with each other on the rainbow. First he sees 'the faces of old women', who 'raised their heavy eyes / Like the shadows of magical figures'. These are symbols of the past. When he ties the earth another set of images comes out:

> Beyond the red boundaries
> Is the new lightning of children
> Who will grow above
> The shadows of old women.
> When they have conquered them
> They may rest and create new forms
> That inspire new life
> Making knots for eternity
> From which new generations will arise . . .

So the past will be conquered and a new generation will rise. This concept of a new generation recurs in 'A Great Generation', a dramatic poem in three voices. The poem, one of several in this mode, takes the form of a dramatized conversation in different voices. The conversation is in the question and answer form and centres on two characters, Mathungo and Bhekani, who left home promising to return the following day but have now taken too long to come back. We shall quote the entire poem:

Others: When shall Mathungo and Bhekani return
So long ago they departed, promising their return
the day after?

One: They will return
When the walls thunder with beetles.

Others: What holds them in this long absence?

One: It is the days obstructing them in their return,
Blocking the gates in the land of setting suns;
Demanding from them the fruit of life.

Others: Where will they find it, since the world
decays with the years?

One: It is they alone who hold the truth.

All: They will bring life to a great generation,
A generation that will rise from the ruins.

One: I hug their deafness in the dark
The voices begin to speak their first syllables
Giving their messages.

Without stating it explicitly the poem clearly alludes to the South African liberation struggle. Mathungo and Bhekani represent the new generation of fighters who left the country and have taken long to come back. This is a way of expressing the idea of a protracted liberation struggle. But there is optimism in the minds of the majority of the South African people symbolized by the voice of 'All'. This optimism in 'the new generation' is confirmed by the voice of the 'One' who is foresighted, who hears the fighters beginning 'to speak their first syllables / Giving their messages'.

The last example we shall quote from this group is a beautiful little poem which shows in just eight lines how ingenious Kunene can be in employing traditional Zulu modes of expression to portray a modern theme. This is 'The Spectacle of Youth', a poem in which the struggle in South Africa is portrayed as a struggle between 'the children of the lion' and 'buffaloes'. The former begin to show their skill from a very early age, conscious as they are of 'simulating the ancient heroes'. One sure sign of their skill at this tender age is their ability to leap 'on the tender necks of antelopes'. This is an indication that very soon they will be going for the buffaloes themselves and killing them:

I loved the children of lion
When their manes were beginning to grow,
Simulating the ancient heroes.
I knew the greatness of their future
When they leapt on the tender necks of antelopes
Which so long prided themselves on their fleetness.
I praised the skilfulness of their power,
Knowing how soon they will be killing buffaloes.

One of the strengths of Kunene in the group of poems just discussed is his ability to use allegory in order to speak at two levels and convey two meanings, a superficial one and a deeper one. These poems have no emotional appeal but they give pleasure because of the author's ability to speak quite simply about a serious matter in what appears to be a casual manner. In the last quoted example the theme is one of violent confrontation but it is depicted in a gentle and graceful manner.

In the last group of poems the poet is more direct in his treatment of the theme of resistance to apartheid. Included in this group are poems such as 'Thought on June 26', 'Time Will Come', 'Vengeance' and 'The Political Prisoner'.

The last-mentioned poem presents the hopes of a political prisoner desirous of reaching 'The other side of the fortress of stone', anxious to be free. Then in the second stanza we are presented with the image of someone who brings dreams of hope, a widow who passes the prisoners carrying firewood. It is this woman who fills the prisoner protagonist with dreams of future freedom until there is a vision of someone else opening the gate.

One day someone arrives and opens the gate.
The sun explodes its fire
Spreading its flames over the earth,
Touching the spring of mankind.

Hope is portrayed in the image of the sun 'Spreading its flames over the earth' to revive the life of humanity. This vision is given more concrete expression in 'Time Will Come' where time is endowed with powers of healing, bringing about hope for tomorrow. The optimism of the poet becomes evident in the use of apocalyptic imagery which gives a powerful description of future victory for 'the children of the sun'. Before a new South Africa is born there will be an eruption of violence because the arms of time 'Will kindle the flame of the volcano / Erupting with light onto our paths'. This is a poem which has both a specific reference to South Africa and, possibly, a wider frame of reference, indicating the poet's hope for a better world:

Time will come
Bringing the gifts of her secrets
These arms that are bound into infinity
Will kindle the flame of the volcano
Erupting with light onto our paths.
Imagination shall overpower the children of the sun
Making them burst forth with our tomorrows.
They shall give birth before their innocence has been consumed.

In 'Vengeance' Kunene employs an oral technique in which the speaker uses rhetorical questions to address an enemy. The poem is a monologue in which the protagonist gives vent to his indignation at the injustice of the enemy. The skilful use of repetition and parallelism results in a forcefulness which strengthens the emotional appeal of the rhetorical question and answer of the poem:

How would it be if I came in the night
And planted the spear in your side
Avenging the dead:
Those you have not known,
Those whose scars are hidden,
Those about whom there is no memorial,
Those you only remembered in your celebration?

Then the structure changes from a rhetorical question to a statement; images of fire and flames appear again and we have a forceful portrayal of feelings of revenge:

We did not forget them
Day after day we kindled the fire,
Spreading the flame of our anger
Round your cities,
Round your children,
Who will remain the ash-monuments
Witnessing the explosions of our revenge.

The technique of the rhetorical question is perfected in one of Kunene's most well-known poems, 'Thought on June 26'. The poem was written in commemoration of South Africa Freedom Day and would seem to have been designed to be read aloud to a public audience. From the first line to the last this twenty-six-line poem consists of a series of rhetorical questions on whether or not it is wrong to take revenge and use force against the enemies of the people of South Africa (although there is no direct reference to South Africa). Though unanswered, the question 'Was I wrong?' is clearly intended to elicit the answer 'No'. The rhetorical question is used together with images and idioms taken from Zulu culture. Thus, in the fourth line, we have the expression, 'The rope of iron holding the neck of young bulls'. In the seventh and eighth lines there is a reference to 'the orphans of sulphur' rising from the ocean. In the twelfth and thirteenth lines we are presented with the image of 'towns of skeletons, / Sending messages of elephants to the moon'. The poem proceeds from a generalized statement which does not mention the object of criticism to specific targets that are cited towards the end. At the same time the cumulative effect of the rhetorical question comes out most strongly in the last nine lines:

> Was I wrong to erect monuments of blood?
> Was I wrong to avenge the pillage of Caesar?
> Was I wrong? Was I wrong?
> Was I wrong to ignite the earth
> And dance above the stars
> Watching Europe burn with its civilisation of fire;
> Watching America disintegrate with its gods of steel,
> Watching the persecutors of mankind turn into dust
> Was I wrong? Was I wrong?

Obviously Kunene does not confine his anger to apartheid South Africa here. The whole imperialist world comes in for an angry attack with Europe and America being specifically cited. The voice of anger becomes evident and so does the justness of the cause.

All the poems discussed in this section reflect a forward-looking attitude on the part of the author, who is constantly looking forward to a new South Africa. By the time we come to *The Ancestors & the Sacred Mountain*, there is a new shift, though not a fundamental one. First, the dialectical thought that characterizes the earlier poems is modified by a greater emphasis on the past. Many of the poems in the second volume express the need to return to the ancestors or 'forefathers' including ancient Egyptian ancestors. This is true of such poems as 'The Return of Inspiration', 'In Praise of the Ancestors', 'My Forefathers' and 'The Years of Silence'. It becomes clear that Kunene now puts greater emphasis on the inspiration of dead poets and the achievements of past generations of Africans than he did in *Zulu Poems*. His own achievements as a poet and those of the present generation are a gift from the forefathers. In 'In Praise of the Ancestors,' he says:

They have opened their sacred book to sing with us.
They are the mystery that envelops our dream
They are the power that shall unite us.
They are the strange truth of the earth.
They came from the womb of the universe.

The concept of the new generation, which features quite prominently in *Zulu Poems*, is still there but is now largely overshadowed by the idea of continuity between the past, the present and the future. Thus the backward look to the ancestors is in part advocated in order to stress the importance of continuity. But historical and cultural continuity is not all for Kunene. The search for continuity must include a search for the link between humanity and the cosmos, a theme which is explored in a number of poems, including 'Cyclic Movement', 'Cycle of Fortunes' and 'Images of the Cosmos from the Earth'. All this serves to show that Kunene is a philosophical poet who is guided by a particular conception of the interrelatedness of tradition, humanity and the universe. It also indicates a new idealism in the second anthology which one does not feel in the first.

Some Key Features of Kunene's Aesthetic Ideology

As stated earlier, *Zulu Poems* represents a wide variety of themes and styles. There are a number of elegies, for example, in which, following traditional Zulu poetry, the poet has used the technique of understatement. There are poems about beauty, about gold-miners, about relationships between people. There are also several poems about poetry and art which demonstrate Kunene's depth of understanding of the subject, such as 'Triumph of Man' and 'Dedication to a Poet'. The salient point, however, is that Kunene has developed a distinctive style through which all these themes are explored. The style is a direct product of the author's abiding interest in Zulu culture and cosmology. The poetry is replete with images of the planets and the constellations – sun, moon, earth, stars and sky. These occur again and again but do not, as in the European convention, symbolize romantic love. They have a direct bearing on the traditional Zulu interpretation of the universe. Kunene says in the Introduction, 'Again, according to the Zulu cultural tradition, the moon, the sun and the stars are physical phenomena which primarily express the nature of distance and the quality of light, while also being symbolic of (physical) power.'[12]

Another important category of imagery is drawn from the animal world. In some of the poems analysed in this chapter, including 'The Spectacle of Youth' and 'Thought on June 26', animal imagery is a central feature of the style. There are references to the lion, antelope, buffalo, elephant and bull. While images of the constellations and planets allude to Zulu cosmology and philosophy, animal imagery is used with reference to fighting. In some of the poems, particularly later poems of struggle, animal imagery is sometimes replaced by images of birds of prey with the eagle representing the forces of liberation and vultures the oppressors. This is true of, say, 'The Rise of the Angry Generation' and 'A Heritage of Liberation'.[13] In 'Anthem of Decades' Kunene uses a particularly powerful image of 'the bluebird of heaven', which symbolizes the wrath of the gods:

> But Sodume's voice, round and powerful, shook the heavens.
> Often he emerged with her in relentless pursuit.
> Both cherished the bluebird of heaven
> Whose tail was deep blue, whose wings were blue
> Whose body was blue but whose feet were burning red.
> Wherever they were they let it fly before them like a cloud.

An extremely important set of images is the category of images which project the poet's optimism and dialectical thought. Like the poetry of T.S. Eliot, Kunene's poetry teems with words that refer to time. Such words as 'time', 'generation', 'tomorrow', 'birth' and 'pregnant' recur over and over again. Associated with these words are images like 'the rainbow', 'lightning', 'dawn' and 'the setting sun'. These words, particularly the first set, relate to the poet's idea of time bringing about a better future, time resolving present problems.

The dream motif is also linked to the idea of the healing aspect of time. It occurs in 'The Political Prisoner', 'Conquest of Dawn', 'The Idealist' and other poems. The motif seems to symbolize what a dream is in real life – hopes and wishes which cannot be fulfilled. In 'The Political Prisoner', for example, the dream turns into an illusion.

The last feature we shall take note of has to do with the new developments that occur in *The Ancestors*. In this later collection Kunene's poetry is much more lyrical and reads more like English poetry than the poetry in *Zulu Poems*. This positive development can be exemplified by the first eight lines of 'Tribute to Mshongweni' with its enchanting rhythms:

> After the festival, after the feast
> After the singing
> After the voices faded into the night
> And the sounds of talking have ceased
> And the angry winds have shed their manes
> And the people have stopped the dance
> Your voice and your voice only
> Shall rise from the ruins.

The poem achieves even greater power and concentration in the remaining thirteen lines. Kunene's achievement in this collection is that of capturing the attention of the reader even in very short poems such as 'On Light', 'The Years of Silence' and 'At the Shore'. Consider, for example, the lyrical quality and imaginative appeal of the last-mentioned poem, which we shall quote in full here:

Empty shells, black stones, seashore,
Witness against the blue sky;
Mother of the red sand and white tails of oceans.
'Follow me' I said to the little crabs and they did.
Now we possess the whole wide world
The soft things of water, the holes, the sea plants
The ability to see the green stones.
We are the bread awaited for these thousand years
We don't need a dream, we don't need a paradise
We are the dream, the crossway of the rainbow
The dawn that breaks all round the earth
We shall plant motherhood on all things
And through us the season shall see the world's awakening . . .

Translation, Traditional Idiom and Communication in Kunene

We noted earlier that Kunene writes his poems in Zulu and then translates them into English. The question that arises is: to what extent does his experiment succeed in *Zulu Poems*? No doubt translation has its limitations even when the poet does his own translation. In the case of Kunene it is clear that in some poems the use of Zulu idioms and grammatical structures presents difficulties in respect of intelligibility and consistency. 'The Political Prisoner' is a case in point. The poem proceeds very well from the first stanza to the fourth. The reader can see a logical thread of thought running through the first four stanzas. The fifth and last stanza is however confusing. The widow is abandoned; she is not able to give birth; she only prides herself 'in the shadows of yesterdays'. This gives rise to a number of questions in the reader's mind: is the widow meant to represent a positive idea or is she a negative symbol? Why is she abandoned? And why is she unable to give birth? The conclusion of the poem is rather puzzling.

In 'The Civilisation of Iron' the reader is thoroughly baffled by the association of 'milk' and 'blood' as images. Is milk meant to have a negative connotation like blood? Most of Kunene's readers would come from cultures where milk is regarded as a source of nourishment. In the same poem the idea of love being 'for sale in the wide streets / Spilling from bottles like gold dust' clearly fails to come off. The whole poem becomes a mishmash of discordant images, as the following lines demonstrate:

They wandered on the roads
Preaching the religion of iron,

Pregnant with those of blood and milk,
I saw milk flowing
Like rivers under the feet of iron.
The earth shrank
And wailed the wail of machines.
There were no more people,
There were no more women,
Love was for sale in the wide street
Spilling from bottles like gold dust.
They bought it for the festival of iron.
Those who dug it
Curled on the stones
Where they died in the whirlwind.

'The Civilisation of Iron' is a typical example of a poem which, judged by its content and ideological orientation alone, is by all means an important work of art, but put to the test of effective communication it is an utter failure. There is a limit to which the idioms of one language can work in another, particularly where such vastly different languages as Zulu and English are involved. To some extent the poem also exemplifies one of the major weaknesses of *Zulu Poems*. Much of the poetry in the volume is too sombre, almost dull. It lacks the freshness and liveliness of Okot p'Bitek's poetry. Much of it manages to appeal to the imagination but not to the emotions. Lewis Nkosi, himself a Zulu speaker, has criticized Kunene quite harshly for some of his unintelligible lines, but more particularly for using as his model a type of poetry that is meant to be recited before a public audience. Nkosi has this to say:

> The Zulu praise-poetry on which a large proportion of these poems is modelled is a type of poetry which is singularly unsuited for the withdrawn meditative voice, working in isolation from an immediate audience; even when the poet is soliloquising, the requirements of a public audience, however 'invisible', are too great for us not to sense a deep internal disorder in the poetry. This feeling of tension, even embarrassment, such as we feel when we overhear an individual talking aloud to himself can only be ameliorated, never completely dispelled in a poetry that cries out to be chanted or performed while it is simultaneously written for the silent page.[14]

In reaction to Lewis Nkosi's comment, I wish to emphasize that, while Kunene's method gives rise to some major difficulties, there is however no doubt that he has been reasonably successful in his rendering of Zulu images and concepts. His use of images taken from Zulu cosmology gives some of his poems a concreteness and vividness lacking in the works of many an African poet. Images of birds and animals have a similar effect, as explained earlier in this chapter. Kunene's method is particularly effective in poems like 'Vengeance' and

'Thought on June 26' where Zulu idioms and concepts are strengthened by such poetic devices as repetition, parallelism and rhetorical questions, which lend these poems a certain forcefulness lacking in some of the others. Furthermore, as Nkosi himself admits, Kunene can be very successful in his short poems. Poems like 'Time Will Come', 'The Spectacle of Youth' and 'Dedication to a Poet' are major achievements in very few lines. It could therefore be argued that Nkosi's criticism is too severe as an overall judgement, though regarding a poem like 'The Civilisation of Iron', discussed above, it is justifiable.

Kunene seems to have come to the realization that his method needs to be perfected. He tells us that the poems in *The Ancestors & the Sacred Mountain*, like those in *Zulu Poems*, were translated from Zulu. However, many of the poems in the later collection, like the two cited in this chapter, have a certain quality which suggests that, in his more recent poetry, our poet does not merely translate, but also endeavours to capture the natural rhythms and idioms of the English language.

Conclusion

In assessing Kunene's achievement the reader is left in some doubt as to whether the poet has developed much in authorial ideology. This is because the dialectical approach to the analysis of social phenomena that is one of the strengths of *Zulu Poems* seems to have been weakened by the incipient idealism that one senses in *The Ancestors & the Sacred Mountain*. However, Kunene's contribution to African poetry is substantial, particularly if we take into account the two epics, which we have not discussed in this chapter. In the context of this book, the importance of Kunene's contribution lies mainly in his attempt to reconcile the world view and linguistic repertoire of a traditional society with the structures and rhythms of a foreign language, which he is using to convey the concerns and hopes of a modern and complex society. His method has problems that we have already referred to, but his aesthetic ideology is encouraging. In the second volume, he probably loses something of the force of Zulu idioms and modes of thinking in the struggle to express them in English, but his poetry communicates better with the reader. This is a positive development in his aesthetic ideology.

Notes

1. Mazisi Kunene, *Zulu Poems*, London, André Deutsch, 1970, pp. 19–20.
2. Ibid.
3. Ibid., p. 11.
4. Ibid.
5. M. Kunene, *Emperor Shaka the Great: A Zulu Epic*, London, Heinemann Educational Books, 1979.
6. M. Kunene, *Anthem of the Decades: A Zulu Epic*, London, Heinemann Educational Books, 1981.
7. M. Kunene, *The Ancestors & the Sacred Mountain: Poems*, London, Heinemann Educational Books, 1982.
8. See K.L. Goodwin, *Understanding African Poetry: A Study of Ten Poets*, London, Heinemann Educational Books, 1982.
9. *Zulu Poems*, p. 26.
10. Ibid.
11. Barry Feinberg (ed.), *Poets to the People: South African Freedom Poems*, London, Heinemann Educational Books, 1980.
12. *Zulu Poems*, p. 17.
13. Both poems are included in B. Feinberg, op. cit.
14. Lewis Nkosi, *Tasks and Masks: Themes and Styles of African Literature*, Harlow, Longman, 1981, p. 149.

PART THREE

POETRY
& THE AFRICAN
LIBERATION STRUGGLE

8

Myth, Pan-Africanism
& the Liberation Struggle
in Wole Soyinka

Soyinka the Poet and Mythmaker

Soyinka is one of Africa's foremost writers and one who has likewise made an impact in the world. Unlike most other African authors he is an all-rounder, who has established himself as dramatist, novelist and poet. His claim to international acclaim as a poet rests on the publication of poems contained in two volumes, *Idanre and Other Poems*[1] and *A Shuttle in the Crypt*.[2] These two volumes show Soyinka's unusual talent for using difficult words and complex constructions. Also, and this is particularly true of *Idanre*, Soyinka is a poet of grand conceptions who employs myth as a poetic device. In fact, the composition of *Idanre* marked a major turning point in Soyinka's career as a poet and as a writer generally. *Idanre* was written after a dramatic experience which brought back memories of Soyinka's visit, three years earlier, to a rockhill which bears the name 'Idanre' and is regarded as the legendary dwelling place of Ogun, the Yoruba god of war, creativity and metals. Soyinka seems to have had some revelation, calling him to fulfil a vocation, in a manner similar to the experience of Christopher Okigbo, who suddenly felt a call to function as the priest of the Igbo river goddess, Idoto. Soyinka dramatizes his own experience as follows:

> Three years later and some two hundred miles away, a rainstorm rived apart
> the intervening years and space, leaving a sediment of disquiet which linked

me to lingering, unresolved sensations of my first climb up Idanre. I abandoned my work – it was middle of the night – and walked. *Idanre* is the
record of that walk through wet woods on the outskirts of Molete, a pilgri-
mage to Idanre in company of presences such as dilate the head and erase
known worlds.[3]

From that time on, Ogun has become the central symbol in Soyinka's
writing and he, Soyinka, has become the god's priest. His next long
poem, *Ogun Abibiman*,[4] was named after the god and this is the poem
we shall focus on in this study.

First, I want to make two important observations about Soyinka the
poet. The first is that his stature as a poet has been exaggerated, particularly in the West. I will add my voice to the voices of those African
critics who have decried Soyinka for his inability to communicate.[5]
Most of the poems in *Idanre and Other Poems* and *A Shuttle in the
Crypt* either are simply impenetrable or have no emotional appeal.
There is verbal dexterity but it is observed by the author's obsession
with difficult words and complicated constructions. As if obscurity
were not enough, Soyinka's poetry fails also to appeal to the emotions,
the imagination or the intellect. It is much too abstract, all dry bones
without any juice and no flesh. Such poetry does not speak to the
reader or listener and cannot be classified as good poetry. We must
repeat the comment made in Chapter 2 that if art has no appeal it is not
art.

The second issue is that of his use of African myths. This might at
first give the impression that Soyinka is a traditionalist. However, the
embracing of Ogun as his central symbol in *Idanre* and other poems
does not signify an African nationalist consciousness on the part of the
author, like that of Achebe or Okot p'Bitek. For the use of such a myth
to signal a nationalist or revolutionary consciousness it has to arise
from the poet's acceptance of his or her own culture and a reaction
against the dominant ideology of the ruling class or colonial power.
Achebe's use of Igbo modes of expression, for example, was motivated
by a desire to assert the positive aspects of African culture which had
been negated by colonialism. There was therefore a cause-and-effect
relationship between his negation of cultural imperialism and his
affirmation of African values. Not so with Wole Soyinka: his use of the
Yoruba god Ogun as an artistic motif was not commensurate with a
search for an African identity.

There is no suggestion here that the use of myth and modes of
expression from African tradition is the only indication of a revolutionary or nationalist consciousness on the part of a writer. In this
author's scheme of things, a truly revolutionary consciousness trans-
cends nationalism and advocates a socialist world view. Nonetheless,
in countries that have gone through the process of colonization a

nationalist consciousness is the necessary first step in that direction. Soyinka's use of traditional myths in his first two volumes of poetry is not an expression of a new and progressive ideological orientation. At this stage of his development his poetry does not show the tension between African and European cultural values that we encounter in the poetry of Okot p'Bitek or Gabriel Okara. Soyinka's search for a myth was really a means of placing him in the tradition of such poets as Yeats, Eliot and other western poets.

Be that as it may, I maintain that an objective and dialectical analysis of Soyinka will not condemn him totally on this score, because it will show that he has developed both in political consciousness and in aesthetic ideology. Two publications signal this development, the novel *Season of Anomy* and the poem *Ogun Abibiman*. In *Stylistic Criticism and the African Novel* I explained that in *Season of Anomy* we see Soyinka tending towards a revolutionary and socialist consciousness. *Ogun Abibiman* shows a definite development in the direction of a committed Pan-Africanism and a determination to communicate effectively with the reader. In *Ogun Abibiman* Soyinka has found matter for his myth and a manner of putting his verbal dexterity to good use. It is this welcome development in Soyinka's poetic career that this chapter sets out to demonstrate. And because *Ogun Abibiman* is an important poem that celebrates Africa's determination to liberate itself from the destructive tentacles of apartheid it is only appropriate that this chapter should serve as a prologue to our analysis of the poetry that articulates the embattled voice of the people of southern Africa.

Ogun Abibiman and the Liberation Struggle

Ogun Abibiman falls into three parts. In Part I, titled 'Induction', Soyinka seizes a moment in African history, when Africa is getting ready for the final onslaught against racial domination. Soyinka saw this moment when the late President Samora Machel of Mozambique closed the border with Rhodesia on 3 March 1976, as a concrete indication of Mozambique's decision to support the guerrilla war against Rhodesia. To Soyinka, that moment was 'more profoundly self-evident as the definitive probe towards an ultimate goal, a summation of the continent's liberation struggle against the bastion of inhumanity – apartheid South Africa'.[6]

For Soyinka then, this is the moment for the affirmation of black power and this affirmation is articulated in the form of the reincarnation of the Yoruba god of war, Ogun.[7] Part I has the subtitle 'Steel Usurps the Forests; Silence Dethrones Dialogue'. This symbolizes two principles running through this section and the entire poem. Steel refers to arms of war, to Africa's acceptance of an armed liberation struggle; while the dethroning of dialogue by silence signifies the rejection of the policy of dialogue with South Africa which had been advocated by some members of the Organization of African Unity (OAU). Silence also lends weight to the tense atmosphere created in this part of the poem, an atmosphere which symbolizes a moment in African history charged with tension and emotion, indicating Africa's preparedness for the final onslaught. An atmosphere of tension is partly achieved through the use of apocalyptic imagery – imagery that symbolizes a violent eruption or transformation. Thus we get images of birds, storms, rivers, floods and blood. Accordingly, Africa's protracted struggle, which is nevertheless certain of final victory, is portrayed in the following terms:

> The boughs are broken, an earthquake
> Rides upon the sway of chants, a flood
> Unseasonal, a power of invocations.
> Meander how it will, the river
> Ends in lakes, in seas, in the ocean's
> Savage waves. Our Flood's alluvial paths
> Will spring the shrunken seeds;
> Rains
> Shall cleanse the leaves of blood.

The green forests of West and Central Africa are now being replaced by 'tracks of steel / And iron frames' borne southwards by Ogun's fighters who are shedding 'green hopes / Of nature paths', giving rise to a new hope of a united front. The moment is so tense with the spirit of fighting that the earth feels it, and time shudders as Ogun kindles the flame in the Blacksmith's shop where, as god of metals, war and creativity, he silently shapes the weapons of war:

> Earth
> Rings in unaccustomed accents
> Time
> Shudders at the enforced pace
> Ogun
> In vow of silence till the task is done,
> Kindles the forge.

As we enter Ogun's farmstead we become witnesses to the revolutionary creativity that has been generated. The Blacksmith's hand hatches the revolution between 'Hammer and anvil', the Craftsman's hand 'unclenches' in the act of creation, the singer's tongue is loosened and the drummer's armpits 'Flex for a lyrical contention'. All arts, all forces are bringing about a new creative unity; there is a strong feeling of oneness, of Pan-Africanism, as all forces move together towards the hour of resolution of the conflict. Now the poet, Ogun's acolyte, 'medium of tremors from his taut membrane', celebrates the great impact of this phenomenal motion of the forces of liberation:

> A cause that moves at last to resolution
> Prediction folds upon prediction till
> The hour-glass is swallowed in its waspish
> Waist, the sun engorged within
> The black hole of the sky,
> Time and space negated, epochs impacted
> Flat, and all is in the present.

Like a professional poet and musician singing songs to the greatness of Sundiata, founder of Ancient Mali, Soyinka the poet assumes the role of a *griot* announcing the imminent coming of Ogun, to assert himself as the god of black people, he 'Whose prostrate planet is Abibiman' – the Land of the Black Peoples. The god of black people is now ready to go to war with the god of the usurpers of the black land and black power, hence 'Let gods contend with gods'. As singer of the black people's new-found determination, Soyinka denounces the option of dialogue with South Africa, embracing the 'vow of silence'. He reminds us that the Sharpeville massacre occurred after dialogue with the racists. The racists will therefore return dialogue with violence. Dialogue, the poet warns us, is ineffectual protestation, the bark of a feeble dog.

Like a *griot* praising the military prowess of his king, Soyinka sings to the power of Ogun, using various poetic devices, including parallelism, repetition and animal imagery, designed to have a cumulative effect, and ending with the portrayal of Ogun as the greatest of gods, who is now ready to spill blood for the total liberation of Africa:

> We speak no more of mind or grace denied
> Armed in secret knowledge as of old.
> In time of race, no beauty slights the duiker's
> In time of strength, the elephant stands alone
> In time of hunt, the lion's grace is holy
> In time of flight, the egret mocks the envious
> In time of strife, none vies with Him
> Of seven paths, Ogun, who to right a wrong
> Emptied reservoirs of blood in heaven
> Yet raged with thirst – I read
> His savage beauty on black brows,
> In depths of molten bronze aflame
> Beyond their eyes' fixated distances –
> And tremble!

In Part II, the focus is on Shaka and on the union between Shaka and Ogun. That union is celebrated in the refrain *Rogbodiyan*, which Soyinka translates as follows:

Wole Soyinka

Turmoil on turmoil!
Ogun treads the earth of Shaka
Turmoil on the loose!
Ogun shakes the hand of Shaka
All is in turmoil

Ogun is, of course, a god and superior to Shaka and it is he who comes down to Shaka's land. Shaka recognizes him as a god and a kindred spirit. He realizes that their union is a historic moment for it signifies the union of the forests and the savannahs, the merging of tropical and sub-tropical Africa as one continent and one nation, fulfilling his prophecy that his land would never be ruled by aliens:

Our histories meet, the forests merge
With the savannah. Let rockhill drink with lion
At my waterholes. Oh brother spirit,
Did my dying words raise echoes in your hills
When kinsmen matched broad blades
With Shaka's shoulders? *The whites have come,*
And though you seize my throne, you will never
Rule this land.

In Soyinka's design Shaka ranks the noblest of the rulers of Abibiman, and the meaning of Shaka's nation, the Amazulu, becomes a generalized one – the Amazulu become the inhabitants of the Land of the Black People. But there is a stern warning against pretenders to the throne of Shaka. In the glossary Soyinka says, 'The professional apologists of our time did try, uncritically, to place in the same category of leaders as Shaka, that murderous buffoon who lately straddled territory where once the great Shaka trod.' Soyinka may have a specific despotic ruler in mind when he says this, but it could equally be argued that the poem makes a collective attack on all African despots and those who are not genuine leaders of the people. Thus any or all of the following could be included in the criticism – Idi Amin, Bokassa, former self-styled 'Emperor' of the Central African Republic, Haile Sellassie of Ethiopia, who called himself 'King of Kings, Lion of Judah' – as suggested by the line 'Will you make a pinhead, bloated leech a lion too?'. The criticism could even include Gatsha Buthelezi, the South African-backed leader of the Kwazulu Bantustan, who is not recognized by the South African Liberation Movement and the Organization of African Unity as a genuine representative of the Zulu people.

In Part III, Soyinka returns to Shaka's war cry, *Sigidi!* which he translates as 'The song of the spearblade as it bites: *I have eaten!*'. The acceptance of this war cry symbolizes an acceptance of the necessity for violence in the struggle for the liberation of southern Africa. Hence the poet and *griot* rejects the claim of those who plead non-violence, those 'chimer(s) of peaceful times'. After all non-violence is returned with violence:

Will love survive the epitaph –
Another Kaffir gone, saves us the sweat?
Can love outrace the random bullet
To possess the heart of black despair?
Remember Sharpeville – not as aberrations
Of the single hour, but years, and generations.

However, the poet/singer/*griot* proceeds to explain that it is not violence that he celebrates, but the end of a long spell of despair. The poet celebrates Africa's new-found hope and determination to fight so that Shaka may again rule the Land of the Black People:

If then we claim – the poet now is given
Tongue to celebrate, if dancers
Soar above the branches and weird tunes
Startle a quiescent world – Vengeance
Is not the god we celebrate, nor hate
Nor blindness to the loss that follows
In His wake.

Nor ignorance of history's bitter reckoning
On innocent alike. Our songs acclaim
Cessation of a long despair, extol the ends
Of sacrifice born in our will, not weakness.
We celebrate the end of that compliant
Innocence of our millennial trees.

Soyinka ends the polemic on violence and non-violence with a reference to Yeats's poem 'The Second Coming'. Just as in Yeats the coming of the 'rough beast' that 'slouches towards Bethlehem to be born' symbolized the end of an era, the end of Christian civilization, so in Soyinka the second coming of Ogun and Shaka signals the end of white rule in Africa. But Soyinka is engaged in a debate with Yeats and the opponents of violent revolution here. While Yeats and those who preach non-violence see 'mere anarchy' being 'loosed upon the world', it is the same Yeats who, in another poem that celebrates an act of violence, 'Easter 1916', says 'A terrible beauty is born'. Soyinka reminds the arm-chair proponents of non-violent change that the African revolution is also giving birth to beauty:

When, safely distanced, throned in saintly
Censure, the prophet's voice possesses you –
Mere anarchy is loosed upon the world et cetera
Remember too, the awesome beauty at the door of birth.

Part III ends with a repetition of the closing lines of Part I which portray the military powers of Ogun in animal imagery. But before he comes to that the poet explains the function of poetry and the arts in the struggle. Now is the time for song, we are told, now is the time for the drummer to play his drum because, 'The drummer's / Exhortations fortify the heart'. The fighter is like a dancer. The dancer is given more courage by song and drum, and so the fighter's heart is fortified by the artist. Now is the time for the artist to sing and celebrate the courage of the black people as he sees the clans 'massed from hill to hill / Where Ogun stood', with their weapons 'from the kilns of Abibiman' dancing to the ancient war cry of *Sigidi*! The *griot* celebrates the ascent of Ogun.

Conclusion

In *Ogun Abibiman*, Soyinka has created a minor epic which is of direct relevance to the African predicament. His prophecy that Samora Machel's act of 1976 was 'a summation of the continent's liberation struggle against the bastion of inhumanity', namely, South Africa, has been partially fulfilled. Four years after Soyinka wrote the poem, Rhodesia became Zimbabwe and the struggle with South Africa became even fiercer. Samora Machel himself ended a victim of the conflict in a mysterious aircrash on South African territory on 19 October 1986. Meanwhile, Mozambique has become the primary target of Renamo or the MNR (Mozambique National Resistance Movement), which is directly supported by South Africa. Southern Africa is a fierce battlefield and the situation is tense. Gods are indeed contending with gods as the god of apartheid musters support from the major imperialist forces of the world. For Ogun and Shaka the going is tough yet, but 'Meander how it will, the river / Ends in lakes, in seas, in the ocean's / Savage waves'. Epic poetry is the most appropriate medium for depicting this titanic struggle of the African people against the worst of human enemies.

The epic form of the poem is evident in its grand design – gods contending with gods – and in its elevated and declamatory style. It is evident in the poet's assumption of the role of *griot* in the tradition of such great epics as *Sundiata*. For the first time, Soyinka genuinely turns to African tradition to seek poetic inspiration and suitable motifs. Thus, not only does he employ the Ogun–Shaka myth to express a new Pan-Africanist consciousness, but he also uses a Yoruba refrain to dramatize the union of Ogun and Shaka, and two Zulu war cries, *Sigidi*! and *Bayete*! While there are still allusions to Yeats these are used dialectically to convey a progressive African ideological standpoint. The imagery used to evoke Shaka and Ogun mirrors their precapitalist world view. Thus the white marauders are referred to as 'termites' while Shaka is 'the black soldier ant'. To describe the warped colonial mentality of some of his descendants, Shaka talks in terms of the termites having 'First built their nest / In the loin-cloth of the king'. Finally, the animal imagery at the end of both Parts I and III, expressing the supremacy of Ogun, is very much the kind of language we would expect a true *griot* would use. Thus in both form and content *Ogun Abibiman* reflects a new and genuine Africa-centred consciousness in Soyinka. This is an important step in writing socially committed literature.

Notes

1.   *Idanre and Other Poems*, London, Methuen and Co., 1967.
2.   *A Shuttle in the Crypt*, London, Rex Collings/Eyre Methuen, 1972.
3.   *Idanre and Other Poems*, p. 57.
4.   *Ogun Abibiman*, London, Rex Collings, 1976.
5.   See, for instance, Lewis Nkosi, *Tasks and Masks*, London, Longman, 1981, p. 161, and Chinweizu, Jemie O. and Madubuike, I., *Toward the Decolonization of African Literature*, Volume 1, Washington D.C., Howard University Press, 1983, pp. 187–188.
6.   See 'Preface' to *Ogun Abibiman*.
7.   For Soyinka's theory on Ogun see Wole Soyinka, *Myth, Literature and the African World*, Cambridge, Cambridge University Press, 1976, pp. 140–160.

9

Revolutionary Practice & Style in Lusophone Liberation Poetry

Introduction

In Chapter 3 we noted that the poetry that was produced before the fighting phase in Angola, Mozambique and Guinea Bissau shares some common characteristics in both content and form with Negritude poetry. We also noted that like that of David Diop much of the Lusophone poetry of the period was characterized by realism. But, however practical and committed they were to the fight for justice, some of the poets were bound to engage, at least to some degree, in theoretical abstractions. This is certainly true of Noémia de Sousa, who declares in the poem 'Black Blood':

> Oh my mother Africa
> Great pagan, sensual slave
> mystic, charmed
> to your transgressing daughter
> Give forgiveness![1]

Even Agostinho Neto in 'The Blood and the Seed', a very down-to-earth poem, refers abstrusely to 'cries', 'voices' and 'hymns':

> Our cries
> are drums heralding desire
> in the tumultuous voices, music of nations,
> our cries are hymns of love that hearts
> might flourish on the earth like seeds in the sun
> the cries of Africa
> cries of mornings when the dead grew from the seas
> chained
> the blood and the seed

Poetry & the African Liberation Struggle

For the future – here are our eyes
for peace – our voices
for peace – our hands

from Africa, united in love.

These are poems by members of the intellectual elite using revolutionary language that is divorced from practice. Very often the resistance to Portuguese oppression was 'passive' resistance, consisting of theorizing without concrete action. All that was to change in the 1960s after the launching of the armed liberation struggle by the People's Movement for the Liberation of Angola (MPLA), the Independence Party for Guinea Bissau and Cape Verde (PAIGC) and the Front for the Liberation of Mozambique (FRELIMO).

The fighting phase gave birth to a new category of poetry. In Mozambique and Angola the poetry of this period is completely free of mystification and subjective idealism. It is a poetry that reflects the concrete reality of a people fighting for freedom, independence and social justice. Although written in Portuguese, the poetry reflects the concerns and wishes of a whole society in which class barriers have been broken down, as the people's sense of unity and purpose grows in their determination to defeat colonialism and build a new and just society.

The poetry of this phase is characterized by the unity of theory and practice. In other words, the philosophy that the poetry articulates is not based on abstractions, but is the result of participation in an actual struggle. One indication of this is the pattern of imagery that runs through Part 2 of Margaret Dickinson's collection, *When Bullets Begin to Flower*. Contrary to the earlier period when the poet used the protest language of 'voices', 'songs', 'drums', 'hope' and 'progress', suggesting a purely theoretical involvement in the struggle,[2] now there is a new set of images which signify a concrete liberation struggle. The images can be put in the following major categories: images of blood and pain; images of cultivation and planting; and images of fertility – flowering, water and rain. In addition, there are constant references to struggle, revolution, unity and hope. Hope is now for something achievable, based on the observable progress of the struggle and not on speculation and wishful thinking, as in the previous phase.

Imagery and Language

Images of blood and pain run through such poems as Agostinho Neto's 'February', Sampadjudo's 'Our Sure Road' and Helder Neto's 'We shall not Mourn the Dead', to name but a few. In these and other poems the necessity for suffering, for shedding blood for the sake of freedom, is accepted without regret. There is now a firm realization that independence cannot be given on a platter; it calls for suffering, endurance and sacrifice. To Sampadjudo pain and blood are the prelude to the joy of freedom:

> Pain and blood
> Pain and blood is the road,
> the ticket we must buy
> to reach our independence along the endless path of our work and our joy
>
> Our sure road is pain and blood
> straight road to the sun
> to the sun of our freedom.

These words are echoed by Helder Neto, who repeats again and again in 'We shall not Mourn the Dead':

> The liberation of our country calls for
> blood
> The blood of her best sons.

These images of blood and suffering bespeak a concrete revolution, a people's real struggle and the poet's participation in it. That the war is a people's war, a collective war waged by the masses, is evident in the constant reference to 'we' and 'the people', as in Antonio Jacinto's 'The People Went to War' and Marcelino dos Santos's 'To Point a Moral to a Comrade'. In the latter poem the individual, the 'You' or 'I', is consciously and openly subordinated to the collective:

> What matters is not what I want
> or YOU want
> but what WE want

And again:

> Each of us
> has a private wish
>
> but what WE want
> is not what I want or you want
> but what WE want

It is in this collective spirit that we see the people of Angola and Mozambique 'planting' the revolution, making it grow. Images of planting, cultivating, creating and building take various forms. Marcelino dos Santos adopts the image of planting as the heading of one of his poems, 'We Must Plant', where the new tree of independence is to be planted everywhere:

> everywhere
> we must plant
> the certainty
> of tomorrow's good
> in the endearments of your heart

where every child's eyes
renew their hope

Yes, mother
We must plant,
We must plant
Along the road of freedom
the new tree
of National Independence.

In Helder Neto the liberation of the country is associated not only with blood but also with rain which enables the wild grass to grow 'as high as the savannah'. In dos Santos's 'To Point a Moral to a Comrade' the guerrillas:

Create hospitals
Create schools

Their task is to
dig the basic soil of Revolution
and make a strong people grow

The protagonist points out time and time again:

We must cultivate
the shamba of the Revolution
a hard future
of sweat, of toil, of blood

And the poem closes with these words in block capitals to make the message loud and clear:

. WE ARE FRELIMO SOLDIERS
ACCOMPLISHING THE PARTY'S TASK
DIGGING THE BASIC SOIL OF REVOLUTION
FOR AN END OF EXPLOITATION MAN BY MAN
TO BUILD COMPLETE NATIONAL
INDEPENDENCE

Images of planting are naturally associated with those of flowering, indicating the fruitfulness of the revolution. Hence, as the Frelimo soldiers 'dig the basic soil of Revolution', they see 'the first young shoots proclaimed / in Cabo Delgado and Niassa Province'. And rightly so because

To expect rice
without sowing it
is not the history of man.

It is through labour and the armed struggle that planters and fighters can make flowers grow, as Sampadjudo tells us in 'Our Sure Road':

Listen Caboverdian,

the siren of the future must sing
in the factories of our land
Look, Caboverdian
how the flower of the future opens all things
in the garden of our land.

There is a clear philosophy behind these images of cultivation and building. First, they are concrete images which bespeak a materialist non-metaphysical conception of life and social struggle. Secondly, through these images the poets proclaim the Marxist philosophy of the dignity of labour, the centrality of work in any endeavour to wage a revolution or to embark on a programme of development. That is why in the poem 'To Point a Moral to a Comrade' which is packed with ideological content Marcelino dos Santos proclaims:

TODAY
We must cultivate
the shamba of the Revolution,
a hard future in the bush

wearing out our hands and eyes
in the great sustained effort.

It is through labour that struggling people will eventually see themselves 'gathering the first fruits' of freedom. It is by carrying guns that fighters will see their revolution flower into independence and sovereignty.

An important feature of the poetry of the liberation phase in Angola, Mozambique and Guinea Bissau is simplicity. There is neither complicated stylization nor artificial adornments; the poets make no show of intellectual erudition. The poems are simply written, so as to be accessible to all classes of people. They depict the people's struggles and their sufferings, achievements and hopes. Margaret Dickinson's collection appropriately ends with Jorge Rebelo's 'Poem', of which the final words are a fitting epilogue:

Come tell me these dreams become war,
the birth of heroes
land reconquered,
Mothers who, fearless
send their sons to fight.

Come, tell me all this, my brother.

And later I will forge simple words
which even the children can understand
Words which will enter every house
like the wind
and fall like red hot embers
on our people's souls

In our land
Bullets are beginning to flower.

Lusophone Poetry and Frantz Fanon's Categories

In *The Wretched of the Earth* Frantz Fanon sees the literature of colonized nations developing as part of national consciousness. In the first stage of its literary activity, the intelligentsia seeks to appeal to or denounce the colonial master. Later, the writer turns to and addresses his or her own people, and finally engages in a literature of combat which calls on the people to fight for their existence as a nation:

> The continued cohesion of the people constitutes for the intellectual an invitation to go farther than his cry of protest. The lament first makes the indictment; then it makes an appeal. In the period that follows, the words of command are heard. The crystallization of the national consciousness will both disrupt literary styles and themes, and also create a completely new public. While at the beginning the native intellectual used to produce his work to be read exclusively by the oppressor, whether with the intention of charming him or of denouncing him through ethnical or subjectivist means now the native writer progressively takes on the habit of addressing his own people.[3]

While it is true to say that Frantz Fanon developed these categories at a particular juncture of history, they nevertheless have a certain generality which illuminates our understanding of the development of poetry in Portuguese-speaking Africa. In our analysis we have identified two distinct phases. First, there is the phase (the second in Fanon's categories) when the poet writes about the people, highlighting how they have been affected by slavery, colonialism or segregation. This poetry is marked by a degree of objective realism, by an appeal to the history, sufferings and struggles of the people. Many of the poems of Agostinho Neto, Viriato da Cruz, Noémia de Sousa and others belong to this precombat phase which is characterized by much theorizing about the struggle against colonialism, and sometimes by language that is highly charged with emotion, as in Noémia de Sousa. Then there is the poetry of combat, written under the influence of the armed liberation struggle, when the writer has advanced ideologically through theory and practice. This poetry is frequently sad and moving, but it is almost free of feelings of hatred, presenting facts objectively. In this poetry the focus is no longer on the oppressor, but on the prosecution of the armed liberation struggle, and on the people who have now become the subject of history.

Simplicity of Style and Artistic Value – Conclusion

As already indicated, much of the poetry of the fighting phase is written in a simple and direct style. In the case of Mozambican poetry, the simplicity is sometimes overdone, as in Marcelino dos Santos's 'We Must Plant'. If we accept the view that 'good' poetry should stand the test of time and remain effective even after the war has been fought and won, then the extreme simplicity of style in dos Santos and others would appear to militate against this. We have to remember, however, that liberation poetry, like liberation songs, is meant to have popular appeal and make an immediate impact on the listener or reader. Putting aside the fact that it was written in Portuguese, which many of the masses could not understand, Mozambican and Angolan liberation poetry is otherwise an example of this kind of popular poetry.

Notes

1. This poem and all the poems cited in this chapter are quoted in Margaret Dickinson (ed.) *When Bullets Begin to Flower*, Nairobi, East African Publishing House, 1972 (Reprinted 1980).
2. See ibid., pp. 28–29.
3. Frantz Fanon, *The Wretched of the Earth*, Harmondsworth, Penguin edition, 1967 (Reprinted 1980), p. 193.

10

Ideology,
Craft & Communication
in Zimbabwean Freedom Poetry[1]

Introduction

In this chapter we shall examine poems that were influenced by the Zimbabwean war of liberation, focusing on three aspects, authorial ideology, craft and communication. Much of the poetry was written during the struggle for an independent Zimbabwe, but some of it was composed after independence.

Of the three poets discussed below, two did not actually participate in the physical fighting, while the third was a guerrilla who composed some of her poems at the height of the war. Of the two who were not combatants, one was in the country throughout the armed conflict while the other was incarcerated by the Rhodesian regime and subsequently forced into exile. We may therefore expect to discern differences in ideological orientation and style between a patriot (Zimunya) reflecting abstractly on the struggle; a keen observer of the conflict (Hove) writing from close quarters; and an active participant in the revolution (Nyamubaya), whose poetry issues from the actual experience of fighting a war of liberation.

A feature of Zimbabwean war poetry which distinguishes it from Lusophone liberation poetry is that it was not written by senior party people. While people of the status of Eddison Zvobgo and the Reverend Canaan Banana, the first president of the Republic of Zimbabwe, have published poems on the struggle for Zimbabwe, there are no senior party officials who exerted anything like the degree of influence that Marcelino dos Santos, Jorge Rebelo and Agostinho Neto did in Mozambique and Angola. What this means is that the poetry of the Zimbabwe revolution is not likely to show the degree of ideological clarity that we discern in Lusophone liberation poetry. It also means that the programme of action that Mozambican poetry in particular articulates is not a significant feature of Zimbabwean freedom poetry, for the Zimbabwean poets wrote principally as individuals recording their own experiences and reactions to the war of liberation, and not as party leaders whose intention might be to influence the course of the revolution through the medium of poetry.

In my discussion of the three dimensions of poetry referred to above, I shall focus on four volumes by three poets : Musaemura Zimunya's *Thought-Tracks*,[2] Chenjerai Hove's *Up in Arms*[3] and his *Red Hills of Home*[4] and Freedom Nyamubaya's *On the Road Again*.[5] I have selected these four because they represent the best poetry that has been published by Zimbabweans in English since independence. I shall not venture to include poetry written in African languages in my discussion and this means that I am leaving out some of our best poets such as the late Joseph Kumbirai. I am also aware that a comprehensive treatment of Zimbabwean poetry written in English since 1980 should make mention of Kristina Rungano, Hopewell Seyaseya and Elfigio Muronda. There are, of course, numerous other poets whose poems are included in *And Now the Poets Speak*.[6]

Musaemura Zimunya

The collection of poems in *Thought-Tracks*, the best of this poet's published collections, covers a wide range of themes and stylistic stances, as can be seen from its seven sub-divisions. Rather than summarizing each section, I shall give a few examples.

Part I contains poems that act as a window on to Zimunya's home area and his experience as a child. We are given a view of children's life in this rural setting, the games they play and their struggle with domestic animals and the elements. Some of the poems describe the mountains that abound in the eastern districts of Zimbabwe, the homes Zimunya and his contemporaries lived in, the ever-threatening menace of drought, people's reaction to their environment and their interpretation of the universe. In Part II the dominant theme is the plight of the political prisoner in white-ruled Rhodesia. In many of the poems the poet is the protagonist and he speaks as a prisoner, contemplating the cruelty of white prison officials, recalling the humiliation he was subjected to when he was imprisoned and writing to his mother in an effort to console her. Part IV is dedicated to freedom fighters and Part V to Great Zimbabwe and the nation of modern Zimbabwe.

A striking feature of this collection is its patriotism. Whether Zimunya is describing the scenery, longing for home from across the seas or singing songs to Great Zimbabwe, he is ever conscious of his duty to his country. At the centre of Zimunya's vision as a poet is the concept of Zimbabwe as a nation, imbuing the whole collection with a strong spirit of nationalism. This reflects the prevailing spirit among patriotic Zimbabweans during the war of national liberation. The writing of poetry became for Zimunya part and parcel of the search for a Zimbabwean identity, symbolized by Great Zimbabwe. Zimunya has this to say in the Introduction:

> At the height of the war of liberation, Great Zimbabwe seemed to speak eloquently timelessly to all who sought and fought for the freedom of this land. It was a living myth. At the same time the message which it seemed to communicate was proportionally impossible to capture . . . I realised that while we were looking for Freedom, we were also engaged in a quest, a quest for an individual accommodation with existence and for the meaning of Great Zimbabwe.[7]

Great Zimbabwe is, therefore, the central symbol in some of the best poems. Other symbols include mountains and the Zimbabwe Bird. These images are linked, so that the mountains of the eastern districts merge into the Rock of Great Zimbabwe and the Zimbabwe Bird in turn symbolizes the nation.

Zimunya's later poetry is predominantly joyful in mood. In this, his first collection, the mood of the poet changes quite significantly from one section to another, and at least three of the sections are quite distinct in this sense. In Part I the dominant mood is that of jollity and celebration. In 'Children's Rain Song' the poet seeks to capture the joyful mood of rural children playing in the rain:

> I see little children
> fling their small clothes away
> like merry flying termites
> after their rainy wedding flights
> skipping, hopping and screaming in the rain
>
> Rain fall fall
> we will eat berries
> rain fall for all
> We will eat mealies
> we will eat cucumbers
> rain fall fall

In 'Kisimiso' he describes the happiness of a family that has gathered together for Christmas festivities:

> Kisimiso means feasting
> dozens of bread loaves, drums of tea, mountains of sadza,
> rock-size pieces of meat of the he-goat
> in lakes of thousand eyed-soup
> and of course, large pots of fizzing frothy beer.
> Nothing about the book themes of good will and peace
> of course, good will was always here;
> an old man well-known to me lost half his hair

while pulling a tourist out of a blazing car wreckage
in June,
six moons before last Christmas.

The lightheartedness of this part of the book is probably best
exemplified by the poem 'Ifulaimachina', which gives an amusing
account of an old African man's wonder at seeing an aeroplane:

pulled a fine long whistle
to fill his heart with this wonder
and in half-empty voice
said 'Ifulaimachine',
following the trail of smoke
with his squinting eyes
and an innocent gumful smile

until the black dot sank into the horizon,
'These men of the white skin,
even puffing into the face of God,
I swear through Chaminuka,
they will finish us all off.'

This is very different from the contemplative mood of the prison
poems, where the protagonist is compelled to think deeply and calmly
about the trials and torments of incarceration. In the poems addressed
to his mother (Mai) there is a great deal of filial love and tenderness as
the imprisoned poet attempts to console his parents back home. Here
are the first two stanzas of 'To Mai':

Dear Mai,
as long as I can still cough and spit
as long as I can still hold this pen
I am alive, Mai.
I hope you are well also.
Please do not let your mind fill with darkness
do not gnaw your heart away with grief
I am alive, Mai,
it will be over before long.

Calm your heart, mother,
do not trouble yourself
that you cannot come to see your lost son.
I am not in the leopard's mouth
as you said in your last letter.

At times feelings of self-pity overcome the prisoner, as in the poem 'In
Prison', which brings echoes of Hopkins's 'terrible sonnets'. There is a
cry of anguish for freedom and a momentary sense of hopelessness:

I am here,
here!
No song of a bird;

no coo of a dove;
not a moo of a cow;
shadowy sunshine,
no sunrise, nor sunset.
I am now here,
half-living for most of the time
until the soul is jarred
from its quest for salvation from foreign places
or from battlefields
by this man's sudden shouts.

This jungle is home now,
this home is jungle now.

In Part V the contemplative mood still persists but there is a whole new dimension to it. The poet not only contemplates Great Zimbabwe and the Zimbabwe Bird, he invests these symbols with deep meanings – he becomes poet-philosopher. In 'Zimbabwe' we are invited to reflect on the significance of three central motifs: Stone, Silence and Rock:

I want to worship Stone
because it is Silence
I want to worship Rock
so, hallowed by its silence

In 'Rock of Zimbabwe' the poet invites his son to comtemplate the timelessness of the rock that is Great Zimbabwe and its ability to defy time and all efforts by the 'time-enslaved' human mind to penetrate its secrets:

Son,
approach time like the stone
capturing time – dead
telescoping the Zero, the Alpha and the Z
of time
before the hands of the clock do so;
watch the sky tire the sun
and the night weary the star
and do not look
do not move
but be a ruin of stones – eternal unto yourself

Many of the poems in *Thought-Tracks* are very easy to understand, some are quite difficult, but there is one thing they have in common – they all appeal to the reader. Zimunya's power of communication in this volume is quite considerable. Several factors contribute to this. First, Zimunya's sense of rhythm and appreciation of the music of poetry give some of the poems a lyrical quality, such as 'Children's Rain Song' and 'No Songs'. Sometimes the power of his verse comes from a combination of repetition, rhythm, change of tone and pace and striking images. A poem which exemplifies this is

'Rooster', undoubtedly one of his best. The word 'Rooster', which is capitalized throughout the poem, is a poetic rendering of the cock, the election symbol of the Zimbabwe African National Union (ZANU), the party that has ruled Zimbabwe since independence. The poem may well have been written in anticipation of ZANU–PF being swept to power after the 1980 elections, to urge the Party to win the support of all Zimbabweans, from the Vhumba Mountains in the east, to the Matopo in the west, and usher in a new era:

> So stand on one leg on the mountain of Chitungwiza,
> erect and cloud-high on the boulder's fontanelle
> suspicious even of the sun with your eagle-searching eye
> as true as the Zimbabwe bird,
> herald at the edge of time, Rooster, Rooster,
> awaken thunder with your wings
> throw your eyes to the sky
> and seizing the anguished moment in a throat
> echo the overdue Hope
> until Vhumba and Matopo answer:
> else what dawn would you let us hear you announce?

Part of the force of the poem comes from the rhetorical questions in the first two and last stanzas. The questions and the repetition of the word Rooster produce effects very similar to those of Blake's 'The Tiger'. While in Blake the poet expresses wonder at the terrible beauty of the tiger, in Zimunya there is a tone of excitement arising from the very real prospect of seeing Rooster achieve victory. This excitement and expectation is intensified in the last stanza, in which the pace of the verse quickens and the various images coming in quick succession one after the other have a cumulative effect which is irresistible.

One of the strengths of Zimunya is the appeal of his poems to the imagination. This is true of poems like 'Fighter', 'The Mountain' and 'Climbers' in Part IV, and, in particular, of the Zimbabwe poems in Part V. As stated earlier, these are also the poems in which Zimunya uses very powerful symbols and motifs. In 'The Mountain' the struggle for Zimbabwe is expressed through the image of a steep mountain which the fighters have to climb and conquer. Their preoccupation with the struggle is transformed into dreams that haunt them every night, dreams about the steep 'stonehouse brooding over this place'. The second and third stanzas project a vivid picture of the impossible task facing the fighters:

> Each time we return to the dream
> the mountain is steeper
> the summit is higher
> and the fear is more intense
> under the howling cliffs.

We have the terror of waiting at the bottom
knowing there are such head-spinning heights above.
Vaguely, we anticipate the claws of an unknown shadow
if we do not climb to the homely height to freedom
aware that when the dream returns again tonight
the heart has deeper depths to sink under.

In 'Fighter', where he is inspired by freedom fighters, the poet rises to
great heights as he paints a vivid picture of the blood of the fighter
streaming in the firmament and bearing fruit:

And though his flesh bears a crater
And a hob-nailed cynic leers at his tragedy,
See, see his blood streams in the firmament
And behold it whispers dew, dawn and day,
And, more, too, a new thing.

Zimunya makes his appeal to the imagination not only through the use
of vivid images and symbols. As stated earlier, Zimunya the poet is a
philosopher as well, a poet of ideas. He is not, for example, content to
use Great Zimbabwe simply as a symbol that stands for the nation of
Zimbabwe. He seeks to explore the nature and significance of the
monument – hence the importance attached to its silence, the
exhortation to his son to 'approach time like the stone', which is not
time-enslaved, and the attempt to define and characterize the timelessness of the stone in 'The Stone Speaks':

I am old and age-less
young and youth-less
living and life-less
dead without death.

Chenjerai Hove

In *Up in Arms*, Hove has set out to portray the sufferings, experiences
and heroic deeds of the common people during Zimbabwe's war of
national liberation and at other times during the colonial era. He has
not set out to sing songs of praise to the heroes of the war. His main
concern is with the effect of the war on the common people and on the
fighters as victims of war's cruelty. He therefore emphasizes its
brutality, and the harshness of those who perpetrate it. These qualities
are personified in 'The Armed Man', whose gun 'mates with his
hunchback', and those who, in the poem 'When I Behold', dismember
and disfigure his sister, leaving:

scattered fingers
charred hair
mangled teeth
mashed tongue
sprinkled with dust.

He recalls the frustrations of a war-torn wife who is tired of a husband who never sleeps, 'guarding the home or on call-up, / Never sleeping!' He tells the story of the heroic grandmother who cooks for and feeds the fighting guerrillas despite the danger to herself, but whom national anthem makers relegate to oblivion. He tells of the treatment of the black worker by his white employers in 'A Boy' and 'To Father on Retirement'. In the former, we are told that although the poet's brother has fathered and husbanded, although he has been on his unpensioned job for thirty years, young white bosses and 'weak-boned madames' insist on calling him a 'boy':

> A 'boy' you are called
> by milk-plastered lips
> and you undo your hat
> to bare that musty dome,
> Yet a 'boy' you remain.

And when in the second poem the protagonist's father retires from his job after twenty-five years of 'spotless service', which has taken its toll of his health and reduced him to 'an empty tortoise shell', all he gets as reward is:

> A pat from my tenth boss
> (the first of its kind)
> plus some tinkling clock
> for my withering wrist;
> And that's all with me

What else can the exploited worker do but go home, to listen to his lungs and watch the place on the anthill to which he will retire on his death?

Hove is the voice of the people. He therefore sets out to use his pen to fire against the civilization that brings such suffering and humility on the common man and woman in the city street and the communal areas. This is the theme of the poem 'Uprising', which gives the volume its title:

> I have been up in arms
> with this rinsed civilization,
> civilization that walks naked
> and roasts brother for sister's lunch

He is at war with this cut-throat exploit-or-you-are-exploited capitalist society with its glaring contrasts:

> In this civilization,
> brother by the corner
> eats till baobab fat
> and sister behind the hedge
> thins like living biltong.

Hove is explicitly partisan in these poems – he speaks for the dispossessed peasant, the exploited worker, the butchered freedom fighter and all the downtrodden. In *Up in Arms*, he lives up to the philosophy he recently articulated in a seminar paper:

> As the sensitive point of the community, the writer cannot withdraw from the concerns of the dispossessed peasant, the malnourished child lying in the squatter camp, the peasant worker's hungry and growling stomach. This is the crowd that appeals to the writer for him to listen. So to write is to listen to that clamour of fury of the people in their daily struggles for a decent livelihood in dignity and freedom.[8]

In *Red Hills of Home*, the emphasis has shifted from social and political issues to personal and family tragedies. There is a tendency to dwell on the tragic side of life in this collection. In the title poem, 'Red Hills of Home', there is indeed concern for the peasant whose way of life is being destroyed, but the social message is overshadowed by the misery of the protagonist, who laments his plight and the plight of his dead father:

> I grew up here,
> father died underground seven rainless seasons ago
> and the burial news
> was all we had to bury.
> Now the featherless eagle, like roast meat,
> recites the misery of the dusty sky.

The focus on the self rather than society comes out clearly in poems like 'Once Partners', 'Since You Left' and 'Delirium in the Street'. In these poems, the protagonist is a dejected, miserable individual contemplating death and despair. In 'Once Partners', for example, the protagonist yearns for a lost marriage partner in a mood of hopeless despair:

> We swam and sank and swam again,
> but tomorrow I sit alone
> alone on the doorstep
> of a home without a fireplace
> not fearing the storm
> nor the silent thunder in my heart.
> The distance left behind is gone,
> the clouds pass me
> without even a drop of dew on my head.

In 'Since You Left' the remaining partner is haunted by

> dreams of wondering and death
> smelling dreams that scar the nose
> dreams of massacres of survival.

In these and other poems Hove makes rather depressing reading. There is too much said about the tragic side of life and little about the joys and delights of living in the world. While misery and tragedy are a fact of life, people do not want to be told that misery is all there is.

From the point of view of craft, however, some of the poems in this collection indicate that Hove has acquired a greater mastery of poetic technique than in the earlier volume. While 'Red Hills of Home' is a sad poem, it is artistically a fine piece of work. Consider, for instance, how in the third stanza the poet portrays the effects of technology and the new way of life on the peasants:

> Red Hills have come
> with wounds whose pus
> suffocates the peasant.
> The peasant's baby sleeps
> knowing only thin dreams of moonlight joy.
> Dying too are the songs
> of the seasons that father once sang
> Red hills and the smoke of man-made thunder
> plunder the land under contract.

There are also some beautiful images in the second stanza referring to the death of the protagonist's father and to his own miserable recollection of it.

However, *Up in Arms* too is the product of a talented artist. Hove uses language in surprising and novel ways, employing ingenious and original images. Consider, for example, some of the metaphors used to express the predicament of Rhodesian society in the first poem:

> Ah, yes!
> Here we are, travelled this long
> on the road to our day
> when we will drink blood for coffee
> and eat our bleeding fingers for sausages.
> Hot steam, our breath,
> While our mouths resemble ancient chimneys,
> that rot with the soot of dying fires.
> We shall swallow blades for supper
> when the people spill
> with red-hot hate

Similar combinations occur in 'Uprising' and other poems. Every now and then the reader is struck by witty expressions and clever combinations of words. In 'The Armed Man', the soldier's rude gun 'mates with his hunchback'. In 'Retiring', the retiring man wishes he 'were a dog / or even its dung'. Talking about the same thing in 'To Father on Retirement', the poet refers to his retiring father as 'an empty tortoise shell', whose offspring will inherit 'only an ancestral name'.

Hove's masterly use of language reminds one of the wit of the metaphysical poets. Charles Mungoshi hits the nail on the head when he says: 'Juxtaposing seemingly incompatible words on lines to force the reader's eye to focus on something beyond, beneath, or in between the words is a device Hove exploits extensively, with devastating effect.'[9]

Similarly distinctive is the poet's tone of voice in both *Up in Arms* and *Red Hills of Home*. There is no raging anger, no shouting and ranting about exploitation, suffering or fighting. Hove treats these and other subjects with admirable sympathy and characteristic calmness. This quality contributes to the considerable appeal of *Up in Arms*. This is not to say, however, that Hove is an easy poet to read and enjoy. It takes a great deal of effort to uncover the meaning of many a poem in *Up in Arms*. Sometimes the attempt to use ingenious combinations of words strikes the reader as flat, communicating little or nothing. This occurs especially with translations of Shona idioms. In 'The Way We Fed', I find several lines to be simply ineffective, because they either are meaningless in English, or are simply rendered as clichés that do not add much to the communicative effect of the poem. In the first stanza we are told: 'The huts seem broken-hearted, barren: / Yet, there morsels abound'. In the third stanza, 'The side pot smiles / like a baby on mother's back'. Similarly, the last stanza contains several lines which fail to have any impact on me as a reader. The following extract contains some of these:

A rude blunt thorn
breaks the tawny, thorny hide
Comforting itself in the old, drying blood!
Oh! she winces. An old rugged face
suppressed, lest some grim-faced cowboy hears!
She off-loads: she must care,
the load unshirkable, flesh begets flesh,
hungry wilds must feed.
She winces yet again!
A jerky, heart-pricking pull!
The thorn breaks within, half-rotten,
and no blood; but tonnes of pain, thunderous!

In my judgement, Hove lacks a feel for rhythm. His poetry is rugged and uneven. This is where I differ from the suggestion made in the Introduction to *And Now the Poets Speak* that Hove has something in common with William Blake.[10] If the suggestion is that the poet's vision is inspired by Blake's poetry, yes, I would agree, for both Hove in *Up in Arms* and William Blake are concerned with the lot of the exploited and downtrodden. From the point of view of form, however, Blake and Hove are worlds apart. In *Songs of Innocence* and *Songs of Experience* Blake is very much concerned with form – with rhythm, rhyme and the symmetry of stanzas. His poetry has an unmistakably lyrical quality and a mellowness I do not discern in Hove. In 'The Journey,'

Hove contrasts the influence that T.S. Eliot and Blake have had on him in a very striking manner. In his search for a model he dismissed Eliot and welcomed Blake:

> Eliot's rugged cigarette stubs scatter,
> marring his career in the trade.
> But the tiger still walked the journey
> Awaiting my arrival.
> I read Blake for a poetry partner
> his lines mauling my schooled heart.
> Shaking the reverend's God by the collar,
> So we shook hands after the victory.

My own reading of Hove's poetry suggests some affinity with Eliot's early poetry. Hove makes use of clever images, intellectually conceived, similar in effect to Eliot's notion of an 'objective correlative' – a concrete object or set of events which evokes appropriate feelings. The difference lies in what Helen Gardner has observed about Eliot, that he blends 'this oblique manner with a highly passionate and dramatic style, which constantly escapes from the regions of wit, irony and sensibility into a dramatic intensity of feeling'.[11] Unlike Eliot, Hove has not quite found a way of producing 'a dramatic intensity of feeling'. He certainly wins the reader's sympathy in *Up in Arms*, but, while he, as poet, may have very strong feelings about his subject, he fails to communicate these feelings to the reader, and so his poetry remains largely cerebral and does not touch the emotions. The relative absence of rhythm and of a strong lyrical element reduces the appeal and readability of the poetry. However, *Up in Arms* does have an appeal for Zimbabwean readers, partly as a result of its social vision. The poems in *Up in Arms* are the songs of a community. The reader is aware that, when Hove praises the bravery of an old woman who cooks and feeds the guerrillas in 'The Way We Fed', he is not talking about a particular individual. The poem is in fact written in memory of all those grandmothers and women who sacrificed so much, risking their lives in support of the freedom fighters. Similarly, when he writes about an old man on his retirement, he is expressing a general concern for the lot of the black workers who were exploited at their work places and died without the benefits which accrued to white workers on retirement.

Freedom T.V. Nyamubaya

On the Road Again, the title of Freedom Nyamubaya's first volume, signifies the author's perception of the nature of the human struggle for freedom, independence and social justice. Nyamubaya participated actively in the struggle for the independence of Zimbabwe. She carried a gun, lost and buried friends and marched to victory with the rest of the fighters in 1980. Now Zimbabwe is an independent country, but Nyamubaya knows only too well that the victory of the freedom fighter was not the end of the struggle. She knows that the 'struggle goes on and on' as she declares in the title poem, and so she is 'Still on the road, an endless journey'. She makes her intention very clear in 'Introduction', which acts as the prologue to what she has to say in the book:

Now that I have put my gun down
For almost obvious reasons
The enemy still is here invisible
My barrel has no definite target

now

Let my hands work –
My mouth sing –
My pencil write –
About the same things my bullet aimed at.

This is one of the major themes that run through this simple and enchanting collection of poems. The fight against the enemies of freedom, both external and internal, has to be seen as an on-going process. In 'Defeated Victory!!!' Nyamubaya analyses Zimbabwe's struggle for independence in the context of the struggles that have taken place elsewhere in Africa – in Guinea Bissau, Kenya, Angola, South Africa and Namibia – and she sees a common pattern: the endless fight against imperialism. It is in this context that she assesses the victories we have scored in Africa and comes to the following verdict:

We surely won all battles
But lost nearly all wars.
We cured all symptoms
But not the diseases:
A defeated victory
Africa past, present and future.

The same sense of a revolution that has not been a complete success informs one of her best poems, 'A Mysterious Marriage', where the idea of independence which does not bring about genuine freedom is expressed in terms of a story about a boy called Independence and a girl called Freedom who, after being forced to leave their home by armed robbers, decide to go back and get married at the end of a big war. Using marriage as a motif Nyamubaya successfully captures the mood of optimism and expectation that gripped the entire population of Zimbabwe at the end of the war of national liberation and during the preparations for independence. Indeed 'Freedom and Independence / were more popular than Jesus' but alas what was the outcome:

Independence came
But Freedom was not there.
An old woman saw Freedom's shadow passing,
Walking through the crowd, Freedom to the gate.
All the same, they celebrated for Independence.

Freedom Nyamubaya can afford to be so forthright in her assessment of the fruits of independence because, unlike most other Zimbabwean writers, she is an ex-combatant; she was there in the struggle and what she says she says from the bottom of her heart, from direct experience and with an authority that no one can question. When she writes about incidents that occurred during the war, for example, when she recalls the sufferings and experiences of the guerrilla fighters, she does so accurately, convincingly and effectively. In 'Daughter of the Soil', she recalls the death of a female comrade who died in a bomb blast. She recalls the horror, the courage of the dying fighter and the pain:

One of the warriors Africa provided
Her blood spurted above the trees
Like the gushes of a bomb fire
I saw her cry – like a woman dying in agony
Yet she was laughing the laughs of pain
Screaming: long live the suffering masses.

The fighting mood and determination of the dying heroine to whom the poet pays tribute is inspiring to the reader in the same way as young Zimbabwean freedom fighters inspired the population and earned themselves the admiration of all lovers of freedom:

A sister of the motherland,
Who sought freedom
Justice for her people
In the hot air, her soul burnt away
Above the angry mountains, her voice echoed away.
Yet she had ventured to join the brave
Who had given their lives
In the dark smoke that swallowed my sister.
Feeling defeated but sure of victory
I saw her die kicking in protest
In the flames disappeared the freedom fighter.

The same spirit, the same attitude, the same determination are evident in 'Loving and Struggling', in which Nyamubaya recalls her companionship with a close friend who died in the war after sharing experiences, sufferings, dreams and hopes, a friend who was married to the struggle and to the poet 'in a triple union'. This friend too died a shocking death, but courageously and with hope for a free and independent Zimbabwe:

Your last words still ring a bell,

'I am dead and gone, take my gun.
Dying to dish justice and freedom for all!
On my blood my nation shall prosper!
I loved you in the name of struggle!
Weep not for me, struggle continues!'

Writing after independence, Nyamubaya seems to have some regrets about the outcome of what her friend fought and died for, hence: 'This land has shattered your dream: / Lancaster House to buy our own land'.

Freedom Nyamubaya is so far the most authentic spokesperson of ex-combatants in Zimbabwean literature. She speaks for them, depicts their experience, defines their role in the struggle and portrays their hopes and fears. And yet she does not speak for freedom fighters only. She writes on behalf of the downtrodden, the exploited and all those struggling for freedom, justice and human dignity. Her sympathy with the downtrodden and exploited is manifest in images like that of the unequal relationship between the Dog and the Hunter, and of knife and fork who work hard till they are blunt and bent from toil but never taste the food.

Nyamubaya's use of direct language, simple images and a prosaic style facilitate direct communication with the reader. She is at her best when she employs allegory and anecdote as in 'The Dog and the Hunter', 'A Mysterious Marriage' and 'Knife and Fork'. In these poems she is able to speak successfully at two levels, that of objective reality, and that of social analysis. She is also adept at describing violent and touching incidents of the war, as in 'Daughter of the Soil', 'Loving and Struggling' and 'Rest My Sister'. In the last three poems, her sympathy for a friend who died in action touches the heart and is capable of drawing tears from the eyes of the reader. Nyamubaya has achieved a high level of readability in this collection which grips the attention with the immediacy of a collection of short stories or even a novel. Despite these qualities, she still has some way to go in perfecting her craft. While her prosaic style is effective, hers cannot be called 'great' poetry at this stage. She still has to attain a density of texture which will lift her art to the realm of poetic excellence. While she employs striking symbols and motifs she has yet to maintain consistency in the flow of ideas from one stanza to the next. In some of her poems the flow becomes diffuse, as though she has lost her train of thought, and the conclusion is therefore disappointing or unexpected. Such poems as 'Fuss Over Nothing', 'On the Road Again' and 'The Native Intellectual' demonstrate this weakness. The last-mentioned poem, to take one example, proceeds very well from the first to the third stanza, showing the vacillations of the African petty bourgeois intellectual, who joins with the people during the national liberation struggle, and reverts to his old ways after independence, profiteering and misusing the authority given to him by the masses. But the fourth and last stanza becomes confused, so that the reader cannot tell precisely what the verdict is on the native intellectual: does he stand condemned or vindicated? Is the poet's last word one of approval or disapproval? In addition Nyamubaya does not strike the reader as a painstaking perfectionist. Some of her poems seem to have been hurriedly written without much care being taken about their form. As a result there are a number of poems, 'Introduction' included, which may be quite impressive in what they say, but disappointing in how they say it. Thus from the point of view of craft Nyamubaya is still learning the trade and should rise to greater heights.

On the other hand, this young poet is ideologically very advanced. She has reached a very high level of consciousness and is capable of a discerning social analysis and a clarity of vision unparalleled in Zimbabwean poetry. She gives the reader insight into the war of national liberation, the contradictions of our society and the machinations of imperialist forces. And unlike many Zimbabwean writers today she seems totally free to write as she feels and sees things. This ideological clarity and the confidence to declare her vision without hindrance can only be the result of putting theory into practice. As a freedom fighter she not only learnt about revolution. She lived revolution. She therefore speaks with the voice of authority.

Conclusion

One of the major concerns of this chapter is to explore the contribution of authorial ideology and craft to the ability of the poet to communicate effectively with the reader. I have shown that the appeal of Zimunya's *Thought-Tracks* is considerable. This is due both to the subject matter the poet deals with and to his ideological orientation. Zimunya demonstrates a progressive attitude to the political scene in pre-independence Zimbabwe, writing from a nationalistic standpoint. Much of the poetry in the volume is about the struggle for the birth of a new nation. While there is no indication of the kind of society the writer would like to see established, there is nevertheless a strong element of commitment to an important and progressive cause. His main achievement here is that he captures the mood of the epoch. Apart from the writer's ideological outlook, there is also evidence of philosophical contemplation. The poet communicates his feelings and involves the reader in his object of contemplation.

Zimunya's achievement in this regard becomes more apparent if one puts *Thought-Tracks* side by side with his subsequent publications, *Kingfisher, Jikinya and Other Poems*[12] and *Country Dawns and City Lights*.[13] In these two volumes, the element of intense feeling and thought is no longer there and the writer's commitment to his subject matter is of a somewhat superficial nature. The subject matter itself is not one that is likely to be of great interest to the reader. In fact, *Country Dawns and City Lights* makes the reader wonder what has become of the poet's social vision, as the book belabours a theme that was exhausted in the 1960s, rather than addressing other issues of greater social relevance to the new Zimbabwe.

In *Up in Arms* Hove seeks to give expression in poetic form to the struggles and sufferings of the people of Zimbabwe during the war of national liberation. He takes a partisan position and aligns himself with the downtrodden and the struggling masses of Zimbabwe. This progressive stance helps him to win the sympathy of the reader.

I have already discussed the strengths and shortcomings of Hove and Zimunya in handling verse forms. I shall now comment very briefly on their use of images. It would seem to me that Chenjerai Hove tends to focus on images as words, as verbal expressions, confining himself to the significance of an image purely as a linguistic form. Zimunya, on the other hand, rises to greater heights as the struggle with images and symbols becomes a struggle to grapple with an idea – the creation of images about Zimbabwe becomes part and parcel of the poet's desire to capture the mood of the epoch, to recreate the struggle for Zimbabwe. To that extent Zimunya's style is conceptual, infused with ideas which have an ideological import. This elevates the poet's object of contemplation. Hove's style on the other hand remains descriptive, for he is content to portray a sympathetic picture of his subject. Furthermore, Hove's mode of communication remains private. He does not create images that have a general appeal, like Zimunya's in the poems on Zimbabwe. The Rock, the Zimbabwe Bird, the mountain and the rooster are all public symbols with definite connotations, which therefore readily communicate a message to the reader.

The strength of Nyamubaya lies in the convincing manner in which she records the experiences of the freedom fighters, the frankness with which she analyses the contradictions of her society and the ideological clarity that informs her vision. Her style is simple and yet forceful. This forcefulness comes from the genuineness of the position she takes and from the seemingly natural manner in which the language flows out of her. There is no artificial tinkering with words in Nyamubaya's poetry. This, of course, means that her art is not perfect, and from the point of view of craft she is the least accomplished of the three poets discussed in this chapter. On the other hand, she is the voice that speaks most directly and convincingly about Zimbabwe's experiences during the war, the contradictions of Zimbabwean society today and about the various forces, both internal and external, that militate against our progress. Her vision is clearly informed by the Marxist–Leninist view of life as a continuous struggle to overcome the forces of reaction and to establish a happy society for all. In Nyamubaya we have the makings of a powerful poet, a social critic and a committed revolutionary.

Notes

1. This chapter is an amended version of a paper read at the Colloquium on Zimbabwean Literature held at the University of Zimbabwe in April 1987, under the title 'Ideology, Craft and Communication in Zimbabwean Poetry Since 1980'.
2. Musaemura, B. Zimunya, *Thought-Tracks*, Harlow, Longman, 1982.
3. Chenjerai Hove, *Up in Arms*, Harare, Zimbabwe Publishing House, 1982.
4. Chenjerai Hove, *Red Hills of Home*, Gweru, Mambo Press, 1985.
5. Freedom T.V. Nyamubaya, *On the Road Again*, Harare, Zimbabwe Publishing House, 1986.
6. M. Kadhani and M. Zimunya (eds.), *And Now the Poets Speak*, Gweru, Mambo Press, 1981.
7. See Zimunya, op. cit., p. x.
8. Chenjerai Hove, 'The Creative Writer and His Social Responsibility', a paper presented at the University of Zimbabwe, 1985.
9. See Hove, *Up in Arms*, p. 2.
10. See Khadani and Zimunya, op. cit., p. xv.
11. Helen Gardner, *The Art of T.S. Eliot*, London, Faber and Faber, 1949, p. 71.
12. M.B. Zimunya, *Kingfisher, Jikinya and Other Poems*, Harare, Longman Zimbabwe, 1982.
13. M.B. Zimunya, *Country Dawns and City Lights*, Harare, Longman Zimbabwe, 1985.

11

Vision
& Form
in South African Liberation Poetry[1]

Introduction

To talk of 'liberation poetry' is to suggest that poetry has a role to play in liberation struggles. In the two preceding chapters we have analysed poetry from countries that have since gained their independence and freedom, although reactionary forces, both external and internal, are bent on disturbing the peace process. In this instance, the struggle for freedom and social justice in South Africa is still raging, so that for the committed poet the question of theory and practice in the creative process is a very relevant one, as is the issue of social vision. This in turn challenges the critic and student of poetry to probe more deeply into the forms and functions of the genre so that the study of poetry can be more relevant to the concerns and objectives of the creative artist.

In his introduction to *Poets to the People: South African Freedom Poems*, an anthology that is dedicated to South Africa's political prisoners and to the African National Congress (ANC) and its allies, Barry Feinberg has articulated the relevance of poetry to the liberation struggle in the following words:

> Undoubtedly poetry and song are the most popular and accessible means of creative expression and communication in South Africa. Indeed, to the vast majority of South Africans, these art forms are often the only means of expressing feelings about life under apartheid; a life where human concern and assertion have been systematically stifled and stamped upon by the most outrageously ruthless and exploitative state system since Nazi Germany. It is this brutal oppression, with its unique codification of racial discrimination, which has generated the immense popular engagement and passion of South African song and poetry – most often in circumstances where other forms of

political expression are too hazardous but, also, as an increasingly conscious component of revolutionary action.[2]

In Mozambique and Angola poetry clearly had a role to play in the struggle against Portuguese colonial domination. Poets were moved to action and politicians to artistic expression during the wars of national liberation in those countries. Similarly, in the words of Barry Feinberg quoted above and the dedication to the African National Congress, we see an eloquent expression of the view that poetry has a role to play in the struggle for freedom and social justice in South Africa.

In South Africa, as elsewhere in Africa, women have played a prominent part in the quest for freedom. Consequently female militants have contributed to the development of liberation poetry in South Africa, and it is salutary to pause and consider the value of their contribution lest we minimize their achievement or fall into the pitfall of vague generalizations. Three of the women poets, namely, Lindiwe Mabuza, Ilva Mackay and Rebecca Matlou, are represented in Barry Feinberg's anthology, in which men poets feature much more prominently. So much importance do South African women place on the role of poetry in the struggle that their liberation movement has allowed them to publish an anthology of poems in its name. The anthology is entitled *Malibongwe ANC Women: Poetry is also their Weapon*.[3] This implies recognition of the power of poetry by the South African liberation movement.

However, in order to discover in more precise terms the role that South African liberation poetry does and can play, and in order to assess how effectively it performs that function, we need to analyse it and let it speak for itself. In the process of our analysis we should bear the following questions in mind: What do the poems say about the ideological orientation and class sympathies of the authors? What do or could they mean to the oppressed masses of South Africa? What does the poetry reveal to us as readers about the hopes and fears of the poets and the liberation movement they represent? Is there a limit beyond which politically motivated poetry stops being art and becomes mere sloganeering? And do poets have something special to offer to the liberation process in South Africa that the physical struggle and day-to-day political activity cannot offer? All this we can discover by examining the preoccupations of the poets, the themes that run through their poetry, the social vision that emerges from the poetry and the forms used to express the poet's vision and concerns. Our analysis will be based on the two anthologies referred to above, starting with *Poets to the People*.

Poets to the People: From Protest to Socialist Consciousness

A suitable starting point in a critical analysis of South African liberation poetry is Oswald Mtshali, author of *Sounds of a Cowhide Drum*.[4]
While there are only five of his poems in Barry Feinberg's anthology,
Mtshali is an important poet from the point of view of vision and style.
His poems are about the underprivileged – workers, black township
children, drunkards in the streets of Johannesburg, chimney sweeps
and the like. Some of these poems do not easily fit the label 'liberation
poems', but there is one feature that characterizes them – they are
poems of protest against the inhumanity of apartheid, the exploitation
of black workers, the brutalization of black prisoners and the
dehumanization of the oppressed. These themes are sufficiently
captured in the five poems that represent Mtshali in *Poets to the
People*.

The young black boy in 'Boy on a Swing' is representative of all the
urban black children who, even at such an early age, have experienced
the alienating effects of segregation, deprivation and exploitation, and
have consequently learned to ask:

> Mother!
> Where did I come from?
> When will I wear long trousers?
> Why was my father jailed? (p. 144)

While the first two questions may be perceived by the reader as simple
questions by a simple boy, the last, which constitutes the final statement of the poem, is indicative of a high level of political consciousness
on the part of the young protagonist and is clearly a voice of protest,
which is echoed in the last lines of 'A Roadgang's Cry':

> 'Abelungu ngo'dam – Whites are damned
> Basibiza ngo Jim – they call us Jim.' (p. 146)

The image of black people portrayed in these two poems is
complemented by two other images – that of physically incapacitated
and imprisoned people as in 'Men in Chains' and 'Handcuffs', and that
of a proletarian 'cog' in a big wheel which is rolling under an oxwagon,
showing how unimportant and helpless the worker is in the South
African social formation. But, while the worker sees himself as having
been reduced to the status of a mere cog who, like the handcuffed man
in 'Handcuffs', is so helpless that he cannot even scratch the itch in his
heart, because:

> How can?
> my wrists
> are manacled.

My mind
is caged.
My soul
is shackled (p. 147)

he nevertheless hears a voice which tells him, 'Have hope, brother, /
despair is for the defeated' (p. 147). As a result of their alienation, the
oppressed blacks are forced to contemplate resistance. However, while
there is hope in these words, the voice of the protagonist is a cry of
hopelessness, the lament of someone who has become the object of
history.

What emerges from this is that Oswald Mtshali is a partisan writer,
the voice of the voiceless. In his quiet tone, in his apparently simple
manner of representation, he depicts for us the image of black South
Africans who once accepted oppression in silence but have now woken
up to the need to resist. His class position is fairly clear – he is the voice
of those at the lower echelons of society, particularly workers and
other oppressed blacks: he is a proletarian writer. This is evident not
only in his subject matter, the social background of his commonest
protagonist, but in his style, which is colloquial, devoid of erudition,
simple but evocative and full of ironic overtones. But, while his is a
voice of protest, it is a feeble voice, for Mtshali depicts Africans who
are powerless against the forces that dehumanize them. While there is a
ray of hope in 'Handcuffs' and other poems, the voice of Mtshali's
protagonist is a cry of hopelessness, the lament of a slave who has no
idea of how to end his slavery.

A much stronger and more eloquent voice is that of Dennis Brutus.
In manner and temperament, Brutus is the very antithesis of Oswald
Mtshali. The dispassionate voice, the gentle criticism and the deceptive
simplicity of Mtshali are not features we find in Brutus's poetry. In his
prison poetry, for instance, Brutus depicts the violence and inhumanity
to which the prisoners are subjected with characteristic power and
intensity of feeling. For this passionate poet, 'sirens, knuckles, boots'
are symbols of the harshness and brutality that harass and haunt the
prisoner, and the poet attempts to recreate the effects of this violence in
the very sound and tone of his work. No perceptive reader can miss the
intensity of feeling in the following poem:

The sounds begin again,
the siren in the night
the thunder at the door
the shriek of nerves in pain.

Then the keening crescendo
of faces split by pain
the wordless, endless wail
only the unfree know. (p. 2)

131

This obsession with 'cries and sirens' is an eloquent expression of the traumatic experience that political prisoners are subjected to in South African prisons. It bears witness to the fact that the poet himself, who was once shot in the back while trying to escape, knows what it is to be incarcerated under the apartheid system. This is exemplified by 'Today in Prison', which gives us a glimpse of the kind of stubborn resistance that takes place in prison when, with suppressed passion and pent-up feeling, the prisoners sing 'Nkosi Sikelela Africa', the anthem of the African National Congress (p. 3).

With Brutus, then, we move to higher levels of protest. There is more than the first-step realization that oppression should be rejected that we find in Oswald Mtshali. There is, instead, a declaration of intent, an explicit confirmation of the necessity to confront apartheid. The brutality depicted in 'The Sounds Begin Again', in 'There was a Girl', a poem which aims to demonstrate that apartheid is so ruthless that even innocent little children are not spared cruel death, and in many other poems – that brutality is, for Brutus, no reason to despair, as he boldly declares in 'To Those Who Persuade Us':

> To those who persuade us
> to purchase despair
> we must say No: (p. 9)

The refusal to succumb to despair is couched in a tone that bespeaks anger, impatience and a firm determination to fight. Those who persuade him to despair only provide him with an opportunity to resolve to take action, for experience has shown him that the oppressor cannot be trusted:

> While my brothers rot:
> we will be fobbed off
> with promises
> and gestures
> no longer:

> it is time to prove our resolve
> our sincerity
> in action. (p. 9)

In 'At a Funeral' the thought of someone being buried evokes the spirit of rebellion in Brutus and he defiantly declares: 'Better that we should die, than that we should lie down' (p. 3).

From the point of view of authorial ideology, Brutus is much more radical than Mtshali. His revulsion towards apartheid finds expression in the violent and angry tone of his poetry. Unlike Mtshali, Brutus does not display a discernible class position. He is a poet of the oppressed, the incarcerated and the brutalized, but he does not come out clearly as a spokesperson for workers and peasants. His voice is the voice of an embittered intellectual whose class sympathies are not clearly defined.

This is true of many of the poets represented in *Poets to the People*.

A group of poets who do not present a class analysis of the South African situation but whose style portrays the class origin of the authors are those poets who have been influenced by the ideology of the Black Consciousness movement. To these poets, colour is a major determinant of the relations of domination and subordination that characterize the South African social formation. One of the most outstanding leaders of the movement, the late Steve Biko, defined Black Consciousness as follows:

> Briefly defined therefore, Black Consciousness is in essence the realisation by the black man of the need to rally together with his brothers around the cause of their oppression – the blackness of their skin – and to operate as a group in order to rid themselves of the shackles that bind them to perpetual servitude. It seeks to demonstrate the lie that black is an aberration from the 'normal' which is white – It seeks to infuse the black community with a new-found pride in themselves, their efforts, their value systems, their culture, their religion and their outlook to life.[5]

Unlike the Senghorian school of Negritude, Black Consciousness proceeds from the concrete reality of the South African situation. It neither idealizes blackness nor posits a theory of racial superiority. Its argument is that white racism is the major political force in South Africa and that Africans, Indians and Coloureds are branded 'non-whites' and are therefore oppressed by reason of their colour. In terms of Black Consciousness ideology as defined by Biko, there is no question of a rapport between black workers and white workers because the latter are privileged and are consequently 'the greatest supporters of the system'.[6]

In terms of the ideological content of their work the following can be classified as Black Consciousness poets: Sipho Sepamla, Ingoapele Madingoane (author of *Africa my Beginning*)[7] and Mongane Wally Serote.[8] From the point of view of ideology and style, Sepamla and Serote are among the best representatives of Black Consciousness poetry although the latter may have moved away from its ideology in more recent years because of his active involvement in the activities of the ANC, an organization which officially advocates a policy of non-racialism.

Black Consciousness poets came to the fore in the 1970s and in line with Black Consciousness ideology they are concerned with the plight of black South Africans as black people. Their poetry sets out not only to champion the cause of the oppressed blacks, but also to project a new ideology which questions and challenges the racist ideology on which apartheid is based. The challenge is presented in the form of a fearless and aggressive attitude, which represents the new determination of the black people of South Africa to resist white domination.

This is conveyed in a defiant tone, perhaps best exemplified by some of Sepamla's poems.

In 'On Judgement Day' Sepamla subjects white people's stereotypical images of black people to satirical commentary:

black people are born singers
black people are born runners
black people are peace-loving[9]

The effect of this tedious repetition is to create an image of blacks as people who are naive, unsophisticated and docile. However, the reality of the situation, as the poem goes on to show, is that white people are blind because 'nobody really sees the storm raging within us'. Thus there is a world of difference between the image of black people portrayed by the white oppressor and what black people really are – angry, impatient and on the verge of a violent uprising. Black people's anger is expressed in the following lines, parodying the erroneous image that white people have of blacks:

laughing has become agonizing
    singers
    runners
    peace-loving
        my foot[10]

Their defiance is captured by those two words: 'my foot'. The style is colloquial, reflecting the authentic language of a people that has now resolved to put an end to humiliation. This informal, conversational style is evident in the title of 'Civilization Aha' and in the aggressive and impatient tone of the last three lines of 'Talk to the Peach Tree':

Come on
let's talk to the devil himself
it's about time[11]

This colloquial style is found also in the poetry of one of the younger poets represented in *Poets to the People* – Mongane Serote. There is no attempt to display erudition in Serote's poetry, no complicated stylization. Instead the reader is made to hear the voices of real people, talking in real situations, expressing their determination to resist oppression. In 'What's in this Black Shit' the tone of defiance is evident from the very first stanza:

It is not the steaming little rot
In the toilet bucket,
It is the upheaval of the bowels
Bleeding and coming out through the mouth
And swallowed back,
Rolling in the mouth,
Feeling its taste and wondering what's next like it. (p. 163).

In the last stanza it becomes clear that this informal and unpolished language marks a new form of social consciousness, and signifies a new relationship between whites and blacks. A black worker has decided to reject the humiliation to which black people have been subjected for generations. He has learned to respond to the white master with 'Shit' and feels victorious at being able to stand up to him in this way:

I'm learning to pronounce this 'Shit' well,
Since the other day,
At the pass office
When I went to get employment,
The officer there endorsed me to Middleburg,
So I said, hard with all my might, 'Shit!'
I felt a little better;
But what's good is, I said it in his face,
A thing my father wouldn't dare do.
That's what's in this black 'Shit'. (p. 164).

We have come a long way from Mtshali's sorrowful lamentations, confronted with a worker who is determined to be the subject of history. This new attitude, of confidence to face white people and challenge their superiority, is a characteristic feature of Black Consciousness poetry, and of Mongane Serote's other poems in *Poets to the People*, such as 'The Growing', 'Hell, Well, Heaven', and 'My Brothers in the Streets'.

The optimism of the Black Consciousness poets is raised to greater heights in the poems of Keorapetse Kgositsile, Christopher Van Wyk and Scarlet Whitman, in which the eventual victory of the oppressed over the oppressor is articulated with clarity and confidence. These poets move beyond the critical attitude of Mtshali, beyond Brutus's declaration of intent, beyond the boldness and nonchalance of the Black Consciousness poets, to an assured statement of future victory. This is the tone of Scarlet Whitman's last two poems, which are also the last in the anthology, 'Freedom Day Song' and 'All Will Be Ours Again'. They depict the dialectical relationship between the eventual defeat of the oppressor and the ultimate victory of the oppressed. Each freedom day brings freedom nearer to the downtrodden, but to Vorster it brings his 'long night nearer', and is the former South African leader's 'nightmare now'. Consequently, in 'All Will Be Ours Again' the poet reclaims the ancestral fields, mountains, hills, forests and lakes held captive by foreigners. In other words, the land will come back to those who toil and suffer for freedom's sake.

To those the patient
to those that endure
to those pitted with scars
who prise clenched nights for crimson stars
it will come

it will come back
all will be ours again (p. 189)

This is a powerful expression of hope and faith in the efficacy of the liberation struggle. This optimism, which is so graphically articulated in Mazisi Kunene's poems, especially in 'Unfortunate Adventure', in which Kunene declares 'Certain, by such magic our triumph is assured' (p. 80), is indicative of a revolutionary consciousness. How the triumph is to come about is suggested by Kunene in 'The Rise of the Angry Generation'. Kunene portrays freedom as the result of a violent revolution waged by a new generation of radical politicians and freedom fighters. The poem portrays the revolution as a great and fierce eagle that hovers with terrible beauty over 'the once proud planet' of apartheid, which now 'shrieks in terror'. The violent revolution and the determination of the fighters are symbolized by a series of powerful images. As the great eagle lifts its wings, 'shells of childhood are scattered / Letting the fierce eyes focus on the morning'. The revolution becomes 'the beautiful bird' which 'builds its nest with old leaves'. The apartheid state, symbolically portrayed as 'the earth' and 'the once proud planet', is terrified by 'the merciless talons of the new generation'. The last six lines summarize very forcefully the qualities which the new generation of freedom fighters has acquired:

They who are not deterred by false tears
Who do not turn away from the fire
They are the children of iron
They are the fearless bees of the night
They are the wrath of the volcanic mountains
They are the abiding anger of the Ancestral Forefathers (pp. 78–79)

While the poetry of Kunene, Scarlet Whitman, Christopher Van Wyk and others is infused with the spirit of combat that goes beyond protest, hardly any of these poets seem to have worked out a guiding philosophy for a free South Africa. The concern is with the demise of apartheid and the end of oppression. Their poetry does not ask the crucial question, what kind of social and economic system should be established when freedom comes at last. Kunene's new generation is a generation of fighters who have no clearly articulated vision of the society they are going to build. This is indicative of the poet's authorial ideology, his limited social vision.

A significant exception to this 'ideological blind alley', as it were, is Keorapetse Kgositsile, whose poetry shows that the author has thought through questions of ideology, has done some class analysis and consequently has an idea of the political system that he hopes to see developing in a liberated South Africa. Three features characteristic of socialist art are discernible in Kgositsile's poetry. First, the struggle is seen in class terms and not in terms of race. Second, idealism is replaced by objective realism. Third, there is optimism about future victory though current problems are not overlooked. Kgositsile is one of the few poets represented in the anthology who specifically extol the virtues of the working class, alongside those of the youth who are given prominence in the works of some of the other poets. Indeed, none of the poets, other than those influenced by Black Consciousness ideology, talk simplistically of the black/white dichotomy in South Africa. The majority recognize that the problem goes much deeper than the question of race, but only Kgositsile and Mtshali focus specifically on the working class. In the case of Mtshali, the emphasis is on the plight of the seemingly powerless working class and other deprived classes, but Kgositsile depicts the working class as a leading force in the revolution. This is clearly articulated in 'New Age' and 'A Luta Continua'. In the latter, dedicated to an ANC leader, the late Duma Nokwe, we are told:

Your name informed by our bloodstains
Was born before your body
To inform us:
A worker's world is ascending
Over the stench and sunken graves
Of these racists rapists goldfanged exploiters (p. 42)

In the closing stanza the poet sings the praises of workers, brotherhood, liberation and peace. The working class is seen as one of two forces that will bring about change, the other being the freedom fighters; by singing the praises of the workers the poet is at the same time glorifying the Spear of the Nation, the military wing of the ANC, of which Duma Nokwe was a symbol, and which is portrayed as a working class movement:

Poet leave him alone you have praised him
If you sing of workers you have praised him
If you sing of brotherhood you have praised him
If you sing of liberation you have praised him
If you sing of peace you have praised him
You have praised him without knowing his name
His name is Spear of the Nation. Mayibuye! (p. 44)

Rather than harp on the race question Kgositsile celebrates revolutionary internationalism and the success of a socialist economy. In 'South Africa Salutes Uzbekistan' he sees revolutionaries in different parts of the world drawing inspiration from the Soviet Union. Vietnam, Cuba, Allende's Chile, the People's Movement for the Liberation of Angola (MPLA), the Palestine Liberation Organization (PLO) and the Independence Party for Guinea Bissau and Cape Verde (PAIGC) are all depicted as pledging support for the socialist programme of the Soviet Union (p. 48). 'South Africa Salutes Uzbekistan' was most probably written in Tashkent, the Soviet Union, during or after the Afro-Asian Writers' Conference held there in September 1976. It says much about Kgositsile's socialist outlook that, while Barry Feinberg wrote the poem 'We Found Common Song' on the same occasion, the latter's poem does not say anything about the Soviet economic and social system, whose virtues are extolled in the eighth stanza of 'South Africa Salutes Uzbekistan':

> Here we have not seen beggars
> We have not seen children
> With ribs like guitar strings
> To condemn the fat-bellied swine
> Who slobber on the dreams of freedom lovers
> We have not seen mothers forced to send
> Their offspring to any stinking street
> To peddle human juice for meal or drink
> Here we have not seen the humiliation of tyranny
> The fear the loathing of oneself
> Which my brother has known and told
> Here man will live and flourish (p. 48)

In the last stanza Kgositsile sees the lessons learned in the Soviet Union being translated into the future economic system of South Africa. This is the sense in which South Africa salutes Uzbekistan, because the African National Congress will fight for people's power and, like the other liberation movements cited above, say 'Yes' to the socialist system:

> History will absolve us
> YES to electrification
> YES to irrigation
> YES to industrialization
> YES to desert reclaimed
> YES to Solidarity
> YES to freedomsong
> YES, Lenin, We shall dream
> We shall turn that dream into reality
> Palpable as this cotton this flower
> This fruit this love
> MAYIBUYE! (p. 49)

Going hand in hand with this praise for socialism is an implicit rejection of the kind of subjective idealism that we find in the Senghorian school of Negritude which falsifies reality by, among other things, suggesting that the black people of Africa are endowed with certain psycho-physiological qualities that other races lack. There is indeed much theorizing about the struggle in Kgositsile's poetry, but there is no over-dependence on philosophical abstractions as in Senghor's. The focus is on the concrete facts of oppression, the struggle and determination of the people to overcome the enemy. Such notions as a utopian past or the idealization of the African race are firmly rejected, as in 'New Age', in which Kgositsile tells idealists not to talk glibly about the glories of the past or the virtues of blackness:

Remember O Poet
When some of your colleagues meet
They do not talk the glories of the past
Or turn their tongues backwards
In platitudes or idealistic delirium
About change through chance or beauty
Or the perversion you call love
Which be nothing nothing
But the Western pairing of parasites (p. 41)

The virtue of the new generation is to know that the past was not without strife. The past was also 'turbulent' and victory can only be achieved through struggle and not by chance. But while the turbulence is highlighted there is also hope. This hope is most emphatically expressed in 'Manifesto', in which Kgositsile proclaims the coming victory in clear and uncompromising terms:

And let no choleric charlatan tell you
It will be by chance
Our voice in unison with our poet's proudly says
CHANGE IS GOING TO COME (p. 47)

There is a sense in which Kgositsile's style can be said to be abstract as his poetry does not depict concrete events or situations. He is to that extent a poet of ideas. However, his ideas are based on the reality of the South African social formation and on the ideological transformation which the people of that country have undergone through struggle. Keorapetse Kgositsile displays a high level of political consciousness and ideological clarity. He analyses the dialectics of the conflict in South Africa from a radical materialist standpoint. He is a poet with a clear vision of the kind of society he sees emerging after the demise of the apartheid system.

Form and Communication in *Poets to the People*

There is a wide divergence of form and style in the poetry we have analysed and this brings about different effects in terms of communication with the reader. Oswald Mtshali's poems are short; very few of them are more than a page long, and none of those found in *Poets to the People* fills one page, which is typical of the poet.

In terms of the modal, or external structure, each of Mtshali's poems starts with some kind of observation or descriptive statement which acts as the springboard for the protest voiced by the poet's protagonists. In 'Boy on a Swing' there is first a description of a black boy moving to and fro on a swing, and, in the concluding stanza, the boy asks the crucial questions:

> Mother!
> Where did I come from?
> When will I wear long trousers?
> Why was my father jailed? (p. 144)

In 'Men in Chains' a train stops at a country station. In 'Going to Work', the worker starts by narrating in an apparently innocent manner how he goes to work five days a week 'with a thousand black bodies / encased in eleven coaches'. In each case the simple opening statement leads to a revelation about the conditions under which the oppressed live and this in turn leads to a questioning of the way things are in South Africa. In one of Mtshali's most successful poems, 'The Washerwoman's Prayer', which was excluded from *Poets to the People*, a black woman, who has toiled 'for countless years' and 'drudged murmurless', ends up offering a prayer of protest to God in a bitter and sarcastic voice:

> Thank you Lord! Thank you Lord.
> Never again will I ask
> Why must I carry this task[12]

The poem is simple; there is no complicated stylization, and no ranting, yet, how poignant!

Another poet of few words is Dennis Brutus. Some of his poems, such as 'The Sounds Begin Again', 'On the Coming Victory' and 'There was a Girl' are no more than twelve short lines, but they are extremely powerful. Brutus's short, terse poems encapsulate the determination of the fighter to end the oppressive system. The reader has a sense of a poet boiling with anger, whose voice is stifled but who, when he does manage to speak, forcefully denounces the violence of apartheid. With Brutus, poetry becomes the vehicle for an effective and genuine portrait of the ugly face of apartheid. In his longer poems, such as 'For Chief' and 'The Guerillas', this force is weakened and the reader's interest wanes. This is one of the weaknesses of A.N.C. Kumalo, Barry Feinberg and, as we shall see, some of the women poets. Poems such as Feinberg's 'Statue Treatment' and 'A Counterpoint of Marching Feet' overtax the reader before they deliver their message.

I must hasten to add that it is not necessarily only very short poems that communicate effectively. Scarlet Whitman's poems are quite long, compared with a typical poem by Mtshali or Brutus, and yet they are quite delightful to read. In 'Woman's Day Song' and 'Freedom Day Song' Whitman's poetry attains a lyrical quality through the use of such devices as repetition, alliteration and parallelism, such as we find in the first stanza of 'All Will Be Well Again':

To us the progeny
to those that toil
to those with raging hearts
to us the looted heirs united in yearning
it will come
it will come back
all will be ours again (p. 188)

In tone and diction Scarlet Whitman's poetry, like that of Keorapetse Kgositsile, is couched in the idiom of conventional English. This is a far cry from the style of the Black Consciousness poets. What is fascinating about this group is that while there is a strong protest element in their poetry their criticism of apartheid evinces a degree of confidence that surpasses the gentle satire of Mtshali and the angry optimism of Dennis Brutus. There is no self-pity in typical Black Consciousness poetry, no sorrowful mourning for the victims of apartheid as we find in, say, 'There was a Girl' or Mtshali's 'Boy on a Swing'. On the contrary, there is a tone of nonchalant defiance, coupled with a lighthearted colloquial style, such as we find in Serote's 'The Growing', 'My Brothers' and 'Hell, Well, Heaven'. The following are the closing lines of the last-mentioned poem:

I do not know where I have been,
But Brother,
I have a voice like the lightning thunder over the mountains.
But Oh! there are copper lightning conductors for me!
To have despair so deep and deep and deep
But Brother,
I know I'm coming.
I do not know where I have been
But Brother,
Was that Thoko's voice?
Hell, well, Heavens! (p. 166)

The repetition of key lines is a feature Serote's poetry shares with African oral poetry. While the repetition may appear tedious on paper, it increases the impact when Serote reads his poems aloud to audiences sympathetic to the struggle for a free South Africa. This is in keeping with one of the characteristics of Black Consciousness poetry, that it is easily intelligible and very accessible. A further virtue of the poetry of this group is its ability to make use of idioms from everyday language and to evoke the mode of speech of 'the people', or the lower-class urban Africans. The poetry is as robust as township Africans themselves, who, despite the oppressive machinery of the South African social formation, are as lively a group of people as you will meet anywhere in the world. In this sense, poets like Sipho Sepamla and Mongane Serote deserve the label 'people's poets', for they have succeeded in creating an authentic black South African style which captures the mood of the times very effectively.

The ironic twist to this observation is that the Black Consciousness poets do not present a class analysis of South African society, and instead tend towards populism. Paradoxically, the style of the poet who most exemplifies a perception of the class struggle can be criticized for being out of tune with his subject. While Kgositsile sings the praises of the proletariat, his style is marked by a high degree of erudition and complicated stylization. His is the kind of poetry that is more likely to appeal to an educated elite. Furthermore, because of its density of texture and complex syntatic structures, Keorapetse Kgositsile's poetry lends itself more to private reading. It is a credit to Kgositsile's talents as a poet that despite its complexity it is very readable, rising to great heights artistically and capable of moving the reader to reflection. The reader cannot but enjoy coming to grips with the meaning of, say, the last stanza of 'New Age', in which repetition and imagery combine to produce a cumulative effect and to convey a forceful message:

Tell those with ears to hear tell them
Tell them my people are a garden
Rising out of the rancid rituals of rape and ruin
Tell them tell them in the dry season
Leaves will dry and fall to fertilize the land
Whose new flowers black green and gold
Are a worker's song of fidelity
To the land that mothered you (p. 42)

Malibongwe – Militant Feminism

Three of the contemporary South African women poets, namely, Lindiwe Mabuza, Ilva Mackay and Rebecca Matlou, are represented in *Poets to the People*. For the purpose of this chapter we shall discuss their poetry in the context of *Malibongwe*, a more recently published anthology. The best poems in the anthology are those by Baleka Kgositsile, Ilva Mackay, Gloria Mtungwa and some of Lindiwe Mabuza's poems. These and the other women poets address a variety of themes which have a bearing on the South African liberation struggle. They sing about Soweto, about children going to the war, about South African heroes, such as Nelson Mandela, legendary leader of the African National Congress (ANC), and Oliver Tambo, its President; Solomon Mahlangu, a young freedom fighter hanged by the South African government; Dorothy Nyembe, who served a fifteen-year jail sentence; and other heroes. The anthology puts more emphasis on the contribution of women and children than does its predecessor, *Poets to the People*.

Some of the poems in *Malibongwe* express the authors' resolve to fight and, in a number of cases, to avenge a fallen hero. In 'Fallen

Hero', for instance, Gloria Nkadimeng mourns a comrade who has fallen in the war and swears to 'mobilise my will', to be silent like the fallen hero who is now silenced, but with a difference:

> i'll be silent like the silenced that (now) you are
> but i'll ricochet in fury
> boomerang to bury this death once and for all! (p. 39)

These lines from Nkadimeng's poem are an example of the tone that informs the anthology. They show the anger of black South African women poets and their resolve actively to engage the enemy alongside their male comrades. Their determination to fight is summarized in Lindiwe Mabuza's poem, 'Faces of Commitment', in which she recalls a friend who for her symbolizes the way deep involvement in the struggle is changing the relations of domination and subordination in the country, as the fifth stanza of the poem shows:

> I thought of you comrade
> Daring the enemy underground
> In the struggle's workshops
> There making history flourish
> Right there where the enemy's hatchet
> Hovers over those who dream
> Then step by step build
> The greatness of man
> Amid the ashes fertilizing spring (p. 107)

The poems in *Malibongwe* constitute a bold challenge to the South African social system. There is no cry of lamentation for the victims of the brutal system, no sense of self-pity, but a refusal to accept subjugation and domination by those who control political power. In terms of social vision, however, the women poets have some limitations. Many of the poems in *Malibongwe* were evidently written some considerable time after those that appear in *Poets to the People*. There were more concrete battles and acts of heroism to refer to, such as the Soweto uprising of 1976, or the heroic death of Solomon Mahlangu. The poetry in *Malibongwe* is therefore less abstract and more practically oriented than the poems in *Poets to the People*. One also notices that writers like Oswald Mtshali, Dennis Brutus and Keorapetse Kgositsile speak as individuals whereas the voice that speaks in *Malibongwe* is a communal voice. Women fighters are portrayed as a social group, as are children and the youth. The anthology captures the mood of the 1976 Soweto uprising more effectively than does *Poets to the People*, as can be illustrated by citing such poems as Fezeka Makonese's 'I Must Go: Do Not Mourn', Lindiwe Mabuza's 'Soweto Road', Baleka Kgositsile's 'The Years of the Child' and others.

Individually, however, the women poets do not seem to have reached the level of ideological consciousness that the best of their male counterparts have attained, though their poetry is characterized by a nationalist consciousness, focusing on individual heroes like Mandela, Tambo and others. This, however, can be seen as glorifying the individual at the expense of the collective. What is more, there is no clear identification with the working class or the peasantry as revolutionary classes, except in a very few poems, principally Baleka Kgositsile's 'Umkhonto' and Lindiwe Mabuza's 'Mangaung'. Even then, the reference to the working class is rhetorical, and there are no poems which focus on the plight of the worker in the manner of Oswald Mtshali, and no projection of the proletariat as a force, as in Keorapetse Kgositsile.

While the poems in *Malibongwe* show the determination of the women poets to fight and to play their role in the struggle, there is no evidence of a guiding social and political philosophy, and little indication of a socialist consciousness. However, they are conscious of their sex and of making a contribution to the struggle as women, and equally conscious of the necessity to reject a western liberal concept of feminism in favour of a more revolutionary feminism which elevates the aspect of militant beauty. A militant beauty is one in which the quality of physical beauty is not what matters, but 'justice for humanity, person to person', as Gloria Mtungwa puts it in 'Militant Beauty':

Flowering in natural beauty
through progressive ideology
she overcame imposed passivity
and became essence of militancy

Her beauty is not her criterion
but justice for all humanity, person to person (p. 51)

Form and Communication in *Malibongwe*

The issue of revolutionary feminism brings us to some significant features of style. The anthology contains a number of poems that show considerable craftsmanship and a conscious effort on the part of the poet to compose a well-constructed poem. Among these we may cite Baleka Kgositsile's 'For My Unborn Child', Fezeka Makonese's 'I Must Go: Do Not Mourn', and Gloria Mtungwa's 'Militant Beauty'. Baleka Kgositsile's 'For My Unborn Child' combines symbolism with repetition and rhyme, as here in the first stanza:

Mound of life
    rise like the tide of revolution
Mound of life
    come join us
    as sure as the day of liberation (p. 25)

Makonese's poem successfully captures the tone of a youth whose experience of the brutalities of apartheid has led him to the conviction that he must join the ranks of the guerrillas, and is now bidding his mother farewell:

Weep no more
Mama dear weep no more
How importune the lightning
The stroke of the hour of parting
My age urges me
I will go
So please mother dear
Weep no more (p. 35)

These poems, together with a number of other short ones as well as some longer ones including Lindiwe Mabuza's 'Faces of Commitment', have their shortcomings. For instance, there is no consistency in the structure of the stanzas of some of the poems and the rhythmic flow tends to be rugged and jerky. But on the whole they are engaging and make the reader feel the poet's involvement in the subject. Poems like 'Militant Beauty' and 'For My Unborn Child' move the reader to reflection. However, many of the poems lack the craftsmanship of those referred to in the discussion on *Poets to the People*. The prevalent rhetorical style lacks the terseness and density of texture of Dennis Brutus and Keorapetse Kgositsile, the cutting edge of Mtshali's gentle irony and the lively and colloquial tone of Black Consciousness poetry. In many cases, the poems are inordinately long, wordy and formless and consequently without much force. Though she is quite an experienced poet, with some good examples of her work in both *Malibongwe* and *Poets to the People*, Lindiwe Mabuza is prone to this weakness, which reduces the overall impact of her poetry.

Many of the poems in *Malibongwe* also lack the conviction and genuineness that one discerns in the best poems by Oswald Mtshali, Dennis Brutus and Keorapetse Kgositsile. At times the reader gets the distinct feeling that the rhetoric that bedevils so many of these poems is not reflective of a genuine feeling – the poems seem contrived, as if the emotion expressed in them does not come from the bottom of the poet's heart.

Despite these shortcomings the best of the poems show some praiseworthy stylistic features. One of these is the choice of imagery and symbolism. We shall examine one striking set of images which clarifies the poets' authorial ideology. These are images of motherhood, childbearing and childhood. In writing about the formation of the African National Congress and its military wing, UmKhonto We Sizwe, in portraying the emergence of a new, liberated South Africa, our women poets often express themselves in terms of motherhood and fertility. In 'For My Unborn Child', Baleka Kgositsile refers simultaneously to the birth of a human child (her own child), the

emergence of a new generation of young revolutionaries and the creation of a new South Africa. The dominant motif is that of an expectant
mother going through the various stages of pregnancy and finally
delivering a baby with great joy after experiencing agony and exhaus-
tion. In the first two stanzas the expectant mother calls upon the
unborn baby to come, to be born 'like the tide of revolution' and join
the struggling people of South Africa 'as sure as the day of liberation'.
In the third stanza she portrays the highest and most painful stages
of the people's struggle in South Africa by referring to her own nerve-
racking experience of labour:

My screams go up
the labour of my people
The pain
the struggle
the blood
The cry of determination
from the bottom of the pile
the women of our land
Life on the beautiful land (p. 25)

In the fourth stanza she goes on to show that the attainment of justice,
like childbirth, is accompanied by blood, and so the birth of a new, free
and democratic society cannot be bloodless, for ' "There is no birth
without blood" / There is no blood without pain'. The pain referred to
is the pain of all the women of South Africa whose children have lost
their lives at the hands of the inhuman system, as becomes clear in the
fifth and sixth stanzas where the screams of a woman in labour are
transformed into a potent scream that 'splits fascist eardrums'. The
culmination of the struggle of a woman in labour is the glorious
moment of birth itself, which, in the closing stanza of the poem,
symbolizes the achievement of liberty through struggle:

Exhausted by the battle of labour
with untold satisfaction
I kiss you welcome
With dreams and hopes
born with each determined kick and move
with each ripple on my stomach
like the anger of my people
Mound of life
come join us
Together we must hunt the fascist down
cut his deaf head off
and let life flow in our land (p. 26)

In 'A New Child is Born' Gloria Mtungwa depicts the same process, not
quite as dramatically, but in a manner which captures what she calls,
'The sweet-sorrow of childbirth'. In this poem it is UmKhonto We

Sizwe which is born in the manner of a human child. The first stanza
dramatizes the contradictory nature of the birth of the fighting force,
the military wing of the ANC:

Pushing and kicking
violently –
causing sometimes
    pain
at times
    joy
sometimes
    curses (p. 21)

In the first stanza the birth cry is heard of the fighting force, born with
stubborn determination:

Born out of sorrow
the liberator
the victor
over squalor grief and subjection
the harbinger
of
love, sunshine and equality.
M.K.
our M.K. (p. 22)

A similar set of images occurs in 'Mangaung', in which Lindiwe
Mabuza chronicles the formation and growth of the ANC in terms of
the birth and growth of a human child. In the first stanza the child proclaims his birth: 'I was born on January the eight'. Later he boasts that
he was born with features of leopards and lions, but his behaviour was
like that of a human being or, at any rate, a living thing:

But I'm an extraordinary spirit
A power, a force, a home
A shield
A spear
A child
Yes, a child born with stubborn leopard spots
of racism
All over
But born nonetheless
Breathing, kicking stretching (p. 12)

In the closing stanza the child, now grown up, gives his true identity
and tells us he gave birth to yet another child, the military wing of the
ANC:

And
What's my name?

Poetry & the African Liberation Struggle

The AFRICAN NATIONAL CONGRESS
of South Africa. Born January
8, 1912.
I gave birth to UMKHONTO
WE SIZWE on the 16th December
1961 (p. 14)

In writing about the Soweto uprising of 1976, the women poets naturally use images of childhood as it was a children's struggle. Even so, childhood is seen in relation to motherhood, to the physiology of women and the processes of childbearing and suckling. Thus in 'Years of the Child', Baleka Kgositsile addresses South Africa as a mother with 'anxious breasts' that itch and give nourishment to brave children who are going to overcome the evils of apartheid:

Mother
Home
your children
of whom your richness
stripped you
let your anxious breast
knead you together
let them itch
with the salt of
your sweat and tears
let our future burn in them
that they create
years of the child
let their hunger
bear their anger
let our children live
and live (p. 45)

When the youth of Soweto resolve to go to the bush and join the fighting forces they reveal their resolve, not to their fathers or elder brothers, but to their mothers, as in Fezeka Makonese's 'I Must Go: Do Not Mourn', which ends with a reference to childbearing. It becomes clear in the last stanza that the mother poet makes her youthful protagonists speak the language of mothers, who think in terms of children born and unborn, thus fusing the psychology of the children of Soweto with that of their mothers:

That the unborn child
May not see what I see
Or taste what I've tasted
This is my journey

Stay well, ma! (p. 36)

Mother symbolism is a common feature of African poetry. Africa is referred to as 'Mother Africa', a common expression of African nationalism which also occurs in Lusophone poetry of the pre-combat phase, as in some of Jose Craveirinha's and Noémia de Sousa's poems. This nationalist consciousness comes through forcibly in *Malibongwe*, in which both Africa and South Africa are frequently referred to as 'Mother'. In the very first poem, Africa is called 'Masechaba', a Sesotho expression for 'Mother of the nation' or 'Mother of children'. In this particular poem, Mother Africa's children are portrayed as having acquired a new consciousness, having rejected their former garments 'of indifference / of docile acceptance' and become fearless fighters who defend the motherland. The poem rejects Mtshali's mournful protestations and recalls David Diop's poem 'Africa', which is discussed in Chapter 3 of this volume. The fourth stanza of Ilva Mackay's 'Masechaba' captures the optimism of David Diop's great poem with even greater force:

> Africa
> the voice of your children
> erodes the mist-shrouded mountains
> like hungry rain
> and cuts through the valleys
> like the pounding rivers
> that ravage and rape your fields (p. 8)

Poetry and the Liberation Process – Conclusion

South African liberation poetry is a very broad subject, and such conclusions as we might draw cannot do complete justice to the topic, considering that there is a very large number of poets involved. It is, however, possible to make observations that throw more light on the comments made in the main body of the chapter.

An obvious feature of South African poetry is the wide variety of ideological stances adopted by the poets. If we contrast the gentle and undeveloped critical realism of Mtshali, the passionate protest temperament of Dennis Brutus, the confident and nonchalant arrogance of Mongane Wally Serote, the revolutionary feminism of, say, Gloria Mtungwa and the socialist world view of Keorapetse Kgositsile, we see a substantial development in ideological consciousness, from Mtshali, whose poetry depicts black people as objects of history, to Kgositsile and the women poets, who see black people becoming the subjects of history. However, this development is not necessarily chronological. While Black Consciousness poetry and the feminism of the poets represented in *Malibongwe* are more recent developments, they do not show the clarity of Kgositsile's vision. Therefore, different levels of political consciousness co-exist in South African liberation poetry, a fact that can be traced to the uneven development of the political struggle.

Poetry & the African Liberation Struggle

The wide variety of ideological stances notwithstanding, there is a strong common denominator in South African liberation poetry. Created under apartheid conditions, it issues from the dialectic between domination and resistance, between the repression characteristic of the South African social formation and the struggle of the majority to break that system. In consequence every poem is a negation of apartheid and an assertion of the ideals of freedom, equality and social justice. Whether it be a Mtshali raising a gentle voice of protest, a Brutus crying out shrilly, a Serote shouting 'shit' to a white boss, or an Ilva MacKay denouncing the ravaging and raping of Mother Africa – the basic cause of this rebellious spirit is the aberrant system of apartheid, and it is the refusal of the oppressed to succumb to brutality that gives the poetry its vibrancy.

However, the question of how to represent the dialectic of the South African situation is not adequately addressed by some of the poets. There are two basic questions that I believe the writer of poetry in present-day South Africa should reflect upon. The first is, what role can art play in helping to bring about the demise of apartheid? The second is premised upon the objective of the liberation struggle: what kind of South Africa do we want to see emerging as a result of the liberation struggle?

The question of what role art can play in the struggle is closely related to the issue of the aesthetics of liberation. In other words, what are the forms of art that are likely to play an effective role in realizing the goals of the liberation struggle, or what are the forms of representation that make poetry an effective tool of liberation? This question, to which we shall return in the closing chapter of the book, has been cogently addressed by Njabulo Ndebele in the following paragraph:

> The problem has been that questions about art and society have been easily settled after a general consensus about commitment. This has led to the prescription of solutions even before all the problems have been discovered and analysed. The writer, as a result, has tended to plunge into the task of writing without fully grappling with the theoretical demands of that task in all its dimensions. Armed with notions of artistic commitment still constrained by outmoded protest-bound perceptions of the role of art and of what constitutes political relevance in art, he set about reproducing a dead end. Consequently, the limited range of explorable experience characteristic of writing under the protest ethos, has continued to plague South African writing . . .[13]

This, in my view, sums up the weakness of many a poem in the two anthologies under discussion, and especially in *Malibongwe*. The writer plunges into writing without thinking through the forms of representation and the result is less than satisfactory. It could, of course, be argued that Ndebele's position is that of an armchair theoretician who has the time to develop theories about forms of representation precisely because he is not involved in a concrete way in the struggle. It could equally be argued that those who write combat poetry are schooled in the fire and furnace of the revolution and write poems whose aesthetics are determined by the dynamics of a concrete revolution. This is an understandable position, but the question Ndebele raises is valid unless we adopt a purely mechanistic approach which sees a one-sided cause-and-effect relationship between literature and history, and unless we deny the writer's power to influence the course of a revolution, which contradicts the basis of dialectical materialism. The role of literature and the arts has been the subject of debate in other revolutions. In China, Mao Tse Tung himself found the subject worthy of serious consideration and contributed to the deliberations of the Yenan Forum on Literature and Art in 1942, at the very height of the Chinese revolution, before the People's Republic of China was established in 1949.

We have seen that the poets under discussion resort to a variety of forms of representation. There is, for instance, the passionate outcry of Dennis Brutus, which typifies what Ndebele has characterized as 'spectacular representation',[14] whose aim is to demonstrate and document the external appearance of apartheid in a spectacular manner. The poetry aims at evoking an emotional response to the horrors of apartheid. This is also a characteristic feature of the poetry of some of the women authors: Sono Molefe's 'We Demand Punishment', Ilva Mackay's 'Mandela and All Comrades in Prison' and Lindiwe Mabuza's 'Mangaung' are examples, though the women poets are often not able to evoke the same degree of emotional response as Brutus. On the other hand, some poems in the two anthologies do move the reader, as does Mtshali, despite his blurred social vision, in his best poems and as do the best poems in *Malibongwe*. In Mtshali there is a simple but subtle combination of exteriority and interiority, a concrete depiction of the ugly face of apartheid coupled with an attempt to explore the psychological response of the oppressed to that brazen ugliness. In *Malibongwe* there are poems which seek to represent the psychological reaction of the rebellious women through images drawn from their own physiology. Where there is too much emphasis on exposing the ruthlessness of the South African social system or on highlighting and chronicling the heroism of the oppressed, as is the case with many poems in *Malibongwe*, art tends to be subordinated to rhetoric, and fails to communicate.

The question of what social system should be created after liberation relates to the conscientizing role of the artist and demands of poets that they go beyond protest concerned merely with questioning and criticizing the system without pointing the way to an alternative society. That is the limitation of the world view presented by Mtshali and, to a large extent, Brutus. The women poets and the Black Consciousness poets go beyond pure protest as their poetry is combat poetry, concerned with the destruction of the existing social formation. The crucial question is: where do we go after apartheid? The one poet who attempts to answer this question and does so with a modicum of success is Keorapetse Kgositsile, whose vision is guided by a socialist consciousness and ideology.

The danger of taking on a conscientizing role as an artist is that it can degenerate into didacticism and propagandist sloganeering, which is more properly the function of the politician. The genuine revolutionary artist eschews didacticism in favour of persuading the reader to accept new possibilities, relationships and values. Opening new frontiers in the reader's consciousness is a task which requires both a high level of ideological consciousness and artistic creativity.

A good example of poetry that demonstrates ideological clarity and gives a sense of direction during the course of a struggle is Mozambican liberation poetry. Despite some deficiencies in style, Mozambican liberation poetry gives the reader more than a glimpse of a social vision of the new man and woman moulded by the dynamics of the liberation struggle. In South Africa the struggle has not yet reached the intensity and consistency that the Frelimo war of national independence achieved in the late 1960s and the early 1970s. While South African liberation poetry is truly a literature of combat, it does not tell the story of a highly organized and systematic struggle guided by an ideology adhered to with consistency and tenacity, as was the case with the Mozambican struggle for independence. In South Africa, the struggle is that of an isolated Solomon Mahlangu bravely sacrificing his own life for the freedom of the majority, or Soweto youths announcing their resolve to go to the war front, or exiled revolutionaries recalling the heroism of those whom Lindiwe Mabuza represents in 'Faces of Commitment', and so on. There is no clear and concentrated programme of action as in Mozambican combat poetry. This is a result of the nature of the South African liberation struggle, whose progress and direction is far less discernible to an external observer than was the case with the wars of national indepence in Angola, Mozambique, Guinea Bissau and Zimbabwe. The hope is that, as the struggle for liberation intensifies and as artists reflect more deeply on their role, the poet will acquire a new vision, seek to promote new forms of social consciousness and endeavour to write poetry that shakes the reader with its ideological weight and artistic excellence.

Notes

1. An earlier version of this chapter is published in E. Ngara and A. Morrison (eds.), *Literature, Language and the Nation*, Harare, Association of University Teachers of Literature and Language, in association with Baobab, 1989.
2. B. Feinberg (ed.), *Poets to the People: South African Freedom Poems*, London, Heinemann Educational Books, 1980, p. xi.
3. Sono Molefe (ed.), *Malibongwe ANC Women: Poetry is also their Weapon*, Sweden, African National Congress. Please note that the anthology does not indicate the place and date of publication. It was probably published in 1985/6 to mark the United Nations Decade for Women.
4. Oswald Mbuyiseni Mtshali, *Sounds of a Cowhide Drum*, London, Oxford University Press, 1972.
5. Steve Biko, *I Write What I Like: A Selection of his Writings*, ed. A. Stubbs, C.R. London, Heinemann Educational Books, 1978, p. 49.
6. Ibid., p. 50.
7. I. Madingoane, *Africa My Beginning*, Johannesburg, Ravan Press, 1979.
8. Of these three only Mongane Wally Serote is represented in *Poets to the People*.
9. For Sepamla's poems quoted here see Gerald Moore and Ulli Beier (eds.), *The Penguin Book of Modern African* Poetry, Harmondsworth, Penguin, 1963 (Third Edition, 1984), pp. 265–266.
10. Ibid., p. 265.
11. Ibid. p. 266.
12. Mtshali, op. cit., p. 5.
13. Njabulo S. Ndebele, 'Beyond "Protest": New Directions in South African Fiction', Paper read at the Second African Writers Conference, Stockholm, Sweden, 1986. Published in *High Plains Literary Review*, Vol. 1, Denver, 1986.
14. Njabulo Ndebele, 'The Rediscovery of the Ordinary: Some New Writings in South Africa', *Journal of Southern African Studies*, Vol. 12, No. 2, April 1986.

PART FOUR

NEW DIRECTIONS IN AFRICAN POETRY & POETICS

12

The Artist
as a Chameleon:
Jack Mapanje of Malawi

Mapanje and Other Malawian Poets

The 1980s have seen the rise of some very promising Malawian poets, the most outstanding from the point of view of productivity and quality being Jack Mapanje, Steve Chimombo, Felix Mnthali and Frank Chipasula. Each one of these has now published a complete volume of poetry,[1] and, were it not for the fact that in this part of the book we are focusing on individual pace-setters whose art can serve as a model for future writers, it would have been ideal to devote the chapter to a full comparative study of the four. Such a study of these four poets from a country that is now well known for its repression of literary creativity would yield interesting results. Even a cursory look at the volumes so far published by these poets would seem to suggest a difference in style and approach between the two who are still living in the country, Jack Mapanje and Steve Chimombo, and the other two, who are in exile.[2] The style of the latter is more explicit and direct, suggesting greater freedom to write as they wish. This poses a dilemma for the critic, who, contrary to normal practice, feels he has to err on the side of caution by being a little more cryptic than desirable in case external intervention brings more wrath on the writer. This predicament has a direct bearing on this chapter, which is being written exactly one month after news of Jack Mapanje's detention in Malawi.[3] On the other hand, to exclude him completely from this volume would amount to a betrayal of the cause of African literature and the objectives of the book. Unable to don the colours of the chameleon the critic can only hope to imitate the reptile's stealthy steps.

With the publication in 1981 of his first complete volume of poetry, *Of Chameleons and Gods*, Jack Mapanje has rapidly gained recognition as one of the leading younger poets of Africa. *Of Chameleons and Gods* is divided into four parts, *Of Chameleons and Gods, Sketches from London, Re-entering Chingwe's Hole* and *Assembling Another Voice*. The headings are to do partly with the subject matter and partly with the setting in which the poems were composed. The first group deals mainly with Malawi, while *Sketches From London* are almost literally that. It would appear they were written when Jack Mapanje was a student in London from 1972 to about 1974/5. The clue to the London orientation of these poems is given in 'Handshakes and Best Wishes', where the poet depicts his departure from his friends at the airport in Malawi with someone shouting, 'Oh, well . . . drink from the source!'. This is a frolicsome reference to London or England as the source of knowledge, as Malawi and other British colonies received their university tradition from that country. A number of the poems in the section are a reflection of the poet's impression of 'the source' as can be clearly detected from 'Drinking the Water from its Source'.

Re-entering Chingwe's Hole groups together poems written about Malawi after Mapanje's return from London. Most of these would probably have been written between 1975 and 1978. This brings us to the last section, *Assembling Another Voice*, most of which were probably written later than the rest of the poems in the volume. In this section the poet reflects on both Malawi and the outside world. There is a poem on Steve Biko, the South African Black Consciousness leader murdered by the Boers; there is a poem on Soweto and another one on the massacre by the Portuguese of the people of Wiriyamu Village in Mozambique, an incident which Professor Adrian Hastings, who is mentioned in the poem and is currently at Leeds University, publicized widely in England in the early 1970s. These three poems and the poem 'On African Writing (1971)' in the first section summarize the extent of Mapanje's concern about issues that have no direct bearing on Malawi and on his own experience in Britain.

The summary above shows something of the range of Mapanje's concerns in this 80-page volume, but our focus will be on the two sections that deal with life in Malawi, namely, *Of Chameleons and Gods* and *Re-entering Chingwe's Hole*, because the poet's achievement is best reflected in these two groups of poems.

Authorial Ideology and Social Vision in Mapanje

That Mapanje is a social critic with a strong feeling for art and artistic objects is evident from the very first poem, 'Kabula Curio-Shop'. The poet is angry, almost indignant, at the treatment of art and artists by the modern tourist industry, which commercializes everything. The indignation of the protagonist emerges from the contrast between the first and second stanzas. The first stanza depicts the artist, the carver, hard at work, making it clear that much labour, skill and concentration have gone into the piece of carving:

Black wood between carefully bowed legs
the eyes red over bellows and smoke
the sharpening of axes, adzes, carvers
the chopping, the whittling and such
carving such scooping and scooping
then the sandpapering and smoothing

Then in the second stanza we see the same product broken and abandoned in a tiny corner of the curio-shop:

now a broken symbol thrown careless
in the nook of a curio-shop: a lioness
broken legs, broken neck, broken udder?

There is also a suggestion that the artist was exploited and did not get his labour's worth: 'such energy release and the price / bargained away'.

In 'Song of Chickens' we have the portrait of a leader who was once the champion of his people's freedom, who genuinely protected his subjects, but who has now turned against them. Some African leaders have become oppressors of their people in alliance with the imperialist world, and some have even collaborated with South Africa and with the former white-controlled governments of Mozambique and Rhodesia to oppress the citizens of their own countries. In this poem the master's cruelty, it is suggested, is displayed in order to impress foreign visitors. The contrast between images of bravery in the first stanza and those of cruelty in the second is expertly portrayed:

Master, you talked with bows,
Arrows and catapults once
Your hands steaming with hawk blood
To protect your chicken.

Why do you talk with knives now,
Your hands teaming with eggshells
And hot blood from your own chicken?
Is it to impress your visitors?

As the poet explains, the Chiuta poems are based on a Malawian creation myth and they take the form of an allegory. On the face of it, the poems are about Chiuta, who, we are told in the Glossary, is 'God, The Creator, The Almighty, The Most Powerful One, He who creates rainbows'. The allegory is not easy to decipher for readers who are not familiar with the Malawi oral traditions, but there is no doubt that the four poems are about a powerful politician. The last poem portrays a failed politician who, like Chiuta, becomes a chameleon to disguise his inadequacies. The reference to Dr Kamuzu Banda strikes the reader.

Another little poem, 'The Tussle', presents an interesting mode of protest by simply reversing people's expectations. In any battle between the lion and the hyena we know who inevitably wins but here the protagonist instructs his son to play a game in which the hyena kills the lion. The person concerned grumbles, 'tell him it's only / a game – animal game / you are men'. The story of the lion and hyena is typical of the African oral story tradition and presents an opportunity for the poet to talk about powerful politicians in a language which the ordinary people understand.

'The New Platform Dances' depicts a contrast between traditional dances as authentically performed in the past and what seems to be a caricature of them in modern Malawi. The protagonist would at first appear to be someone in the position of President Banda, boasting about having 'Scattered nervous women' and 'Then enticed them back / With flywhisk's magic', but as we come to the third and final stanza it becomes clear that this is a voice from the past commenting satirically and bitterly, in a manner similar to that of Okot p'Bitek's Lawino, about this deplorably degraded and impoverished imitation of the real thing:

Now, when I see my daughters writhe
Under cheating abstract
Voices of slack drums, ululate
To babble–idea–men–masks
Without amulets or anklets,
Why don't I stand up
To show them how we danced
Chopa, how IT was born?
Why do I sit still
Why does my speech choke
Like I have not danced
Before? Haven't I
Danced the bigger dance?
Haven't I?

The last poem we shall comment on from this section is 'Before Chilembwe Tree'. The poem is addressed to John Chilembwe, who is described in the Notes and Glossary as 'the first Malawian rebel missionary to rise against Nyasaland Colonial Government under the banner of Christianity'. Chilembwe therefore started the tradition of resistance, and, since oral traditions believe that he did not die at the hands of colonialists but went up to heaven through the *nsolo* tree, some may well believe that he will come back and usher in a new era of freedom. For his part, the protagonist is disenchanted by the current state of affairs and so travels to the *nsolo* tree and makes a traditional religious offering, awaiting Chilembwe's second coming, praying to him in the manner of someone talking to a dead ancestor. However, the poem ends on a somewhat pessimistic note. The voice seems now to be addressing the followers of Chilembwe, who have danced and sung for his return but so far to no avail. The question then is who will show the way again as Chilembwe did?

> You've chanted yourselves hoarse
> Chilembwe is gone in your dust
> Stop lingering then:
> Who will start another fire?

In reading *Re-entering Chingwe's Hole* we get a clearer picture of the poet's vision. The first thing that strikes the reader here is that Zomba is portrayed as some kind of waste land. On his return the poet is disappointed by the lack of life that now characterizes Zomba Plateau, the place where the capital of Malawi was once located and where the main campus of the University of Malawi, Chancellor College, is situated. It is clear from 'Visiting Zomba Plateau' and 'Re-entering the Shrines of Zomba' that the place has lost its colour. But what we see here is not necessarily a contrast between the Zomba that the poet knew when he left for London and the Zomba he sees now on his return. The return of the poet from abroad presents him with an event around which to depict the lifelessness of modern-day Zomba as opposed to the Zomba that might have been in the days of old before the gods deserted the noble shrines of the plateau. The contrast between the Zomba of today and that of the past is made forcefully in the last seven lines of 'Visiting Zomba Plateau':

> Where is your charming hyena tail –
> Praying-mantis who cared for prayers once?
> Where is the spirit that touched the hearts
> Lightly – chameleon colours of home?
> Where is your creation myth? Have I come
> To witness the carving and jingling only of
> Your bloated images and piddling mirrors?

Zomba in fact becomes a microcosm of Malawi. This becomes clear in 'Glory Be to Chingwe's Hole', a poem ostensibly about a hole on the Zomba Plateau into which, according to oral traditions, wrong-doers were dropped as a form of punishment. The hole is located just above Namitembo River and it is believed that, although it looks so small and does not appear to be very deep, those who were thrown into the hole were never seen again, as their bodies went right into the river, where they perished. Chingwe's Hole still presents this horrific image of itself to the poet and this has wide-ranging ramifications for people's lives in Malawi.[4] But here Mapanje fuses two myths – the myth of Chingwe's Hole and that of the Frog who carved a beautiful woman from a sacred ebony tree. The Chief who threw prisoners into Chingwe's Hole in the first stanza is associated with the Chief who wanted to deprive Frog of Ebony Beauty as related in the second stanza. The explanation given in the Notes and Glossary is that by sticking a pin into her head Frog turns Ebony Beauty, whom he has carved, into a human being, but when the pin is removed she becomes wood again. According to the myth, the oppressive Chief is defeated by a combination of the song of Dove and the physical force of Hawk. There is an interesting suggestion here about the role of art in liberation, since, without the song of Dove, Ebony Beauty could not have been rescued by Hawk. We shall quote the last paragraph of Mapanje's explanatory note:

> Frog runs into the forest where he assembles birds, animals, and other creatures and with them plans the rescue of his wife. Dove is chosen to lead the attack by singing a melodious song. Hawk is chosen for his speed and the rest follow Frog. The forest crowd soon gathers at the Chief's palace in a great commotion. The Chief decides to see what the crowd is up to. Suddenly all is quiet. Dove sings his most melodious song. The Chief invites his bride to listen to this lovely music. As they come out of their palace, Hawk, with the speed of lightning, swoops down and picks the pin from the Beauty. The Beauty becomes wood again.[5]

A point of interest to note is how Mapanje gives advice to senior government officials in poems like 'On His Royal Blindness Paramount Chief Kwangala', 'Making Our Clowns Martyrs' and 'When This Carnival Finally Closes'. The last two address the issue of people who have been top government officials being dropped and finding themselves having to return to their roots. The interesting thing is that Mapanje depicts what has actually happened in some African countries. For instance, the present writer knows of the case of a member of the Cabinet of the late Chief Leabua Jonathan of Lesotho, whose dismissal, it is said, was announced at a Cabinet meeting, and when he left the meeting he found he had no government car and no driver to take him home any more, and when he found his way home he was greeted with the message that he could no longer live in the government house. This is the sort of thing that happens in 'Making Our Clowns Martyrs' where a politician goes back home with no 'National colours flanking your black mercedes benz'. The politician's home people welcome him but the contrast between the life style he is used to and what he is returning to is shocking:

But welcome back to the broken reed-fences, brother;
Welcome home to the poached reed-huts you left behind;
Welcome to these stunted pit-latrines where only
The pungent whiff of buzzing green flies gives way.
You will find your idle ducks still shuffle and fart
In large amounts. The black dog you left still sniffs
Distant recognition, lying, licking its leg-wounds . . .

Mapanje's poetry is that of a social critic who is dismayed at the way things are going in his society, the loss of freedom and what he sees as a deterioration in cultural and other values. His poetry is protest poetry, performing a similar function to that of novels of disillusionment typified by Ayi Kwei Armah's *The Beautyful Ones Are Not Yet Born*. He puts the question but does not provide the answer. His role is that of opening the eyes of his readers to what is going wrong and of a gadfly in the flesh of political leaders, whom he reminds of their misdeeds. Issues such as imperialism and neo-colonialism are, however, on the periphery of his concerns. In order to acquire a greater appreciation of his vision we should explore his aesthetic ideology.

Aesthetic Ideology, Form and Communication in Mapanje

Mapanje's preoccupations as a poet are essentially cause for satire. But how does he use satire? What forms and devices does he employ to make it work? The key to his artistic method is hinted at in the cryptic Introduction to the volume:

> The verse in this volume spans some ten turbulent years in which I have been attempting to find a voice or voices as a way of preserving some sanity. Obviously where personal voices are too easily muffled, this is a difficult task; one is tempted like the chameleon, who failed to deliver Chiuta's message of life, to bask in one's brilliant camouflage. But the exercise has been, if nothing else, therapeutic; and that's no mean word in our circumstances!

It is clear from this that Malawi has become an oppressive country with a strong system of censorship. Mapanje's voice is muffled, what he has to say is said carefully, indirectly and often in a cryptic fashion. This makes many of his poems extremely difficult to decipher, particularly for the reader who is not familiar with Malawi's oral traditions and political system. However, Mapanje has also gone to great lengths to evolve a consistent aesthetic ideology deriving from the historical and social conditions under which he writes. His poetry reveals several major stylistic features which we shall now consider.

First, Mapanje makes extensive use of myth and oral traditions. This is at work in the poems on Chiuta and on Chingwe's Hole and many others. In these poems Mapanje relies on the Malawian reader's knowledge of the various myths to decipher the meaning of a poem. In fact, Mapanje is not the only Malawian poet who has resorted to this approach. Steve Chimombo uses myth very extensively in *Napolo Poems*, an important volume which contains poems inspired by *Napolo*, 'the mythical subterranean serpent residing under mountains and associated with landslides, earthquakes and floods in Malawi'.[6] While Frank Chipasula and Felix Mnthali[7] can write in more direct language, the pressures on those within Malawi are such that it seems to have been accepted that the writer can only influence his or her readers' consciousness by appealing to popular myths. What this means is that, unlike in, say, Okot p'Bitek, where the use of oral traditions arises from a desire to preserve these traditions, in Mapanje and other Malawian writers myths are used primarily as a way of communicating with Malawi's peasant-based society by appealing to what that society knows of its own culture and history. Oral traditions are thus a medium of communication rather than a means of recapturing the past. Of course, the method gives rise to a dialectical process – for Mapanje the use of oral traditions in poetry has led to an abiding interest in orature, as evidenced by the publication of *Oral Poetry from Africa*.[8] Similarly, by using oral traditions as a means of communication the writer *ipso facto* helps to keep those traditions alive.

This African 'mythical method', as we may call it, allows a poet to be a chameleon, to convert Ebony Beauty from a human being to wood and vice versa. Thus in Mapanje the mythical method introduces an element of allegory, with the poet speaking on two levels, a superficial and a deeper level. This is true of 'Song of Chickens', for example. In 'The Tussle' the protagonist advises his son to tell whoever asks him about hyena killing lion that 'it's only a game – animal game'. The poet could say the same about 'Song of Chickens': 'It's only about chickens and hawks, not people'. Similarly, Banda becomes Chiuta and Malawi Chingwe's Hole.

But myth and allegory alone cannot adequately account for Mapanje's success as a satirist, particularly as they introduce a strong element of obscurity into the poetry. What makes Mapanje's poems so successful as satire are tropes and other devices borrowed from oral tradition. Satire is a very common feature of African orature and one of the forms it takes is apostrophe, the device of speaking as if the poet or protagonist were directly addressing a particular person or audience. This device is used in Mapanje in a manner similar to that of Okot p'Bitek in *Song of Lawino*. But in Mapanje apostrophe has a peculiar punch, driving the point home in a biting manner. This arises from the couching of the apostrophe in the form of a question in most cases. The question is asked, but, as the poem is a monologue, the villain to whom the question is addressed is not given the opportunity to respond, so the view of the satirist carries the day. Consider, for example, how the innocent chicken asks this simple question of its master:

Master, you talked with bows,
Arrows and catapults once
Your hands steaming with hawk blood
To protect your chicken.

Why do you talk with knives now,
Your hands teaming with eggshells
And hot blood from your own chicken?
Is it to impress your visitors?

Of course not all the poems make use of the question as a device. In fact, one of Mapanje's most accomplished satirical pieces, 'Making Our Clowns Martyrs', does not use the question technique at all. It takes the form of 'brotherly advice', which is sometimes more effective than vengeful ire.

To give his satire its bite Mapanje often employs apostrophe in conjunction with the lampoon, as is evident in the contemptuous tone of some of the poems. Take, for instance, the 'brotherly advice' that is given to him who returns home without a chauffeur. Ostensibly the protagonist is sympathetic; in reality he is shedding crocodile tears:

Hard luck my friend. But we all know what currents
Have stroked your temper. You come from a breed of
Toxic frogs croaking beside the smoking marshes of
River Shire, and the first words you breathed were
Snapped by the lethal mosquitoes of this morass.
We know you would wade your way through the arena.
Though we wondered how you had got chosen for the benz.

Or take the last stanza of 'On His Royal Blindness Paramount Chief Kwangala':

No, your grace, I am no alarmist nor banterer
I am only a child surprised how you broadly disparage
Me shocked by the tedium of your continuous palaver. I
Adore your majesty. But paramountcy is like a raindrop
On a vast sea. Why should we wait for children to
Tell us about our toothless gums or our showing flies?

The last quoted example reveals another aspect of Mapanje's satire. There is a certain lively rudeness about it. The poems often end with or include a little impudent and aggressive question or comment that is particularly biting. The last seven lines of 'Visiting Zomba Plateau' will serve as another example:

Jack Mapanje

Where is your charming hyena tail –
Praying-mantis who cared for prayers once?
Where is the spirit that touched the hearts
Lightly – chameleon colours of home?
Where is your creation myth? Have I come
To witness the carving and jingling only of
Your bloated images and piddling mirrors?

The combination of apostrophe and the lampoon gives rise to a vivid dramatic element in the poetry. In 'The New Platform Dances', for example, one can almost visualize the old protagonist raging with anger, just as one can see Chilembwe's follower placing his gourd before the *nsolo* tree in 'Before Chilembwe's Tree'. Though the poetry lacks an effective rhythm, this is made up for by the devices discussed above, which lend the poetry a lively conversational style that at times is irresistibly amusing. Mapanje's apparent lightheartedness is, in some ways, similar to that of Okot p'Bitek, but the reader is aware that, unlike Okot, Jack Mapanje writes under immense pressures. It is a peculiar achievement of the Malawian poets that they can afford to laugh about their fear.

Notes

1. The four volumes appeared in the following order:
   Jack Mapanje, *Of Chameleons and Gods*, London, Heinemann Educational Books, 1981;
   Felix Mnthali, *When Sunset Comes to Sapitwa*, Harlow, Longman, 1982;
   Frank Chipasula, *O Earth, Wait For Me*, Johannesburg, Ravan Press, 1984;
   Steve Chimombo, *Napolo Poems*, Zomba, Manchichi Publishers, 1987.
   Many of the poems in *Napolo Poems* had long appeared in poetry anthologies around the world. There are also other poets in Malawi, like Edison Mpina, who has published a volume of much poorer poetry.
2. Felix Mnthali, who was once detained in Malawi, is now Professor of English at the University of Botswana. Frank Chipasula is in the United States of America.
3. Jack Mapanje was reported to have been arrested and detained on 24 September 1987. At the time this chapter was written, in October 1987, there was no news of his release.
4. Chingwe's Hole is not a fictitious hole. It actually exists in Malawi and the author of this book has seen it with his own eyes.
5. See Mapanje, op. cit., pp. 77–78.
6. See Chimombo, op. cit., Preface.

7. Note that, though some of the poems in Mnthali's *When Sunset Comes to Sapitwa* were written before the poet left the country, the volume was published after he had gone into exile.
8. See Jack Mapanje and Landeg White, *Oral Poetry from Africa: An Anthology*, Harlow, Longman, 1983.

13

The Artist
& the Revolutionary Dance:
Kofi Anyidoho of Ghana

Introduction

One of the most distinguished poets of the new generation is Kofi
Anyidoho, author of *A Harvest of Our Dreams*,[1] which includes
poems originally published under the title *Elegy for the Revolution*.[2]
Anyidoho is a pace-setter, with several literary awards to his credit.

A Harvest of Our Dreams is divided into six parts. Each part has
distinctive features of tone, diction and content. There are significant
variations in tone as the reader goes through the different parts. For
example, the elegiac tone of Part One is markedly different from the
chatty voice of Part Two, where in 'Awoyo' Anyidoho adopts a tone
of voice reminiscent of Lawino in *Song of Lawino*. In Part Four, *My
Mailman Friend Was Here*, the poet moves into pidgin English. The
poems are in the form of letters written from Bloomington in America
to various people in Ghana, who seem to be mainly relatives. In Part
Five we return to a serious voice. Some of the key poems in the volume
are in this section. They include 'They Hunt the Night', 'Long Distance
Runner', 'Our Fortune's Dance' and, most important of all, 'The
Panther's Final Dance'. In the last section, *Elegy for the Revolution*,
there is a mixture of very serious and lighthearted material. Some of the
central poems are to be found here, such as 'Elegy for the Revolution',
'Dance of Death' and 'New Birth-Cords'.

Anyidoho and Revolutionary Consciousness

Anyidoho speaks with the voice of a revolutionary who is concerned
with events in the history of post-independence Ghana. His poetry is a
reaction to a revolution that was betrayed and it speaks with an

assertive firmness and aggressiveness. The first poem, 'Mythmaker', is dedicated to students who 'lost their lives in student risings against the Panther's boast'. The poem asserts in a lyrical, almost mournful voice, that 'These students will / be home / Some Day'. In 'Seedtime' hope for the nation is expressed in a variety of images. The poem shows how attempts to advance the revolution have been frustrated at various stages. 'This land survived the flood of birthwaters', we are told, 'but moonmen came' who misled the people of Ghana, who have now lost 'seedtime in seasons of harvest dance'. The people of Ghana won their independence but lost the opportunity to grow in the very moment of celebrating independence. An important symbol is that of the orphan who lays an egg which the rainstorm comes and sweeps away:

Our orphan laid an egg across the backyard of the skies
The rainstorm came and swept it all away
Again he laid an egg against the backyard of the skies
Again the rainstorm came and swept it all away
Today he sows a mystery seed in the bosom of whirlthoughts
Our predator birds shall have to prey upon
their own anger their own nightmares

The orphan who finally decides to sow 'a mystery seed in the bosom of whirlthoughts' would seem to refer to a new revolutionary consciousness which is difficult for the predator birds to destroy and thus ensures the success of the dream:

We will not die the death of dreams
We will not die the cruel death of dreams

There will be anthems sung for victories reaped in dreams

In 'A Harvest of Our Dreams' the theme of the betrayal of the people's revolution is more explicitly explored. There is the symbol of the honeybee who went across the world gathering fragrance for his Mother–Queen but then some other gatherer came with his own plans: 'Our hive went up in flames'. So 'our honeycomb' went floating through 'seedtime within the soul beyond the reach of Song'. The poet sings to the memory of this honeycomb. But he is not alone in this because he is 'seeking kindred minds / for lost passwords into fiestas of the soul'. It seems that the poet is striving to create a revolutionary consciousness in the minds of other people as a way of achieving the desired goal. The poem ends with hope of future victory and success. There is a reference to 'Uncle Demanya', who is to return. This is probably an allusion to a Ghanaian hero or revolutionary, perhaps Kwame Nkrumah, as he is mentioned in 'Pan Am 188' in reference to a tarmac which 'Our Uncle Kwame built for his murdered dreams'. Uncle Demanya is a redeemer who will come back and bring to fruition the dreams of his lifetime:

Kofi Anyidoho

Uncle Demanya shall come back home
with the bread basket of which
he sang through life across the hunger of our graves.

A central poem in Anyidoho's collection is 'The Panther's Final
Dance'. Three key symbols are employed in this poem, the interpretation of which should lead to an understanding of this poet's rather
obscure use of symbols. The three symbols are images of thunder,
panther and hippo. Thunder or 'the Thunder' is a recurring symbol
and is sometimes referred to simply as 'rumblings' or alluded to in
words or phrases connected with lightning. In these various versions
'thunder' occurs in many poems, including 'Seedtime', 'A Harvest of
Our Dreams', 'Our Fortune's Dance', 'Dance of Death' and 'Elegy for
the Revolution'. The 'panther' image appears in 'Mythmaker', 'Our
Fortune's Dance', 'Kingmaker', 'My Last Testament' and 'Dance of
Death' among others. 'Hippo' seems to be used only in 'The Panther's
Final Dance', which we shall now discuss.

The attitude of the protagonist to thunder is sometimes ambivalent,
as in this poem where 'thunder' is criticized for picking 'a clique of
trickster gods / for councilmen and ministers of state'; but in the main
thunder is portrayed in a very positive light. The attitude of the protagonist to panther is definitely ambivalent. Panther is given a negative
image, except when he 'smote down the rule of demi-semi-dogs' in the
third stanza of this poem. And, in 'Soul in Birthwaters', there is a note
of pathos in: 'The maimed panther is no playmate for antelopes'. The
hippo, however, seems to symbolize something altogether detestable, a
person or group of people whom the protagonist regards with
contempt.

Like some of the poems in Part Five and Part One, 'The Panther's
Final Dance' was written in 1979 when Kofi Anyidoho was studying at
Indiana University at Bloomington in the United States, and Lieutenant
Jerry Rawlings was handing over power to civilian leaders after his first
coup. It is quite plausible therefore to interpret thunder as representing
the power of the people under a genuine leader such as Kwame
Nkrumah. As indicated earlier, Kwame Nkrumah is mentioned in
endearing terms in 'Pan Am 188' as 'Our Uncle Kwame' who had built
the 'concrete road' or tarmac 'for his murdered dreams'. Nkrumah also
had dreams like the poet. Seen in this light, 'panther' could refer to
military rulers, they who came 'in flash of guns'. On the other hand, the
mention of our caretaker gods 'sending back the lame panther / to his
place of birth in the forest zone' could be a reference to the return of the
military to the barracks when Jerry Rawlings handed over power to
civilian rulers around 1979. It is these civilian rulers, like Hilary
Leman, who may be symbolized by 'the hippo'. They were powerless
to stem the tide of corruption or to pull Ghana out of the morass of its
economic problems.

169

The picture that emerges from this analysis of the three key images seems to indicate that Kofi Anyidoho distrusts military rulers, although he may have some hope in such leaders as Jerry Rawlings; that he had no faith in civilian leaders with no sense of direction, and that, while he has some critical comments to make about Nkrumah, he comes close to his idea of a revolutionary leader. It is Nkrumah then, or a leader with the qualities of Nkrumah, who is portrayed as 'Mythmaker', 'Uncle Demanya' and 'the honey bee' who had plans for his 'Mother–Queen', the Mother–Queen being the nation of Ghana. It is that sort of leader who is capable of bringing about the rule of thunder.

In 'Dance of Death', the positive value attached to thunder becomes quite explicit. Thunder conquers lions and panthers and enables the antelope to move about in peace:

> The growls of lions
> are muffled by mumblings of thunder
> The poise of panthers
> baffled by flashes of flaming skies
> The antelope passes through
> on its peace mission to the little stream of life

In 'Dance of Death', Anyidoho advocates the promotion of revolutionary action even at the cost of death. This is in order to put back on course 'a revolution gone astray into / arms of dream merchants', to quote the closing lines of 'Elegy for the Revolution'. 'Dance of Death' is indeed the one poem which encapsulates Anyidoho's vision most passionately and most eloquently. The poet irrevocably and openly declares his support for revolutionary change and calls upon his compatriots to be prepared to make the supreme sacrifice of death so that the nation may be born anew:

> The birth of a new nation
> calls for sacrifice of souls
> and our hearts are filled with
> a passion for life by baptism of death

He rejects peaceful change because it has been tried and has not worked: 'Our minds have laboured in vain / preparing blue-prints for revolutions of peace'. It is therefore incumbent upon the revolutionary patriots to form a united front, to 'link our arms' and do the dance of death which may result in death by firing squad. But even death may be necessary because 'It is on the field of execution / that death embraces life'. In a powerful stanza that demonstrates the poet's talent for lyrical and performative verse, various instruments are called upon to give rhythm to the dance of revolution:

Put the rhythm to the loom
Weave new tapestries for our gliding feet
This rhythm grows too urgent for our peace
Splitting our souls among a thousand desperate loves
The dance of death is a dance of grace
Give us back those old drummers
Give them back those broken drums with nasal twangs
Call them here call the owners of our town
Bring them stools to sit in state and watch
Our feet in this final glide across our twilight zone

The poem closes with words which not only assert the poet's hope for future victory, but give evidence of his profound understanding of the nature of revolutionary change. Revolutionary change involves a dialectical relationship between destruction and construction: destruction of the old and the building of a new system on its ashes:

The god of creation rambles
through the ruins of broken worlds
and
The process of reconstruction
is also
A process of demolition

In a sense, 'Dance of Death' is a response to the question posed in 'Our Fortune's Dance', where the wealth of Ghana is symbolized by 'our honeycomb', while the people are bees that should swarm around the honeycomb and, it is suggested, grab it back:

Our people how soon again in our hive
shall we swarm around our honeycomb?

When will the people of Ghana seize their wealth again, the poet asks. And in 'Dance of Death' the answer is given. It is no longer a question of asking the people when they will do it. He is urging them to seize the moment and triumph. There is, however, a voice of caution in 'New Birth-Cords', which warns those who may be led by 'rogues' to sacrifice their lives 'on the defiled altar of a nation's dreams'. The warning is 'a life is dearer than a wreath of tears', and so 'Do not brother die for a myth'.

Anyidoho is therefore not a fanatic, but a committed revolutionary who has strong patriotic feelings and was bitterly disappointed by the betrayal of his country's revolution in the 1970s. Whether or not his attitude to Ghana's political leaders has changed since the second coming of Jerry Rawlings, the author of this book has no idea.

That Anyidoho's level of political consciousness is highly developed and includes an understanding of the operations of imperialism on a worldwide basis is evident from the protagonist's attitude to America in 'Long Distance Runner', a poem written in America in 1978. The poem is based on a party, real or imaginary, organized for Ghanaian people by one Mike, who is probably an American. At the party the poet is called upon to sing, but the song he sings is of the wounds of his people, who have been betrayed by 'war leaders':

> They call for song and I sing the story
> of our wounds: the failures and betrayals
> the broken oaths of war leaders grown smooth
> with ease of civil joys

When they call for more he changes the tune to that of the failures of America, the problems of the poor black people of Harlem, whose predicament belies the myth of America as a heaven for all, and he sings about Geronimo, an Amerindian leader whose generosity was betrayed by the white rulers of America:

> For a change just for a little change I sing
> your dirge about their land's defeat in the beauty
> of her dawn: the ghost of Harlem standing guard
> across their bridge of mirth their launching pad of
> dream and myth

> I sing also your long lament for grand Geronimo
> Amerindian chieftain who opened his heart a bit too wide
> the lonely horseman who now perhaps only maybe
> still rides his old stallion across their dream their myth

The hosts are of course not amused by this, but all the same the poem ends with America being portrayed as a long distance runner who wins the race by cheating and breaking all the rules of the game:

> We know there is an agony in waiting for the long distance runner
> who breaks the finisher's line for the judges to declare he

> jumped the starter's gun stepped upon some other
> runner's toes threw him off balance and off the race

> And what is a race, Cousin, without the rules
> without other runners?

Form and Communication in Anyidoho

In the introductory section of this chapter, I referred to the differences in tone between one part of the volume and another. The diction also shows corresponding variations. The blurb on the back cover quotes Kofi Awoonor as saying of Anyidoho that 'His clear understanding of the Ewe dirge form has widened his own primary appreciation of the substance of the lyrical form of lament as both a personal and a public statement'. This applies particularly to Parts One, Five and Six, in other words, to those parts of the volume which deal directly with the theme of the revolution. Some of the poems in these sections of the book show an intensity of feeling and a lyrical quality which the reader associates with two other Ghanaian writers – Kofi Awoonor and Ayi Kwei Armah – the latter in his epic novel, *Two Thousand Seasons*. All three have made a special study of the rhythms and idioms of Ewe and other related languages. In Anyidoho the lyricism is achieved through the combination of a number of devices – repetition and parallelism, the use of a refrain, the use of images that have a particularly imaginative appeal, and the organization of the verse in such a way that it has an incantatory and mournful effect. In the first poem, 'Mythmaker', repetition is evident from the very first stanza. This is how the poem opens:

> The children are away
> The children are away
> The children
> These children are away
> away in schoolrooms where the world in book
> distils daydreams into visions
> burns memorials of the past
> in bonfires of the soul

The first four lines are repeated several times in the poem although with some variations in the words and the arrangement of the lines. A typical example of images that have an imaginative appeal occurs in 'Seedtime', in which the combination of strong images, free verbal repetition and parallelism results in very powerful poetry, as the following lines will show:

> Our orphan laid an egg across the backyard of the skies
> The rainstorm came and swept it all away
> Again he laid an egg across the backyard of the skies
> Again the rainstorm came and swept it all away
> Today he sows a mystery seed in the bosom of whirlthoughts
> Our predator birds shall have to prey upon
> their own anger their own nightmares
> We will not die the death of dreams
> We will not die the cruel death of dreams

The last two lines quoted constitute one of the two refrains of the poem and emphasize the optimism that informs it, despite the mournful tone produced by the techniques. Though the poems are an assertion of the will of the people of Ghana to achieve their dream, this assertion is articulated in the form of a dirge. Indeed the refrain of the title poem, 'A Harvest of Our Dreams', defines itself in the line: 'We will hum a dirge for a burden of these winds'. But there is a sense in which this apparent contradiction between intent and tone is not really a contradiction. The mournful voice is appropriate to a song of lamentation for 'a revolution gone astray into / arms of dream merchants', as the poet says in 'Elegy for the Revolution'; but the act of lamenting gives rise to a determination to make a success of the revolutionary process. So there is a cause-and-effect relationship between the lamentation and the determination to bring the revolution to a fruitful end.

As already noted the poems on the revolution are replete with animal imagery and with words associated with thunder, storms and lightning. Anyidoho uses idioms and symbols which are probably taken from the Ewe language and which certainly reflect a traditional, pre-capitalist world view. Though based on the Ewe language, the images and symbols would fit with any African myth and language system. Apart from animal imagery there are such traditional symbols as 'honeycomb' for wealth, 'hunters' or 'hunter-bees' for politicians, 'stool' for state power and 'destoolment' for deposition. These should be intelligible to an African from any part of the continent. The use of force is expressed in terms of the panther's 'claws' or 'paws' or 'teeth'. Other key words are 'dreams', referring to the poet's vision of revolutionary change, and 'hope'. All this is very different from the diction and tone of Part Two and Part Four. Consider, for example, the Lawino-like language of this satirical attack on Awoyo by an unnamed woman:

Awoyo I am not the whore's daughter like you
Your mother went from this village to that village
Shitting babies all along her path across the clan.
Did she ever suggest to you
who your papa could have been?
They say the day she died the elders sighed
and poured a long libation on her grave
praying her soul to come next time somewhat reformed.

You witch daughter with the face of an owl
Come cross my path again
I will spread your shame for you to crawl upon.

Take also this letter from Bloomington in pidgin English:

Old De Boy Kodzo
I write you long long tam, I no dey hear from you.
I say me I go write you somting small again.
Dem tell me say you too you come for Varsity
Me I say tank Gods! Old De Boy too icome for where
dem say all de small peoplo mas come and make dem
big peoplo. But lak I say som tam before de sodza peoplo
come bloody ma mauf, too much book ino go make your
pikin belly full. But I sabi say your own concrete head
be too too fool.

Thus Anyidoho's style involves a return to traditional symbols in the serious poems and an acceptance of current and authentic varieties of English in those poems written in pidgin or those that are meant to be translations of African colloquial expressions, as in 'Awoyo'. The aspect of his style which makes the greatest impact is the lyricism and traditional imagery of the revolutionary poems. In these poems Anyidoho has achieved a density of texture which at first makes the poetry quite difficult to penetrate, but he is in the main extremely successful in articulating a passionate revolutionary vision.

Notes

1. Kofi Anyidoho, *A Harvest of Our Dreams: with Elegy for the Revolution*, London, Heinemann Educational Books, 1984.
2. These were first published by the Greenfield Review Press in 1978.

14

The Articulation
of a Socialist Artistic Vision:
Niyi Osundare of Nigeria

Introduction

Reading the poetry of the three poets discussed in this part of the book, from Mapanje through Anyidoho to Niyi Osundare, is like climbing a mountain with three peaks in order to get a clear view of a city located in a valley below the mountain. The view of the city becomes clearer and clearer as the climber moves from peak to peak until the city stands revealed in its full splendour from the highest peak. We are talking about the city of ideological consciousness.

From the point of view of style and communication each of the three poets has his own strengths not found in the other two, and in regard to content we have to reckon with the fact that the three poets write under different circumstances. While Nigeria has its own problems, creative writers in that country have so far not been subjected to the pressures that Malawian writers have to contend with. However, the fact remains that the poetry in the three volumes analysed in this part of the book represents different levels of development on the ideological spectrum. Jack Mapanje's poetry is of the protest genre – it asserts the necessity for preserving freedom and other humanistic values. The poet is in search of a voice to preserve what he calls 'sanity' in the Introduction to *Of Chameleons and Gods*. It could be argued, of course, that those pressures that prevent him from expressing himself more directly also make it impossible for him to articulate his social vision. Be that as it may, Kofi Anyidoho goes further than Mapanje in displaying a fervent revolutionary consciousness. He is interested not just in civil liberties, but in the transformation of society. However, the nature of the post-revolutionary society he envisages is not clear.

Neither does Anyidoho give any clear indication of a class analysis of the social forces at work in his country. The reader is consequently presented with a blurred vision of the kind of society that the poet hopes to see created. This is where Osundare's poetry reveals a more developed form of social consciousness.

Osundare has published several volumes of poetry, including *Village Voices*, in which he devotes his poetic energies to the service of the exploited African peasantry. But our study of Osundare in this book will be based on the volume that best demonstrates his poetic vision to date, namely, *The Eye of the Earth*.[1] The collection is carefully structured and falls into three parts or movements – *Back to Earth*, *Rainsongs* and *Homecall*, with an intervening section, *Eyeful Glances*, between the first two. The volume is dedicated to 'OUR EARTH and all who struggle to see it neither wastes nor wants'.

That the poet has a clear social vision based on a highly developed ideological consciousness becomes evident in the Preface, where he explains his conception of the relationship between the present predicament of Africa and the European colonization of the continent, and that in his scheme of things the celebration of the greenness of the forests of the past is by no means an indication of a desire to return to some idealized romantic pre-history. The backward look is employed as a means to move forward with a knowledge of what can be achieved: 'For in the intricate dialectics of human living, looking back is looking forward; the visionary artist is not only a rememberer, he is also a reminder.'[2] Accordingly the first movement of the volume takes us back to those rich forests of Africa which are no more – a stark reminder of the devastating effects of deforestation. Osundare thus starts at home, with a focus on the problems of Africa, utilizing the physical features of his own home area of Ikere in Nigeria, where the two rocks of *Olosunta* and *Oroole* are located. When we come to the third and final movement, the theme becomes a universal celebration and assertion of the richness of the earth and of the necessity to preserve our world. A true revolutionary belongs not only to his or her own country, but to the world, and this is true of Osundare. It is with this idea of a revolutionary poet that we now turn to his poetry and let it speak for itself.

Osundare's Poetic Vision

The poem 'Earth' stands as a prologue, announcing the concerns of the rest of the poems. The poem is a song to the attributes of Mother Earth, who is both 'Temporary basement / and lasting roof' of all living things. We live our temporary lives here, but earth is also the permanent roof of life which continues to stand after the dead have gone, and been buried in its bowels. The earth is both 'breadbasket / and compost bed'. It gives us the food we eat and the manure with which we nourish that food. Mothering 'rocks and rivers / muds and mountains', the earth is that which gives silence to the twilight sea. It is indeed 'Virgin of a thousand offsprings'.

EARTH

Temporary basement
and lasting roof

first clayey coyness
and last alluvial joy

breadbasket
and compost bed

rocks and rivers
muds and mountains

silence of the twilight sea
echoes of the noonsome tide

milk of mellowing moon
fire of tropical hearth

spouse of the roving sky
Virgin of a thousand offsprings

The poem celebrates the richness and preciousness of our planet, and the three sequences which follow are an attempt to recreate that natural richness, in danger of destruction by profit-hungry money-makers and leaders without vision. They call upon all the human inhabitants of earth to dress it in its natural beauty and splendour, by working hard to ensure that the wealth of the planet is put to good use for the benefit of all.

The first movement, *Back to Earth*, consists of three poems: 'Forest Echoes', 'The Rocks Rose to Meet Me' and 'Harvest Call'. All three are a reminder of the richness of the past. In 'Forest Echoes', Osundare depicts a dense forest, such as would have existed in days of old, a forest full of every manner of creature – milling trees, with the palm 'Mother of nuts and kernels' standing unchallenged by any other, birds, the squirrel, the chameleon, the praying mantis, the hyena harrying the hare, the elephant trampling on grass, termites on an anthill, snakes, monkeys, the gazelle and all manner of plants. It is a forest where, as the poet puts it in the Introduction, 'each tree, each vine, each herb, each beast, each insect, had its name in the baffling baptism of Nature'.[3] Of course, the forest only exists in the poet's imagination now, but there is no doubt he has portrayed a forest that every sensitive reader will be able to visualize. And what emerges, apart from the poet's ability to present a vivid picture, is the significance of the forest. The forest is a symbol of the earth's treasure – if only those who run the affairs of state had the necessary will and vision. This is the reason for the poet's projection of the palm tree as the Queen of the forest trees – it is a source of life for human beings, and by destroying the forest, people are destroying that which nourishes life:

> Let iroko wear the crown of the roof
> let ayunre play the clown of the fireplace,
> but let no tree challenge the palm,
> evergreen conqueror of rainless seasons.
> Let no tree challenge the palm
> Mother of nuts and kernels
> tree proud and precious like the sculptor's wood
> bearer of wine and life:
> short plump palmlets which pamper
> the belly of unventuring gourds,
> their unreachable parents
> like some faraway land
> now too tall, too thin, too distant
> for the climbing rope
> let no tree mock their aged brows
> pockmarked with the blind bullets
> of wasteful wars.

In 'The Rocks Rose to Meet Me' we rise to a yet higher level of consciousness. The poet says in the Preface that the rocks *Olosunta* and *Oroole* 'Occupy a central place in the cosmic consciousness of Ikere people', but he dramatizes them in the poem 'as a *creative, material essence*, as lasting monuments of time and place'.[4] This is indeed one of the functions of the rocks in the poem. As a symbol of the consciousness of the people who inhabit his surroundings, *Olosunta* sees it as his duty to remind the poet of the necessity to be conscious of his own time and place, which means rejecting foreign world views and developing an Africa-centred consciousness. *Olosunta* therefore rebukes the poet for wearing 'the mud of distant waters' and for seeing things through the eyes of the West:

> 'You have been long, very long, and far',
> said he, his tongue one flaming flash
> of unburnable gnomes
> 'Unwearying wayfarer,
> your feet wear the mud of distant waters
> your hems gather the burr
> of fartherest forests;
> I can see the westmost sun
> in the mirror of your wandering eyes'.

'The Rocks Rose to Meet Me' is therefore a homecoming. By reminding the poet of the receding past, it brings about a changed consciousness in him. This new form of consciousness leads him to a new understanding of the uses to which the treasures of the earth should be put. *Olosunta* (so says the poem) is well known for his religious significance and for being rich in gold, for 'his belly still battle ground of god and gold'. The question is, how is the gold to be used? For personal aggrandizement and for turning certain people into princes while others are paupers? Osundare says no to that: we must dig the gold for the purpose of feeding the hungry and creating a world of equality. The poet's socialist ideology stands revealed:

> The gold let us dig,
> not for the gilded craniums
> of hollow chieftains
> (time's undying sword awaits their necks
> who deem this earth their sprawling throne).
> With the gold let us turn hovels into havens
> paupers into people (not princes)
> so hamlets may hear
> the tidings of towns
> so the world may sprout a hand
> of equal fingers.

In the last poem of this movement, 'Harvest Call', we move on to images of crops. We are taken to three places where harvest time was once a time of plenty. We are taken to Iyanfoworogi:

> where yams, ripe and randy,
> waged a noisy war against the knife;

then to Oke Eniju:

> where coy cobs rocked lustily
> in the loin of swaying stalks

and finally to Ogbese Odo:

> where cotton pods, lips duly parted
> by December's sun,
> draped busy farmsteads
> in a harvest of smiles.

This was in the past, and such plenty is no more. The fourth section of the poem is consequently devoted to the question of where these crops are and how they can be recovered:

> But where *are* they?
> Where are they gone:
> *aroso, geregede, otiili, pakala*
> which beckoned lustily to the reaping basket
> Where are they
> the yam pyramids which challenged the sun
> in busy barns
> Where are they

the pumpkins which caressed earth breast
like mammary burdens
Where are they
the pods which sweetened harvest air
with the clatter of dispersing seeds?
Where are they? Where are they gone?

The answer is that they are still there in the womb of the earth. It is a
question of how we work and use the earth:

Uncountable seeds lie sleeping
in the womb of earth
uncountable seeds
awaiting the quickening tap
of our waking finger.

The second movement, *Rainsongs*, celebrates rain as a life-giving
force, and here Osundare speaks for Africa, which has been afflicted
by endless droughts. When rain does come in such circumstances it is
truly welcome. The healing power of rain is given expression in a very
short poem, 'First Rain':

a tingling tang awakes the nose
when the first rain has just clipped
the wing of the haughty dust
a cooling warmth embraces
our searching soles
as the land vapour rises
like a bootless infantry
and
through her liberated pores
    our earth breathes again.

In the first movement the poet can justifiably be criticized for
idealizing the past, as the picture he portrays is of a past productive
because it lacked any threat of hunger and drought. In the second
movement, however, Osundare is wiser. While he celebrates rain as a
life-giving force, he does not turn a blind eye to its destructiveness. The
destructive side of rain is the theme of 'But Sometimes When It Rains'.
The first stanza is enough to demonstrate the poet's concern:

But sometimes when it rains
and an angry thunder raps earth's ears
with its hands of fire
Sometimes when it rains
and a heartless storm beheads
the poor man's house
like some long-convicted felon,

Sometimes when it rains
you wonder who sent the skies weeping

Osundare's revolutionary vision is most eloquently articulated in the third and final movement, *Homecall*, which calls on us, the inhabitants of the earth, to make our planet what it should be: to make the earth productive, not to impoverish it; to work for the improvement of the quality of life for all, not to oppress others and wallow in our selfish greediness; to plough and not to plunder. In 'They Too Are the Earth', Osundare sings songs to the wretched of the earth – the beggars, the toiling masses, the old and oppressed women 'battling centuries of / *male*ficent slavery'. All these are of the earth. In contrast, there are those who lead a life of pleasure and plunder:

> Are they of this earth
> who fritter the forest and harry the hills
> Are they of this earth
> who live that earth may die
> Are they?

In 'What the Earth Said' we are given contrasting images of the world, from workers to exploiters, from the agents of international capitalism to those whose 'backs creak on heartless machines'. Thus earth has shaken 'hands calloused by wood and steel' and seen 'penuried lives, spent, in ghetto dungeons'. On the other hand, earth has seen 'foremen soulless like their whistling whips' and 'native *executhieves* hold fort for alien wolves', and also 'factorylords roll in slothful excess'. The solution to this unequal, unhappy and unfair world is a call for a revolutionary transformation of the world. This is what the poet says in response to what the earth sees:

> And the earth,
> the earth receives these green fruits
> with dusty tears,
> the earth receives them
> saying:
>> behold these seeds planted so soon
>> in the season before the rains
>> let them sprout in the mouth
>> of daring struggle;
>> let them bloom
>> and kill the killer pests.

Osundare closes the movement and the volume with the poem 'Our Earth Will Not Die', which affirms the future victory of a progressive and productive world. The poet is quite right to end with this poem of affirmation, the last stanza of which is quoted at the end of this chapter, but I believe that the most powerful poem in the whole sequence, and the one which articulates his socialist vision most eloquently and persuasively, is the second last poem, 'Ours to Plough, Not to Plunder'. In this poem, Osundare gives expression to the socialist idea of the dignity of labour. Those trained in the bourgeois ethic loathe manual work, which in their view is below the dignity of the educated and the well-to-do, regarded as the occupation of labourers, the working class and peasants. What such people do not realize is that there is dignity in labour and that, as Chung and I have said elsewhere, 'without labour it would not have been possible to build the pyramids of Ancient Egypt and the monuments of Ancient Rome or to erect the skyscrapers of New York'.[5] What Osundare has achieved, uniquely among African poets, is a celebration of the instruments of labour as fit subjects for poetry, seeing beauty in digging, cutting, winnowing and sweating:

> The earth is ours to plough and plant
> the hoe is her barber
> the dibble her dimple
>
> Out with mattocks and matchets
> bring calabash trays and rocking baskets
> let the sweat which swells earthroot
> relieve heavy heaps of their tuberous burdens

Osundare realizes that it is only work guided by a true understanding of the value of labour and of the riches of the earth which can bring about green wheatfields and swelling pawpaws; it is only labour that can bring gold out of the womb of the earth. He therefore proclaims with joy:

> Let wheatfields raise their breadsome hands
> to the ripening sun
> let legumes clothe the naked bosom
> of shivering mounds
> let the pawpaw swell and swing
> its headward breasts
>
> Let water spring
> from earth's unfathomed fountain
> let gold rush
> from her deep unseeable mines
> hitch up a ladder to the dodging sky
> let's put a sun in every night

Going back to the theme of 'Earth', the first poem in the volume, and introducing a new dimension, the poet reaffirms his conviction that the earth is richly endowed, both a barn and a grainhouse. What we need to do to ensure that we make the grainhouse a living reality is to work, not waste, to tend the earth, not harm it:

> Our earth is an unopened grainhouse,
> a bustling barn in some far, uncharted jungle
> a distant gem in a rough unhappy dust

This earth is
    ours to work not to waste
    ours to man not to maim
This earth is ours to plough, not to plunder

Osundare's vision clearly portrays a socialist view of art. It is guided by a revolutionary materialist conception of the world.

Form and Communication in Osundare

We have already touched on a crucial aspect of Osundare's aesthetic ideology – the use of words referring to labour and agricultural activity to portray a socialist view of art. This is new in post-independence African poetry, although one meets it in the poetry of the liberation struggle, such as Agostinho Neto's 'We Must Return'[6] or 'Poem' by Carlos Chombo of Zimbabwe.[7]

Like other African poets with an Africa-centred consciousness, Osundare finds himself going back to images of nature. But, unlike Soyinka or Okigbo, Osundare is not interested in mythmaking. Gods like Ogun or Idoto have no place in his scheme of things. He writes about nature as we know it, about forests that exist in the objective material world, about rocks that we can actually see with our eyes and touch with our hands. There is no mystification in his poetry, and this is an expression of his materialist view of the world.

In line with his idea of recreating a picture of the treasures of the past for the purpose of informing the present, he fashions out a style – and this is particularly true of 'Forest Echoes' – which captures the greenness, the lushness and the variety of life that existed in the dark forests of pre-capitalist Africa. In singing the glories of that past, he raises his poetry to epic heights of tone and diction. This again is true of 'Forest Echoes'. There is an intensity of feeling, a density of texture and a lyricism which is the stuff out of which an elevated style is created. This, for instance, is how he marks his entry into the forest he portrays:

Here, under this awning, ageless
the clock, unhanded, falls
in the deep belly of woods
its memory ticking songfully
in *elulu*'s sleepless throat
Mauled the minutes, harried the hours;
taunted is time whose needle's eye
gates our comings and goings
time which wombed the moon
to bear the sun,
the hole in the ragged wardrobe
the gap in the ageing teeth

the bud on the ripening tree
Oh time,
coffin behind the cot.

And every toemark on the footpath
every fingerprint on every bark
the ropy climbers flung breathlessly
from tree to tree
the haunting sound and silence
of this sweet and sour forest
dig deep channels to the sea of memory.
And the outcome:
   will it be flow or flood . . .

The intensity of feeling and the transportation of the poet into the
world of the imagination are most evident at the end, when he tells us
that he has been riding high on the waves of poetic remembrance and
must now 'dismount', to come down to our world of pedestrian speech:

And now
Memory,
loud whisper of yester-voices
confluence of unbroken rivers,
lower your horse of remembrance

Let me dismount.

Repetition and parallelism are a recurring feature of Osundare's
style, and, in 'The Rocks Rose to Meet Me' and other poems, these
devices create a rhythmic beat which lends his poetry to public
performance with drums and other musical instruments. This, for
instance, is how 'The Rocks Rose to Meet Me' opens, and, as in all the
other poems of the first movement, there are instructions on the
necessary musical accompaniment:

The rocks rose to meet me
like passionate lovers on a long-awaited tryst
The rocks rose to meet me
their peaks cradled in ageless mists.
Olosunta spoke first
the eloquent one
whose mouth is the talking house of ivory
Olosunta spoke first
the lofty one whose eyes are
balls of the winking sun
Olosunta spoke first
the riddling one whose belly is wrestling ground
for god and gold.

In some of the poems, repetition and parallelism give rise to a lyrical
quality that one associates with nursery rhymes, as in the following
lines from 'Let Earth's Pain Be Soothed':

Let it rain today
    that parched throats may sing
Let it rain
    that earth may heal her silence
Let it rain today
    that cornleaves may clothe the hills
Let it rain
    that roots may swell the womb of lying plains
Let it rain today
    that stomachs may shun the rumble of thunder
Let it rain
    that children may bath and bawl and brawl

In 'Raindrum', the rhythm of the poetry accurately captures the rhythms and sounds of raindrops:

The roofs sizzle at the waking touch,
talkative like kettle drums
tightened by the iron fingers of drought

In poems such as 'Excursion' and 'What the Earth Said', the reader feels that Osundare overdoes his game of repetition, introducing an element of unpleasantness in the style. One wishes there was more density of texture in these poems. The fact that they are meant to be chanted aloud partly accounts for the repetition but on the printed page the repetition weakens the poetry. Take, for example, the following lines from 'Our Earth Will Not Die' where the repetition of the words 'Fishes', 'Birds', and 'Rabbits' at the end of the lines is probably effective when the poem is dramatized, but quite superfluous on the printed page:

Fishes have died in the waters. Fishes.
Birds have died in the trees. Birds.
Rabbits have died in their burrows. Rabbits.

However, Osundare has produced in this volume a poetry with a sweetness and mellowness virtually unparalleled in African poetry to date, and a rhythmic beat which compares well with that of Kofi Anyidoho. His style successfully celebrates the multifarious richness of the earth and invests human labour with the poetic rhythms it deserves. The poet's vision is immensely optimistic, an optimism summarized and celebrated in 'Our Earth Will Not Die', whose closing stanza combines various devices to portray the poet's socialist vision:

Our earth will see again
eyes washed by a new rain
the westering sun will rise again
resplendent like a new coin.
The wind, unwound, will play its tune
trees twittering, grasses dancing;

hillsides will rock with blooming harvests
the plains batting their eyes of grass and grace.
The sea will drink its heart's content
when a jubilant thunder flings open the skygate
and a new rain tumbles down
in drums of joy.
Our earth will see again

this earth, OUR EARTH.

Notes

1. Niyi Osundare, *The Eye of the Earth*, Ibadan, Heinemann Educational Books (Nigeria) Ltd., 1986.
2. Ibid., p. x.
3. Ibid., p. x.
4. Ibid., p. xi.
5. See Fay Chung and Emmanuel Ngara, *Socialism, Education and Development: A Challenge to Zimbabwe*, Harare, Zimbabwe Publishing House, 1985, p. 94.
6. See Michael Wolfers, *Poems From Angola*, London, Heinemann Educational Books, 1979, p. 19.
7. See M. Kadhani and M. Zimunya, *And Now the Poets Speak*, Gweru, Mambo Press, 1981, p. 1.

15

Social Vision, Aesthetics & Liberation: Retrospect & Prospects

The Relationship Between Authorial and Aesthetic Ideology

In this final chapter I wish to look back on some of the findings of the previous chapters, not only with a view to bringing into focus some of the major revelations of the book, but also in the hope that there may be lessons to be learned by intending writers. The first issue we shall address is that of the relationship between authorial ideology and aesthetic ideology, and whether there is any relationship between the two categories.

Wole Soyinka tells us that he was once asked whether he accepted the necessity for 'a literary ideology'. His answer, Soyinka explains, was as follows: 'My response was – a social vision, yes, but not a literary ideology. Generally the question reflects the preoccupation, neither of the traditional nor the contemporary writer in African society but of the analyst after the event, the critic.' Soyinka also adds, 'But then it would be equally false to suggest that contemporary African literature is not consciously formulated around certain frameworks of ideological intent.'[1] Later on in the same essay he concedes that Negritude is a literary ideology.[2]

The distinction Soyinka makes between 'social vision' and 'literary ideology' corresponds more or less to the distinction made in this book between authorial ideology and aesthetic ideology. Our analysis proves without a shadow of doubt that there is a strong link between the two categories of ideology. Negritude, which Soyinka himself takes as an exception to his general rule that aesthetic ideology is a formulation of the critic rather than the artist, is an eloquent example of writers consciously formulating an aesthetic ideology that articulates their social vision. As explained in chapter 3, in its images, its choice of words and its rhythms, Negritude poetry seeks to articulate the philosophy of Negritude as a social vision. Nor is Negritude the only example. The style of Okot p'Bitek derives from his cultural nationalism, as do the diction and idiom of Okara's poetry. As for Kunene, there is clearly a causal relationship between his interest in Zulu traditional thought and cosmology on the one hand and his choice of images, idioms and sentence constructions on the other. We could go on citing poets but the point is sufficiently made in the relevant chapters. An interesting case is that of Jack Mapanje, whose use of myth and oral traditions is at least partly determined by factors other than the poet's social vision – by a desire to find an effective medium of communication with the people. Even so, that aesthetic ideology is consciously formulated. In any case, can Soyinka the poet really tell us that the mythmaking that characterizes his aesthetic ideology is not the result of a conscious decision on the part of the author?

Soyinka has a point in respect of some of the poets, however. The Negritude poets actually went out of their way to formulate a philosophy of artistic creation, an aesthetic ideology, and the same is true of Kunene, Mapanje, and, no doubt, Okot p'Bitek and Christopher Okigbo. In respect of some of the other poets, however, it is not certain whether the use of certain images, symbols, idioms and devices is the result of a conscious decision to fashion a style characterized by these features or whether the style is more or less automatically determined by the authorial ideology, even if the writer is not conscious of the fact. One has in mind here the pattern of images we find in the liberation poetry of Mozambique and Angola, the feminist symbolism of South African liberation poetry and the diction and patterns of imagery employed by, say, Chenjerai Hove. The issue is problematic, and this is where Soyinka's point about the function of critic is relevant.

That there is a link between authorial ideology and aesthetic ideology is certain, but whether the poet is conscious of that link is not always certain. This is where the critic comes in. For a writer at the beginning of a poetic career like Freedom Nyamubaya the issue of an aesthetic ideology may not even arise, as the young poet may only be concerned with expressing his or her experience in the best possible form. It is also probable that most poets are not fully aware of their strengths and weaknesses until somebody else has put their poetry to the test and passed judgement on it.

Stylistic Stances, Ideology and Communication in African Poetry

On the basis of this study it is possible to group many of the poets according to their stylistic stance, which has implications for effective communication and reveals something about the poet's authorial ideology. These groups should, however, be seen in terms of tendencies rather than definite and discrete divisions. What is more, there is no attempt here to place every poet in a particular group; indeed, some poets could fit into two or more categories.

Before I examine the various groups I should like to explain that all the poets analysed in this volume are members of the African petty bourgeoisie, and have chosen to write in English, French or Portuguese. To that extent, their primary audience is not peasants and workers, who have little or no command of European languages. To choose a language is to choose an audience, and by the fact of writing in English, French or Portuguese the poet has chosen to address members of the African petty bourgeoisie and westerners. When we talk of the poet's ability to communicate, we are therefore referring to the relative ability of the author to appeal to the common run of the petty bourgeoisie, i.e. academics, teachers, university students and members of various professions.

The first group we shall isolate is the Negritude group, and their attempt to create a style appropriate to both the subject matter and their philosophy. A central feature of the style is the recurrent use of words like 'black', 'white', 'blood' and others cited in chapter 3, words which project the nationalist consciousness of poets concerned with the dichotomy between bourgeois, western culture and traditional, pre-capitalist African culture, the latter being proffered as the ideal. Another aspect of the style is a bold attempt to relate sign to sense; in other words, to write performative verse which communicates not only through images and meanings, but also through sound and rhythm. This technique is perfected in such poems as Senghor's 'Night of Sine' and 'New York', and David Diop's 'To a Negro Dancer' and 'Rama Kam'. Léopold Senghor and David Diop are in this regard very successful in communicating with the reader, and, while the idealism of the Senghorian school is to be regretted, we should raise our hats to the Negritude movement for developing a philosophy which the poets were able to articulate eloquently in poetic form.

From Negritude, we move on to an Anglophone group, who attempt to be authentically African by employing traditional African concepts and modes of expression in their English-language poetry. Among the chief representatives of this group are Okot p'Bitek, Mazisi Kunene and Gabriel Okara. We also find echoes of their method in Kofi Anyidoho.

As noted earlier, these poets do not resolve the problem of communicating with peasants and workers who have no English, except for Kunene, who writes in Zulu and then translates into English, as Okot p'Bitek did from Acoli in *Song of Lawino*. What they achieve as a group is to make a statement about language: that it carries with it an ideology and a world view. There is no ideological neutrality in the use of idioms, linguistic structures and metaphors. Standard English carries the prejudices of its mother-tongue speakers, whose outlook is dominated by a western bourgeois world view. By using elements of African languages and traditional culture these writers are projecting a world view in opposition to western bourgeois ideology. This becomes quite clear in the contradictions that arise between Ocol and Lawino in *Song of Lawino* and *Song of Ocol*. Lawino's rejection of Ocol's world is not only expressed in terms of an ideological outlook but also in the very language used by the protagonists. Thus, while Ocol's song is couched in conventional standard English, Lawino's language is characterized by traditional idioms and modes of expression. The upshot of this, from an artistic point of view, is that *Song of Lawino* is a much richer poem than *Song of Ocol*, which is as naked as the protagonist's hollow ideology. Similarly, in Okara the contrast between tradition and modernity inheres in images taken from nature and modern technology respectively.

With varying degrees of success, each of the poets who propound this aesthetic ideology has forged a distinctive style, suggesting that their recourse to traditional modes of expression and oral forms lends their poetry a certain freshness and liveliness that marks it off from the flatness and colourlessness of conventional language and English cliché. But the approach is not without its difficulties and limitations. First, from an ideological point of view there are some problems, particularly with respect to Okot p'Bitek and Gabriel Okara, who posit traditional values as those we should embrace. While it is true that certain aspects of tradition can stand the test of time and social change, like any other, African societies develop, and cannot cling to tradition unless it is reconciled with the need for social progress. In the case of Okara, traditionalism at times becomes downright reactionary, when the poet–protagonist rejects modern technology in favour of 'nature', as in the poem 'You Laughed and Laughed and Laughed', which fails to reconcile tradition with technology and projects an ideology characterized by Rousseauesque romantic idealism. Furthermore, a poet who embraces this aesthetic ideology can sometimes fail to translate the African idiom meaningfully into English and consequently to communicate. This is one of Kunene's major shortcomings in *Zulu Poems*, which sometimes fail to convey his message in a coherent and logical manner. The experience of both Kunene and Okot p'Bitek indicates a need for those who are attracted to this method to go beyond the mere translation of African ideas and idioms. As demonstrated by the quality of Okot p'Bitek's *Song of Prisoner* and Kunene's *The Ancestors & the Sacred Mountain*, the method works better when the translation of African modes of expression is combined with an attempt to capture the natural rhythms of English. A more recent version of the method is that of Kofi Anyidoho, whose style epitomizes this attempt at reconciliation. Anyidoho's poetry can be difficult to apprehend, but for a patient reader it rewards the effort.

At the opposite end is the so-called 'euromodernist' style of Wole Soyinka and the early Okigbo, characterized by complicated syntactic structures in the tradition of some well-known English poets. These two are wont to resort to obscure allusion, in emulation of the mythical method of T.S. Eliot, Ezra Pound and other western poets. From an ideological standpoint, they are steeped in western bourgeois ideology, so their aesthetic ideology too is predicated upon western aesthetic values. The difference lies in the fact that, while they drew their inspiration from western models, the African poets sought to make use of African elements of belief, practice and myth to enrich their artistic vision. Soyinka's awareness of his particular time and place brought something new to the western tradition which he seeks to perpetuate in *Idanre*. With regard to communication, their complex syntactic structures and obscure allusions render the works of these two poets, inaccessible. In the case of Wole Soyinka, the situation is aggravated by the fact that his poetry is cerebral, all flesh and no bones, devoid of para-linguistic affective devices to appeal to emotion or imagination. In *Idanre and Other Poems* and *A Shuttle in the Crypt*, Soyinka's poetry operates on a purely intellectual plane, devoid of emotional appeal. As a reader, I also feel that, in these two volumes, Soyinka lacks the sincerity and conviction of Okigbo; for, while Okigbo shares the former's modernist tendencies, *Collected Poems* gives the impression of a genuine search for a poetic vision and an appropriate form. This is evident in *Part Three: Late Poems*, where Okigbo has discovered a new vision, abandoned earlier techniques and learned to communicate better with the reader.

Yet another strand is that of poets who write in conventional or standard English without resorting to modernist techniques. This group is typified by Keorapetse Kgositsile, Dennis Brutus and Musaemura Zimunya. The style of the group can be described as 'classical', in the sense of being formal rather than experimental in their use of language. There may, however, be a tendency towards complicated stylization, which, for example, sets Kgositsile apart from other socialist poets, such as those of the fighting phase in Mozambique.

We shall have occasion to refer to Brutus and Kgositsile later on in the chapter. Suffice it here to make two observations about these three southern African poets. First, they have made effective use of conventional English. Second, while their authorial ideology is marked by some degree of radicalism, their level of revolutionary consciousness is not commensurately advanced. Zimunya's authorial ideology is characterized by a mild nationalist consciousness, expressed in terms of such symbols as Great Zimbabwe and the Zimbabwe Bird, and in the eulogizing of guerrilla fighters, among other modes of expression. Dennis Brutus goes a step further by adopting a more assertive protest position which reflects his active involvement in the struggle against apartheid. As already explained in the chapter on South African liberation poetry, Keorapetse Kgositsile is guided by a socialist world view which goes beyond nationalism and protest and advocates the creation of a socialist society. Thus there is a degree to which poets of different ideological persuasions can write in a similar manner.

In terms of diction, the greater formality of Keorapetse Kgositsile, Dennis Brutus and Zimunya separates them from the Black Consciousness poets, whose poetry has a strong local and informal flavour. In comparison with the art of the Kgositsile group, Black Consciousness poetry is often plain and readily accessible. However, this is not to suggest that Black Consciousness poetry is necessarily more engaging or more effective. On the contrary, Brutus and Kgositsile are in all probability more successful in moving the reader to contemplation than Sipho Sepamla, Pascal Gwala or Mongane Serote.[3] What the Black Consciousness group has done is to depart from petty bourgeois discourse by approximating the speech-style of the urban African, and consequently to address the South African black working class.

The style of the last group we shall consider is the opposite of euromodernism, that is, the style of poets of the fighting phase in Angola, Mozambique and Guinea Bissau. The Nigerian, Niyi Osundare, also partakes of the aesthetic ideology of this group, suggesting that it is not just the war situation but social vision that dictates the style. Their style is direct and free of complicated stylization. Take, for instance, the unpretentious, rich simplicity of Jorge Rebelo's 'Poem', Agostinho Neto's 'February', Armando Guebuza's 'Those Strange Times'[4] and a good number of Osundare's poems (analysed in chapter 14). These poets conceal their artistry and complexity under apparent simplicity, thus exploding the myth that obscurity and complicated stylization are necessary for the creation of great art. Jorge Rebelo's 'Poem' is on the face of it very simple, but it is a profound work of art, rich in imagery, expressive of a very high level of ideological clarity, capable of appealing to the emotions and the imagination, and of causing the reader to reflect. This and the other given examples move the reader by the weight of their message, and the simplicity of their diction. There are, however, two major temptations to which members of the group are prone, and both of these are discernible in Marcelino dos Santos. The first is to carry simplicity and verbal repetition too far, as in dos Santos's 'We Must Plant' (chapter 9). The second is, in the heat of the struggle, to be didactic, even to slide into propagandist sloganeering, as in 'To Point a Moral to a Comrade', in which Frelimo ideology triumphs over artistry.

What this brief account demonstrates is that there is a wide range of stylistic stances in African poetry and that some are more effective in communicating with the reader than others. The point made in chapter 2 must be reiterated here, that obscurity and complexity do not necessarily mean an inability to communicate; nor does simplicity necessarily mean effective communication. Much of the poetry of Léopold Senghor is highly stylized and yet immensely readable. Many of Anyidoho's peoms demand a great deal of concentration and yet are capable of making a lasting impression on the reader, just like some of Kgositsile's complex poems. On the other hand, some South African women poets write in a plain style but their poetry is dull and uninteresting.

It appears communication depends on the interplay of many features: diction, syntax, sound devices, subject matter and such paralinguistic affective devices as tone, irony and humour. Whether the poet resorts to complicated stylization or not, he or she should endeavour to communicate effectively. As George Thomson correctly observed, 'all poetry is in origin a social act, in which poet and people commune'.[5] If, by resorting to private symbols or modes of expression, the poet fails to communicate, he or she has violated the social function of poetry. A poet who does this deprives poetry of its source of life, which is its capacity to appeal to and influence people.

From the point of view of dialectical criticism, effective communication is an essential ingredient of good poetry, but it is not all. The quality of what is communicated is of equal importance. Poets speak not just for themselves, but for humanity, and so should strike a chord in the hearts and minds of their readers by the significance of what they communicate. Consequently, what the poet reveals about social reality is vital, and the value of a poem depends as much on *what* it says as on *how* it says it – which leads us back to the role of authorial ideology. To gain a fuller appreciation of the significance of authorial ideology in literary creativity, we should examine the philosophical basis of authors' interpretation of the world around them. This is the topic of the next section.

Idealism and Materialism as Trends in African Poetry

One revelation that the study has made is that, broadly speaking, two philosophical trends have dominated African poetics since the rise of Negritude. The first trend is idealist and the second materialist.

The idealist trend is based on a subjective metaphysical view of the world which promotes the incorporation of superstitious beliefs in the poet's vision. There seems to be a belief among some African poets that to have an authentically African artistic vision the African poet must go back to the world of primitive beliefs. The idea was first promoted by the subjective school of Negritude. The use of the totem and masks as symbols becomes for Senghor an articulation of his metaphysical philosophy, which also becomes manifest in his lyrical philosophical abstractions about the qualities of black people, as in 'Murders':

> You are the flower of the foremost beauty in stark absence of flowers
> Black flower and solemn smile, diamond time out of mind.
> You are the clay and the plasma of the world's virid spring
> Flesh you are of the first couple, the fertile belly, milk and sperm
> You are the sacred fecundity of the bright paradise gardens
> And the incoercible forest, victor over fire and thunder.[6]

What makes this lyrical poetry metaphysical is that it is not based on reality. It is largely a subjective interpretation of the qualities of black people, which cannot be verified by concrete facts of history.

David Diop also fails to avoid incipient mysticism, as evidenced by his depiction of the black woman in 'To a Negro Dancer', where the black woman is invested with mystical qualities. What this means is that the distinction made in chapter 3 between the subjective and realist schools of Negritude is really a matter of tendencies, not a cut and dried division.

Metaphysics as the philosophical underpinning of an aesthetic ideology is pervasive in Christopher Okigbo's *Labyrinths* and in Wole Soyinka. We saw in chapter 4 how Okigbo's romantic idealism gives his poetry a mystical aura and how the spiritual dominates his search for a poetic vision, particularly in *Heavensgate*. This analysis of Okigbo's idealism helps us to reflect on Soyinka, who also resorts to mysticism in *Idanre and Other Poems*. In the Preface to *Idanre*, the poet is portrayed as 'a pilgrim to Idanre in company of presences such as dilate the head and erase known worlds', and in the poem itself the poet portrays these mystical visions he claims to have had.[7] For the sake of a poetic vision, Soyinka and Okigbo promote a superstitious unscientific view of reality, creating a world populated by preternatural beings. Consider, for example, these two stanzas from Okigbo's 'The Passage':

> Me to the orangery
> solitude invites,
> a wagtail, to tell
> the tangled-wood-tale;
> a sunbird, to mourn
> a mother on a spray
>
> Rain and sun in single combat;
> on one leg standing,
> in silence at the passage,
> the young bird at the passage.[8]

The following stanzas from Soyinka's *Idanre* speak of the same aesthetic ideology:

Later, diminutive zebras raced on track edges
Round the bed, dwarfs blew on royal bugles
A gaunt *ogboni* raised his staff and vaulted on
A zebra's back, galloped up a quivering nose –
A battle with the suffocating shrouds

Opalescent pythons oozed tar coils
Hung from rafters thrashing loops of gelatine
The world was choked in wet embrace
Of serpent spawn, waiting Ajantala's rebel birth
Monster child, wrestling pachyderms of myth[9]

This is a far cry from Niyi Osundare's materialist view of the world. His celebration of the rich African forests of the past does not lead him into fits of phantasmagoria, creating fabulous creatures and flora that have no objective existence. Osundare's earth is the earth we know. The idealist perspective suggests that an African poet must embrace the quaint, the exotic or the primitive. The example of Niyi Osundare demonstrates that poetry can equally be made out of everyday objects like 'dibbles', 'hoes', 'mattocks' and 'matchets'. Gabriel Okara has also shown that the poet does not have to go deep into the world of the unreal to capture the traditional values that are disappearing. The poet can do that by contrasting 'pianos' and 'drums', 'motor car' and 'talking drums', 'ice-blocks' and 'fire', 'the Front' and 'the Back'. The same is true of Kunene and Okot p'Bitek, whose poetry is deeply concerned with preserving traditional values. Their interest in oral traditions does not give rise to an aesthetic ideology that promotes a superstitious world view.

From a Marxist point of view, poetry does not have to be made out of an unreal world. In fact, poetry becomes 'real poetry' when it throbs with the rhythms of our real world, in which the forces of progress are struggling to make the earth a better home for everyone to live in. If anything, this volume has vindicated the definition of poetry by Carlos Chombo, the Zimbabwean poet, in his poem entitled 'Poem':

The Real Poetry
Was carved by centuries
Of chains and whips
It was written in the red streams
Resisting the violence of
'Effective Occupation'

It was engraved in killings in Katanga,
In the betrayals of Mau-Mau,
In the countless anti-people coups

Its beat was the bones in Bissau
Its metaphors massacres in Mozambique
Its alliterations agony in Angola

Its form and zenith
Fighting in Zimbabwe

The Real Poetry
Is sweat scouring
The baked valley of the peasant's back
Down to the starved gorge of his buttocks

It bubbles and boils
In the blisters of the farm labourer
It glides in the greased hands
Of the factory worker

Not a private paradise
Nor an individual inferno

But the pain and pleasure
Of People in Struggle

Viva O Povo![10]

Lest my comments about idealism be construed as the atheist and anti-religious sentiments of a Marxist critic, I should hasten to explain that that is in fact not so. True, historical Marxism decried all forms of religious belief, but the dogmatism of the past is giving way to a new realization that it is possible to believe in a religion and be a revolutionary Marxist. This is one of the lessons to be learned from Frei Betto's interview with Fidel Castro, the Cuban leader.[11] There is no reason why Christians, Moslems, Hindus and people of other religions should not feel free to benefit from the revelations of Marxism without fear of ridicule by doctrinaire Marxists. If Marxism is an instrument of liberation, it should leave room for all people of all races and creeds to benefit from it.

It is true, however, that Marxism liberates people from superstitious beliefs that shackle their minds and make them slaves of supernatural and preternatural beings. A Marxist world view will, similarly, reject an aesthetic ideology based on philosophical abstractions which bear little relation to reality, or one that utilizes symbols such as watermaids, nymphs and mermaids that are but figments of the imagination, because such an aesthetic ideology promotes the perpetuation of false consciousness, detrimental to a scientific world outlook and consequently to progress. The material development of African people should be accompanied by higher forms of social consciousness. This is one of the major difficulties I have with the world view presented in Okigbo's *Heavensgate* and Soyinka's *Idanre*. The question arises as to what extent the poet can incorporate traditional and similar material without running the risk of promoting a superstitious and unscientific view of the world. The question is evidently problematical and does not permit of simple answers, unless one takes the view that any form of religious belief is an expression of false consciousness and therefore superstitious. What might be of relevance for our purpose here is to refer briefly to the poetry of Mazisi Kunene.

In the poems dealing with the theme of the ancestors and the cosmos Kunene tends to portray a metaphysical view of the world. Consequently, his poetry is also marked by a certain degree of idealism. In fact he is in real danger of projecting a very subjective interpretation of the African concept of civilization in the Introduction to *The Ancestors & the Sacred Mountain*, where he theorizes about African philosophy without adducing any convincing evidence, so that his argument is not too dissimilar from that of the Negritude philosophy. In his actual poems, however, the South African poet, though religious and philosophical, avoids the mysticism of Okigbo and the projection of a superstitious and unscientific world view.

There is, however, a manner of using myth in poetry without lapsing into superstitious mysticism. A good example of this is Jack Mapanje, who employs oral traditions extensively in his poetry, not in an effort to mystify, but precisely because he wants to communicate with the population that understands those traditions and myths. Thus chameleons, frogs, gods like Chiuta, Chingwe's Hole and other symbols serve as communicative metaphors, not as symbols of a private mystical world. This is an empirical and materialist view of myth, a technological view which employs myths for a functional purpose. This is the view of myth that seems to be operative in Soyinka's *Ogun Abibiman*, where Ogun and Shaka serve as symbols of Africa's determination to rid herself of the evil of apartheid. In a similar vein, Musaemura Zimunya uses Great Zimbabwe extensively as a symbol of the people of Zimbabwe's nationalist and revolutionary consciousness. Great Zimbabwe does exist objectively, of course, and does constitute a focal point of consciousness for the people of Zimbabwe, but there is a level at which the national monument and the Zimbabwe Bird assume a mythical dimension, and this is perfectly natural.

It would appear that Soyinka's vision has shifted over the years so that his poetry and his novels have become more committed to social change than his earlier art and the author less metaphysical in outlook. This welcome development becomes clear when one reads *Myth, Literature and the African World*, where Soyinka advocates what he calls the 'assertive secular vision' of writers like Ayi Kwei Armah and Sembene Ousmane. He refers to the revolutionary stance of these writers as 'a trend which is likely to be more and more dominant as the intelligentsia of the continent seek ideological solutions that are truly divorced from the superstitious accretions of our alien encounters'.[12]

This trend shows itself not only in the poetry of Niyi Osundare and Kofi Anyidoho but more especially in the poetry of the liberation phase in Angola and Mozambique. In chapter 9, we saw how some poets were transformed during the liberation struggle, embracing a materialist non-metaphysical conception of life and social struggles and reversing their earlier Negritude tendencies. In the poetry of these writers, as in that of Niyi Osundare, images relating to productivity, such as rain, water, planting, seeds and flowering, abound. It should be noted that this is not only liberation poetry, but poetry written by people who espouse a socialist world view. Thus it would appear that images of productivity, flowering and growth are particularly suitable for an aesthetic ideology based on socialism.

Towards an Aesthetics of Liberation and Social Criticism

Having dealt with the issues of authorial and aesthetic ideology, stylistic stances and the philosophical basis of writers' interpretation of the world around them, we must end the book with some observations about the lessons to be learned from the various authors we have discussed. For the writer of poetry there are several messages. First, if we go by the example of such poets as the Negritude poets, Okot p'Bitek, Marcelino dos Santos, Kofi Anyidoho, Niyi Osundare and so on, we should be able to conclude that it is not enough for the poet simply to write. For a writer to be a poet of consequence he or she must have an aesthetic ideology. In other words a great poet does not just let words and rhythms flow at random; a great poet experiments with modes of representation. Thus, the Negritude poets seek to relate sound to sense among other things. Okot p'Bitek finds the material for expressing his ideas in oral traditions as does Mazisi Kunene and also Christopher Okigbo at a certain stage of his development. Jack Mapanje uses the realm of myth as a metaphor of social criticism.

But aesthetic ideology alone is not enough. A serious poet must have a social vision. Thus the Negritude poets were, despite the limitations of some of them, concerned with asserting the humanity and dignity of the African people; Okot p'Bitek was searching for an alternative to the devastating effects of neocolonial culture; Dennis Brutus, the South African women poets, the Black Consciousness poets and Keorapetse Kgositsile are struggling against the inhumanity of apartheid and for the establishment of a free and democratic South Africa. For Niyi Osundare it is not enough to work for a free, independent and prosperous Africa. For him the struggle for the freedom and economic development of Africa must be part of a celebration and assertion of the richness of the earth and of the effort to preserve it.

The genuine poet, therefore, has a social vision expressed and encapsulated in an appropriate style, which enables the reader to participate in an exploration of that vision through the artistic form of the word. Poetry is significant only if what the poet utters touches the reader and effects a response, be it in the form of laughter, amusement, weeping or simply reflection. For the reader to have the experience of being touched by a poem it must evoke something recognizable and meaningful. To quote George Thomson again:

> The poet speaks not for himself only but for his fellow-men. His cry is their cry, which only he can utter. That is what gives it its depth. But if he is to speak for them, he must suffer with them, rejoice with them, work with them, fight with them. Otherwise what he says will not appeal to them and so will lack significance.[13]

What this means is that effective communication is not simply a question of craft. The significance and appeal of poetry is partly determined by its relevance to human life. Thus, poetry has a social function, and for the poet to be able to cry the cry of humanity he or she must strive to keep harmony between poetry and life. This is the lesson Christopher Okigbo learned. As a result of his genuine search for a poetic vision he arrived at the conclusion that the writing of poetry could not be divorced from social obligations in the real world. He paid the ultimate price when he lost his life while fighting for what he considered to be his social obligation.

The case of Okigbo is an example to those involved in writing liberation poetry and the poetry of social criticism and national reconstruction. Christopher Okigbo not only found a new vision. His long search also led to the discovery of a new aesthetic ideology when he embraced critical realism and abandoned individualistic idealism and its attendant obscurantism. In other words, before he died Okigbo had taken the decision to write a poetry of social concern in a manner which enabled him to communicate better with the reader.

For those involved in the struggle for social justice the experience of Okigbo suggests that the poet should engage in practical action of some sort, for through action the poet will become part of the world of the oppressed, the poor, the dehumanized. Through the action of its creator poetry will be able to speak to humanity and to have a profound meaning. The case of Okigbo also suggests that the revolutionary poet must keep searching for a genuine aesthetics of liberation. This means, among other things, that the poet must endeavour to develop a clear social vision, and to create poetry that communicates it effectively, both for the current struggle and for time to come. The poet will inevitably encounter certain cogent questions in the process. What are the goals of a liberation struggle? Is it to punish the oppressor or to liberate both the oppressed and the oppressor? What is the objective of social criticism in post-independence Africa? Is it merely to ridicule and offend political leaders, or to contribute positively to the transformation of society? And how does the poet contribute to the liberation process? Is the poet a party propagandist or is he or she concerned with promoting new and progressive forms of social consciousness? How does the poet achieve the goal of raising readers' social consciousness? By resorting to open didacticism or by leading the reader gently by the hand to an awareness of new possibilities in social relationships and poeple's potential?

It seems to me that committed artists have the obligation not only to draw the attention of the reader to the evils, injustices and abnormalities of the existing social order but also to point the way to a new and more humane society. To perform this function adequately, committed poets must constantly and ceaselessly reflect upon their own social vision and modes of representation with a view to speaking more genuinely for humanity and in a manner which strikes a chord in their readers. This continuous search and exploration is necessary if their poetry is to have a positive and lasting impact both in their own time and for posterity.

Notes

1. Wole Soyinka, *Myth, Literature and the African World*, Cambridge, Cambridge University Press, 1976, p. 61.
2. Ibid., p. 63.
3. I refer here to Serote's earlier short poems and not to recent publications like *A Tough Tale* (London, Kliptown Books, 1987), whose diction is formal and elevated.
4. All three poems are found in M. Dickinson, *When Bullets Begin to Flower*, Nairobi, East African Publishing House, 1972.
5. George Thomson, *Marxism and Poetry*, London, Lawrence and Wishart, 1975, p. 54.
6. See Wole Soyinka (ed.), *Poems of Black Africa*, London, Heinemann, 1975, p. 96.
7. Wole Soyinka, *Idanre and Other Poems*, London, Methuen and Co., 1967, pp. 57 ff.
8. Christopher Okigbo, *Collected Poems*, London, William Heinemann, 1986, p. 20.
9. Soyinka, *Idanre and Other Poems*, p. 67.
10. See M. Kadhani and M. Zimunya, *And Now the Poets Speak*, Gweru, Mambo Press, 1981, p. 1.
11. See Frei Betto, *Fidel and Religion: Conversations with Frei Betto*, Sydney, Pathfinder Press/Pacific and Asia, 1986.
12. Soyinka, *Myth, Literature and the African World*, p. 87.
13. Thomson, op. cit., p. 60.

Index

Index

imagery and symbolism,
145–9
militant feminism, 142–4
Soyinka, Wole, 33, 57, 94–102,
184, 188–9, 192, 195–6, 197,
198
Ogun Abibiman, 95–102
and Pan-Africanism, 96, 101
development in political
consciousness and aesthetic
ideology, 96
obscurity and the use of
myths, 95–6
Sundiata, 98

Tambo, Oliver, 142
Tamuz, 42
theory of language in poetry,
17–19
Thomson, George, 194, 200

Upandru, 36

Van Wyk, Christopher
see South African Liberation
Poetry, *under Poets to the
People*
Virgin Mary, 35

Weston, Jessie, 40
White Goddess, 40, 46
Whitman, Scarlet,
see South African Liberation
Poetry, *especially under
Poets to the People*
Williams, Raymond, 7
Wordsworth, 77

Yeats, 33–5, 96, 100
York, University of, xiii

Zimbabwean Freedom Poetry,
110–127
and ideological clarity, 110
see also Hove, Nyamubaya
and Zimunya
Zimunya, Musaemura, xii, 13,
111–6, 192–3, 198
Thought-Tracks, 111–6
as poet-philosopher, 114, 125
mood of his poetry, 112–4
patriotism and nationalism,
111–2, 125
power of communication, 114
the use of images and
symbols, 115–6, 126
Zvobgo, Eddison, 110